CLARENDON LIBRARY OF LOGIC AND PHILOSOPHY

General Editor: L. Jonathan Cohen

SIMPLICITY

SIMPLICITY

ELLIOTT SOBER

CLARENDON PRESS · OXFORD
1975

Oxford University Press, Ely House, London, W1

GLASGOW   NEW YORK   TORONTO   MELBOURNE   WELLINGTON
CAPE TOWN   IBADAN   NAIROBI   DAR ES SALAAM   LUSAKA   ADDIS ABABA
DELHI   BOMBAY   CALCUTTA   MADRAS   KARACHI   LAHORE   DACCA
KUALA LUMPUR   SINGAPORE   HONG KONG   TOKYO

ISBN 0 19 824407 X

© *Oxford University Press 1975*

*Printed in Great Britain by
Butler & Tanner Ltd, Frome and London*

For
Norma

Preface

THE diversity of our intuitions about simplicity is matched only by the tenacity with which these intuitions refuse to yield to formal characterization. Our intuitions seem unanimous in favour of sparse ontologies, smooth curves, homogeneous universes, invariant equations, and impoverished assumptions. Yet recent theorizing about simplicity presents a veritable chaos of opinion. Here one finds arguments that simplicity is high probability,[1] that it is low probability,[2] and that it is not a probability at all.[3] Indeed, the complexities of the problem of simplicity have led some to question the possibility and the fruitfulness of trying to define the notion of simplicity that seems to be involved in hypothesis choice.[4]

In what follows, I try to show that the simplicity of a hypothesis can be measured by attending to how well it answers certain kinds of questions. I claim that the more informative a hypothesis is in answering these questions, the simpler it is. The informativeness of hypotheses relative to questions is characterized by the amount of extra information they need to yield answers.

[1] In *Scientific Inference*, Jeffreys tries to develop a simplicity ordering for differential equations and then proposes to assimilate this simplicity ordering to an ordering in terms of high probability. Quine's 'Simple Theories of a Complex World' concurs with certain examples cited by Kemeny in his 'The Use of Simplicity in Induction' which tend to identify the simplicity of a hypothesis with its high probability.

[2] Popper's theory of simplicity (see, for example, his *Logic of Scientific Discovery*, Chap. 7) identifies the simplicity of a hypothesis with its falsifiability as does Kemeny's proposal in 'Two Measures of Complexity'.

[3] Goodman's 'Safety, Strength, Simplicity' argues that the notion of simplicity involved in hypothesis choice is distinct from both high and low probability. Goodman's theory of the simplicity of formal systems (see *The Structure of Appearance*, Chap. 3) also is nonprobabilistic. A more recent nonprobabilistic theory is presented by Friedman in his 'Empirical Simplicity as Testability'. This theory has Popper's *Logic of Scientific Discovery* as its point of departure, but offers an alternative construal of the idea of the *dimension* of a predicate.

[4] See, for example, Ackermann's 'Inductive Simplicity' and Bunge's 'The Weight of Simplicity in the Construction and Assaying of Scientific Theories'. Hesse's 'Simplicity' offers a clear survey of recent work on simplicity and its limitations. See also the anthology of articles in Foster and Martin (eds.), *Probability, Confirmation, and Simplicity*, which overlaps with the five articles on simplicity in *Philosophy of Science*, 28(2), 1961.

The more additional information a hypothesis needs to answer a question, the less informative it is relative to that question.

The machinery of the theory is developed in Chapter 1. In Chapter 2, I apply the theory to a host of very general inferential policies that seem to be instances of choosing the simpler hypothesis, and I argue that the proposed theory mirrors and explicates these intuitions to a significant degree. Chapter 3 focuses on the simplicity criterion proposed for phonology by Chomsky and Halle and provides further applications and explorations of the theory I am defending. In Chapter 4, I show how my theory may be applied to perceptual judgements as a way of examining the idea that perception is a kind of lower-level theorizing. In Chapter 5, I present a way of justifying the use of simplicity in hypothesis choice and offer some indications of how the proposed theory is to be evaluated. Breaking the contents down by chapters in this manner may obscure the way different themes tend to recur and interweave. For example, the idea of a natural predicate is discussed in Chapter 1 and is further developed later on, especially in Chapter 3. The idea of perspicuous notation and representation is introduced in Chapter 2, another example is cited in Chapter 3, and it is defined and discussed in Chapter 4. In addition, notions of simplicity applying to formal systems, to pictures, and to inscriptions are shown to flow from the concept of simplicity developed in Chapter 1.

I wish to thank Mary Hesse, who encouraged me to deal with the problem of simplicity and advised me on countless versions and revisions. I also benefited from conversations with C. J. van Rijsbergen and Neil Tennant. Bernard Comrie, Ed Keenan, and Alan Sommertein were kind enough to give me detailed criticisms of Chapter 3. I am glad to mention a similar debt to Daniel Dennett for his suggestions on Chapter 4. Hilary Putnam and Roderick Firth also helped me considerably by their careful reading of the manuscript. I began this work while supported by a University of Pennsylvania Thouron Fellowship for Study in the United Kingdom; I made final revisions while holding a University of Wisconsin Summer Research Grant. Both of these I acknowledge with thanks.

Madison, Wisconsin   E. S.

August 1974

Contents

I

Simplicity as Informativeness

1.1 Informativeness

One of our principal goals in making knowledge claims is to render particular experience redundant. By enabling us to anticipate the course of our sensations, hypotheses make the results of observation less surprising and less informative. It is as if the world and our theories about the world were in a reciprocal balance: the more the latter tell us, the less informative the former is. In this sense, requiring that theories inform us is equivalent to requiring that the world be made that much less able to tell us anything new.[1] On the most elementary level, we can imagine asking whether a given object has a certain property. If we believe a hypothesis which entails an answer to this question, we do not have to go out and look for ourselves (or ask someone else, or consult a book, etc.). However, if we do not believe any such hypothesis, then we must consult with experience to answer our question.

A crucial feature of this relationship between knowledge claims and particular experience is captured in the relationship between general hypotheses and questions about the properties of particular individuals. Suppose that we believe the hypothesis

(1) $$(x)(Fx \supset Gx).[2]$$

Suppose further that we want to know whether some arbitrary

---

[1] Of course, we want our knowledge claims to be true as well as informative How these two desiderata are related will be discussed in Section 1.9.

[2] In the interest of smooth exposition, I will talk about the informativeness of hypotheses relative to questions when, strictly speaking, I should talk about the informativeness of hypotheses of such-and-such a form relative to questions of such-and-such a form. Also, as in statement (1), where distinct predicate letters are used, they are intended to be given distinct predicates in any interpretation. To make this work less unreadable than it otherwise might have been, I omit quotation marks wherever the context makes it clear whether a term is used or mentioned.

individual a has the property of G-hood. We can represent this question as a set, each of whose members is an alternative answer to the question,

(2) $(Ga, \sim Ga).$[3]

Notice that if we believe (1), we can use it to help us answer (2). One way of doing this is to discover the truth of

(3) $Fa.$

If we believe (3), we may conjoin it with (1) to yield an answer to question (2):

$$[Fa \ \& \ (x)(Fx \supset Gx)] \to Ga.[4]$$

On the other hand, if we believe the hypothesis

(4) $(x)(\sim Gx),$

it would enable us to answer question (2) without any outside help, because

$$(x)(\sim Gx) \to \sim Ga.$$

From this, we can conclude that (4) is more informative than (1) in answering question (2), since the former requires less extra information than the latter to imply an answer.[5]

Hypotheses expressed in the form of mathematical equations also display this property. Suppose we believe that

(5) $y = f(x)$

and want to use it to help us answer the question

---

[3] We will follow this notational convention wherever convenient. It will be discussed in Section 1.3.

[4] We will say that $A \to B$ just in case '$A \supset B$' is valid. '$A \to B$' says that A logically implies B, following Quine, *Methods of Logic*, pp. 39–44.

[5] If general hypotheses always required additional information to imply answers to questions about the properties of individuals, then we would have a quite general proof of the so-called 'Duhemian thesis'. See Duhem, *The Aim and Structure of Physical Theory*, pp. 180–220. For Quine's more general formulation, see 'Two Dogmas of Empiricism' in *From a Logical Point of View*, pp. 40–6. But, in fact, such procedures as universal instantiation (in which a perfectly general hypothesis implies a particular one without outside help) provide counterexamples. Suffice it to say that in this world, the nontrivial general laws we believe and the questions that we want answered are such that the general laws require extra information to answer the questions. Examples like universal instantiation show that the truth of the Duhemian thesis is not due to purely formal considerations but is at least in part an artefact of the relatively fine grain of our questions and the relatively coarse grain of our hypotheses.

(6)   What is the value of the variable y in situation s?

If we believe a sentence of the form

$$(7) \qquad\qquad x_a = c,$$

where c is a constant whose value is known, we could conjoin (7) to (5) to imply an answer to question (6). On the other hand, if we want to use

$$(8) \qquad\qquad y = f'(x, w)$$

to answer question (6), it seems that we need in addition a sentence of the form

$$(9) \qquad\qquad (x_a = c) \,\&\, (w_a = c'),$$

where c' is also a constant whose value is known. Sentence (9), when conjoined with (8), also implies an answer to question (6). Thus, we would say again that hypothesis (5) is more informative than hypothesis (8) relative to question (6), because (5) requires less extra information than (8) to imply an answer.

Clearly, there is an inverse relationship between the informativeness of a hypothesis H (relative to a question Q) and the amount of extra information that H requires to answer Q. That is, the more informative a hypothesis is, the less extra information it needs to imply an answer. This inverse relationship recapitulates the inverse relationship between our knowledge claims and our experience: The more informative our knowledge claims are about the properties of the individuals in our environment, the less we need to find out about the special details of an arbitrary individual before we can say what its properties are. Thus, the informativeness of a hypothesis manifests the redundancy of the world it describes.

My theory of simplicity requires that we formalize this notion of a hypothesis needing extra information to answer a question. Some constituents of the explication are already clear. For example, we will say that a hypothesis H answers a question Q with the help of extra information I only if $H \,\&\, I$ implies an answer to Q. Furthermore, the explication must mirror the fact that there are two extremes on the scale of informativeness. On the one hand, some hypotheses and some questions are mutually irrelevant, while on the other hand, some hypotheses answer some questions without any help at all from outside information. But other details remain to be examined. When is a hypothesis relevant to a question? What contribution does a hypothesis make towards answering a question? What extra information does a hypothesis require to yield an answer? Finally, how are we to compare the extra information needed by one hypothesis to answer a question with the extra information needed by another hypothesis? Solving these problems will put us well on the way to understanding this notion of informativeness.

1.2 Relevance

Let us first deal with the problem of when a hypothesis is irrelevant to a question and use the classical law of gravitation as an example:

(10)
$$F = \frac{m_1 m_2}{r^2}.$$

If someone wants to know the value of any variable in (10) for a particular situation, all he need do is find out the values of the rest of the variables and plug them into the equation.

Now consider the question

(11)   What is the temperature of a in situation s?

Could (10) help us here? In one very clear sense, the answer is no. 'Temperature' is not a variable in the equation; hence, the values of other variables cannot be plugged in to yield a value of the temperature of an object. From this point of view, whether equation (10) can answer a question about the temperature of an object is a purely formal issue, to be decided by attending to the variables that essentially occur in it.[6]

In another sense, it is conceivable that (10), together with other information, might help us to answer the question about temperature. Suppose that the object in question happens to be a space ship that is shooting away from the earth and that the interior of the ship changes temperature as a function of the change in gravitational force between space ship and earth. Given this situation, we can easily imagine how (10) could figure into a calculation of the temperature of the object at a given time. Regarded in this way, whether a hypothesis is

---

[6] A term occurs essentially in a sentence S if and only if it occurs in every sentence that is logically equivalent to S.

relevant to a question can be decided only by attending to the current status of human knowledge. Whether (10) can help us calculate the temperature of an object (or the gross national product of Yugoslavia) is wholly an epistemic question, not to be answered by examining the logical form of question and hypothesis alone.

The relation of formal relevance seems fairly clear-cut. Where S is the set of essentially occurring variables in an equation H and where question Q has the form 'What is the value of the variable v in situation a?', H is formally relevant to Q just in case $v \in S$. In the case of logical formulae, if P is the set of predicates that essentially occur in a hypothesis and Q is the set of answer predicates, then the hypothesis is relevant to the question just in case P and Q have a common member. One result of this definition is that logical truths and falsehoods are irrelevant to every question because no predicate essentially occurs in them.

A definition of epistemic relevance is more difficult but need not detain us here. From the point of view of developing a theory of simplicity, formal relevance suffices, since we will find that our judgements of simplicity can be explained by considering the purely formal relation between hypotheses and questions without having to invoke such difficult notions as epistemic relevance. Moreover, epistemic relevance can be defined in terms of our notion of formal relevance (see Section 1.6), once we have characterized the sort of question-relative informativeness at issue here.

In what follows, our use of formal relevance instead of epistemic relevance occasionally may seem to lead to counter-intuitive consequences. This apparent counterintuitiveness will usually be due to the existence of suppressed premises. When a hypothesis seems to be relevant to a question and yet turns out to be formally irrelevant, this is often because we are tacitly assuming the truth of yet another hypothesis, which, if conjoined to the one being considered, would render the entire conjunction formally relevant to the question. Thus, in our previous example, the classical law of gravitation seems to be relevant to a question about the temperature of an object, and yet the law is formally irrelevant to that question. The paradox can be resolved if we conjoin to the law the assumed equation expressing the relation of temperature to gravitational force. The conjunction, which more fully represents the state of our beliefs, is itself formally relevant to the question.

1.3 Questions

In the preceding pages, I have taken the liberty of representing questions as sets whose members are the alternative answers that may be given to the questions themselves. In the case of the simple yes-or-no answer, this technique seems unobjectionable. We represent 'Is P true?' as '$(P, \sim P)$'. But can this procedure be defended in general? Let us consider questions with more than two alternative answers, such as

(12)   What is the colour of individual a?
(13)   What is the position of individual a?
(14)   What is the relative frequency of
            property F in the set of individuals s?

The alternative answers to questions like these may often be formulated as sets of mutually exclusive and collectively exhaustive alternatives. Thus, according to our policy, we might represent question (12) as

(15)   (Red a, Blue a, Green a, . . .).[7]

Admittedly, there is no one privileged disjunction of alternative answers; there are many ways of slicing the cake. Which set is chosen as the 'right' one is dictated largely by the classification system of current theory and the demands of the problem at hand. But given any question like the ones mentioned above, the circumstances often do dictate what the alternative answers are.

This characterization of alternative answers seems to run into problems when the question involves an infinity of answers, as in (13) and (14). When the number of answers is denumerable, the problem is just that we cannot write them all down; when the number of answers is indenumerable, the problem is that there are more answers than there are expressions in our language to express them with. In both cases we will resort to the expedient of identifying a question with its (single) answer schema. Thus, the question 'What is the value of variable v in

---

[7] The alternative answers are collectively exhaustive in the sense that any coloured object will fall under one of these answer predicates.

situation s?' will be represented as '$v_s = k$', where 'k' is a dummy letter. Every alternative answer will have this form: they differ only with respect to the constant that replaces 'k'.

Our criterion for individuating questions is neither linguistic nor typographic. For us, two questions are identical just in case the sets of their alternative answers are identical. In this sense, a question is an epistemic occasion containing a request (implicit or explicit) for information. Construed in this way, the alternative answers to a question are simply the different possible satisfactory responses. Another way in which our notion of a question departs from ordinary usage is that our questions are always about arbitrary individuals. Grammatical questions in natural languages typically contain information about the subject of inquiry as well as requests for further information. In our system, however, a question informally posed about 'this electron' would be represented as a question about some arbitrary individual a. Such a policy enables us to isolate more fully the requests for information in the question and to isolate the information supplied by the grammatical question in the category of extra information. By doing this, we ensure that all of the information used to answer a question is above board and open to inspection.

Our notion of a question is peculiar in still another way. The questions we have singled out to talk about seem to be altogether puerile and scientifically uninteresting. Do physicists spend time worrying about questions like 'What colour is this object?' As mentioned at the outset, one of our goals in formulating theories is to render particular experience redundant. The ability of hypotheses to do this is revealed by their ability to inform us about the properties of the individuals in our universe. So the kind of question we have fixed upon is not an arbitrary one among many; how our knowledge claims succeed in answering questions of this sort is a crucial indication of their ability to anticipate the course of our experience.

1.4 The Contribution

We can now turn to the idea of a hypothesis making a contribution to answering a question. We saw earlier that a universal generalization contributes a certain amount of information about the properties of an individual and that for the hypothesis to answer the question considered, some extra information must be added. One might say that answering a question involves traversing a certain logical distance. The universal generalization covers part of this distance; then extra information is imported to cover the rest.

As a first step towards representing the idea of the contribution a hypothesis makes to answering a question, we can define the *appropriate instantiation* of a hypothesis H (assumed to be in prenex normal form) with respect to a question Q as follows. Suppose that question Q has the form

$$[P_1(a_1a_2 \ldots a_n), P_2(a_1a_2 \ldots a_n), \ldots, P_m(a_1a_2 \ldots a_n)],$$

and that H is formally relevant to Q in that H has the form

$$\ldots [\ldots P_h(x_1x_2 \ldots x_n) \ldots],$$

where $1 \leqslant h \leqslant m$ and each x_i $(1 \leqslant i \leqslant n)$ is bound to a quantifier.[8] Now uniformly instantiate with a_i each variable x_i $(1 \leqslant i \leqslant n)$ that is bound to a universal quantifier, and uniformly instantiate with q_i each such variable bound to an existential quantifier. For any variable x_k $(k > n)$ that occurs in H, proceed in similar fashion with instantiations a_k or q_k as required. The resulting sentence is the instantiation of H with respect to Q. Call this H^+. Note that H^+ is nothing but an instantiation of H with the choice of replacing constants geared to the ones that occur in a particular question. Table 1 clarifies this.

TABLE 1: *Constructing the appropriate instantiation of a hypothesis*

H	Q	H^+
$(x)(Fx)$	$(Fa, \sim Fa)$	Fa
$(\exists x)(Gx \supset Fx)$	$(Fa, \sim Fa)$	$Gq \supset Fq$
$(x)(\exists y)(Hxy \supset Fx)$	$(Fa, \sim Fa)$	$Haq \supset Fa$
$(\exists x)(y)(Hxy \supset Fx)$	$(Fa, \sim Fa)$	$Hqb \supset Fq$
$(x)(\exists y)(Hxy)$	$(Hab, \sim Hab)$	Haq
$(\exists y)(x)(Hxy)$	$(Hab, \sim Hab)$	Haq

The last two hypotheses show that forming H^+ obliterates differences between hypotheses due to the order of quantifiers.

[8] We are making two assumptions here regarding the relationship of H and Q. First, all occurrences of answer predicates in H are attached to the same series of variables. Second, where $P_h(a_1a_2 \ldots a_n)$ is an answer predicate and $P_h(x_1x_2 \ldots x_n)$ essentially occurs in H, $a_j = a_k$ iff $x_j = x_k$ (where $1 \leqslant j, k \leqslant n$). These two assumptions will not affect any of the applications to be made in what follows. However, for the sake of generality, these two assumptions will be removed in the Appendix.

The consequences of this for our theory of simplicity will be discussed in Section 2.7.

It is important to note that the rule for forming H^+ does not guarantee that all of the information contained in H^+ contributes to answering the question; some parts of the instantiation may be irrelevant. Thus,

$$(x)(Fx \supset Gx)$$

and $(x)[(Fx \supset Gx) \& Px]$

do not have the same instantiations relative to the question $(Ga, \sim Ga)$ even though they make the same contribution towards answering it. By combining our notions of formal relevance and appropriate instantiation H^+, we can mirror this fact and complete our definition of the idea of the contribution a hypothesis makes to a question. One merely writes H^+ in a shortest conjunctive normal form and crosses out each clause that is neither formally relevant to Q nor formally relevant to a clause that is formally relevant to Q (nor formally relevant to a clause that is formally relevant to a clause that is formally relevant to Q, nor . . .). What remains is the contribution H^*.[9] Notice that by this criterion the contribution of both the above hypotheses is 'Fa $\supset$ Ga', although that of '$(x)[(Px \supset Fx) \& (Fx \supset Gx)]$' is '$(Pa \supset Fa) \& (Fa \supset Ga)$'.

The same procedure suffices for those questions represented by an answer schema (e.g., quantitative questions) rather than by the set of alternative answers themselves. One merely treats dummy constants in the answer schema as if they were real constants. Thus, 'What is the successor of a?' would be represented by the answer schema

$$s(a) = k,$$

and the appropriate instantiation (and contribution) of the equation

$$(x)(y)[s(x) = y \text{ iff } y = x + 1]$$

would be $s(a) = k \text{ iff } k = a + 1.$

In summary, then, H^* is the contribution of H to answering Q, and is formed by appropriately instantiating H and then

[9] See Quine's 'On Cores and Prime Implicants of Truth Functions' for a discussion of how one derives a shortest disjunctive normal form expression for a schema. The dual of this method suffices for deriving a shortest conjunctive normal form expression, as required above.

eliminating irrelevant clauses from a shortest conjunctive normal form representation of the instantiation. Intuitively, H^* contains all the data that H provides about the individuals and properties about which the question inquires.

1.5 Minimum Extra Information (MEI)

We are now in a position to formalize the idea that a hypothesis answers a question with the help of extra information. Given that the contribution of a hypothesis towards answering a question is the distance the hypothesis traverses in answering the question, we now must say how one defines the minimum amount of extra information that suffices to traverse the remaining distance.

Let H be formally relevant to Q, and let H^* be the contribution that H makes to answering Q. We will say that an answer essentially occurs in H^* just when its answer predicate so occurs. Thus, the answer 'Fa' essentially occurs in 'Fa', in 'Fq', and in '$\sim Fa$'. The rule for generating the *minimum extra information* (MEI) set for H^* relative to Q simply is this:

> For every $A_i \in Q$ that essentially occurs in H^*, such that $(H^* \supset A_i) \not\leftrightarrow A_i$, form the conditional $H^* \supset A_i$. The set of all these conditionals is the MEI set.[10]

Let us see how this rule fits our preformal intuitions.

It follows from the rule that there are pairs of hypotheses and questions for which no MEI set is defined. A special instance of this is truth-functional tautologies and contradictions, which are not defined relative to any question at all. Also, if H can answer Q without outside help, the MEI of H relative to Q is a tautology. We could show that our rule satisfies this self-sufficiency requirement by showing that, if H implies an answer A_i, so does H^*. The argument procedes more easily when the restrictions of footnote 8 are lifted; in the Appendix, it will be argued that the fully general characterization of our rule satisfies the self-sufficiency requirement. Our rule also fulfils the requirement that the conjunction of each parcel of extra information with the hypothesis itself should imply an answer

---

[10] We will represent the MEI set as an unordered list like this: $\begin{pmatrix} A \\ B \\ C \end{pmatrix}$ so as not to confuse the MEI set with the question set.

to the question. Consider the MEI set of any hypothesis H relative to any question Q. If H and Q are irrelevant to each other, then the MEI set is not defined. But suppose that H and Q are mutually relevant. In this case, every member of the MEI set has the form $H^* \supset A_i$, and for every I which is a member of the MEI set, $(I \& H) \to A_i$, since $[(H^* \supset A_i) \& H] \to A_i$.

It also is important that the MEI set be the *weakest* parcel of extra information that suffices for the contribution H^* to yield an answer. An indirect proof that our rule fulfils this minimalness condition runs as follows. For any hypothesis H that is relevant to an answer A_i in question Q, our rule specifies that the MEI set is the conditional $H^* \supset A_i$. Call this I_r. So

$$(16) \qquad I_r \leftrightarrow (H^* \supset A_i).$$

Now suppose that there is a sentence I_w which is logically weaker than I_r and yet suffices for H^* to imply A_i. If I_w is weaker than I_r, we know that

$$(17) \qquad \sim(I_w \to I_r).$$

(16) and (17) together imply that

$$(18) \qquad \sim[I_w \to (H^* \supset A_i)].$$

Furthermore, if I_w suffices for H^* to yield A_i, then

$$(19) \qquad (I_w \& H^*) \to A_i,$$

and (19) is equivalent to

$$(20) \qquad I_w \to (H^* \supset A_i).$$

But (20) is incompatible with (18). Given the truth of (16), it follows that (17) and (19) cannot be true together, so there is no sentence I_w that satisfies them both. This shows that for every answer A_i such that H is relevant to it, the extra information constructed according to our rule satisfies the minimalness condition stipulated previously.

Our rule also requires that the conditional $H^* \supset A_i$ not be equivalent to the answer A_i itself. This ensures that the hypothesis not be *useless* relative to the answer, since if A_i were in fact equivalent to its own MEI, we would have to know that A_i is correct in order to use H to yield the answer A_i. Uselessness and irrelevance are twin concepts, and by excluding them both our rule ensures that an MEI is constructed for all and only the answers that the hypothesis can genuinely help to yield.

TABLE 2: *Examples of MEI construction*

	H	H*	MEI
(21)	$(x)(Fx)$	Fa	$(Fa \lor {\sim}Fa)$
(22)	$(x)(Fx \ \& \ Gx)$	Fa	$(Fa \lor {\sim}Fa)$
(23)	$(x)(Fx \lor {\sim}Fx)$	ND	ND
(24)	$(x)(Px)$	ND	ND
(25)	$(x)(Gx \supset Fx)$	$Ga \supset Fa$	$(Ga \lor Fa)$
(26)	$(x)[(Fx \ \& \ Gx) \lor ({\sim}Fx \ \& \ {\sim}Gx)]$	$(Fa \ \& \ Ga) \lor ({\sim}Fa \ \& \ {\sim}Ga)$	$\left(\begin{array}{l} Fa \ \lor \ Ga \\ {\sim}Fa \lor {\sim}Ga \end{array}\right)$
(27)	$(\exists x)(Fx)$	Fq	$\left(\begin{array}{l} Fq \supset Fa \\ Fq \supset {\sim}Fa \end{array}\right)$
(28)	$(x)(\exists y)(Hxy \supset Fy)$	$Hbq \supset Fq$	$\left(\begin{array}{l} Hbq \supset Fq) \supset Fa \\ Hbq \supset Fq) \supset {\sim}Fa \end{array}\right)$
(29)	$(x)[(Gx \ \& \ Hx) \supset {\sim}Fx]$	$(Ga \ \& \ Ha) \supset {\sim}Fa$	$((Ga \ \& \ Ha) \lor {\sim}Fa)$

Table 2 contains examples of how the rule applies. Under H are listed the hypotheses to be considered, under H^* are the contributions these hypotheses make, and under MEI are the MEI sets of the hypotheses. 'ND' means not defined. The question considered is $(Fa, \sim Fa)$.

Hypotheses (21) and (22) are both self-sufficient with respect to the question. Neither requires any additional information to yield an answer; their MEI sets have a tautology as their only member.[11] Hypotheses (23) and (24) are each formally irrelevant to the question, so their MEI sets are not defined. Hypotheses (25) and (26) both contribute to answering the question, but each needs some additional information to do so. We will call such hypotheses *relevant non-self-sufficient hypotheses*. For (25) to yield an answer, $Ga \lor Fa$ must be conjoined with it. For (26) to answer the question, either $Fa \lor Ga$ or $\sim Fa \lor \sim Ga$ must be conjoined with it. Hypotheses (27) to (29) also are relevant and non-self-sufficient and, as before, each will yield an answer when a member of its MEI set is conjoined.

Our rules for deriving the MEI of a hypothesis relative to a question apply equally to mathematical equations. To show how this may be done, we will call on the classical law of gravitation as an example. We first must define the following three functions, each taking physical objects (at a given time) as arguments and real numbers as values.

$F(a, b)$ the gravitational force between a and b.
$M(a)$ the mass of a.
$R(a, b)$ the distance between a and b.

We will also use two styles of variables: 'ϕ' and 'ψ' range over the physical objects, and 'w', 'x', 'y', and 'z' range over the real numbers. Given this, the classical law of gravitation is

(30) $(\phi)(\psi)(w)(x)(y)(z)\{[M(\phi) = x \ \& \ M(\psi) = y$
     $\& \ R(\phi, \psi) = z \ \& \ w = xy/z^2] \supset [F(\phi, \psi) = w]\}.$

---

[11] A hypothesis that is self-sufficient with respect to a given question will require no extra information to answer that question only if we assume that the use of logical principles of inference does not count as using additional information. We will make this harmless assumption; it is harmless because competing hypotheses may be thought of as formulated within a common background language and logic. Thus, we allow competing hypotheses to help themselves *gratis* to this shared logic, and in doing so we are not prejudicing our assessment of their relative informativeness. Viewing logical truths as uninformative is in keeping with Bar-Hillel and Carnap's 'An Outline of a Theory of Semantic Information'.

(30) says: Take any pair of physical objects ϕ and ψ and any triplet of real numbers x, y, and z. Then the gravitational force between ϕ and ψ will equal xy/z^2 if the mass of ϕ equals x, the mass of ψ equals y, and the distance between ϕ and ψ equals z.[12]

Now consider (30) relative to the question

(31)   What is the gravitational force between bodies a and b in situation s?

Question (31) is represented by the answer schema

(32) $F(a, b) = h.$

To compute the MEI that hypothesis (30) needs to answer question (32), we proceed as before. First, we construct H^*, which is the instantiation of (30) formed by replacing all occurrences of 'ϕ' with 'a', 'ψ' with 'b', 'w' with 'h', 'x' with 'i', 'y' with 'j', and 'z' with 'k'. This instantiation is

(33) $[M(a) = i \ \& \ M(b) = j \ \& \ R(a, b) = k \ \& \ h = ij/k^2]$
$$\supset [F(a, b) = h].$$

Now with (33) as our H^* and (32) as our A_i, we construct the conditional $H^* \supset A_i$, which is equivalent to the disjunction

(34) $[M(a) = i \ \& \ M(b) = j \ \& \ R(a, b) = k \ \& \ h = ij/k^2]$
$$\lor [F(a, b) = h].$$

(34) is the MEI for hypothesis (30) to answer question (31).

Suppose that all of the dummy letters in (34) were replaced with the appropriate constants. Then the left-hand disjunct gives the values of the masses of bodies a and b and the distance between them; and the right-hand disjunct gives the value of the gravitational force between a and b. Roughly speaking, then, if you want to use the classical law of gravitation to tell you the value of the gravitational force between two bodies, you must discover the truth of a disjunction: the gravitational force itself, or the relevant masses and distance.

We may generalize this result by considering any hypothesis in the form of the equation

(35) $y = f(x_1, x_2, \ldots, x_n).$

For equation (35) to answer the question

---

[12] To make the exposition easier, we will not include the gravitational constant G in our representation of the classical law of gravitation. This omission will not affect the outcome of our discussion, however.

(36)   What is the value of y in situation s?,

we must conjoin to (35) a disjunction $A \lor B$, where A gives the value of y in situation s and B gives the values of the variables $x_1, x_2, \ldots, x_n$ in situation s.

It is not immediately obvious that the procedure just followed in the case of the classical law of gravitation will work in the more general case of a hypothesis of the form given in (35) answering a question like (36). The reason is that in (35) the structure of the hypothesis has not been spelled out. In spite of this, the applicability of our method to the classical law of gravitation makes reasonable the supposition that once the structure of an equation is spelled out, the MEI may be calculated in the way indicated.

1.6 Comparing MEI Sets

If a hypothesis H is more informative than a hypothesis H' in answering a question Q, then H requires less extra information than H' to answer Q; so the MEI set of H will be smaller in content[13] than the MEI set of H'. In this section, we will systematically investigate the relationship between the relative informativeness of pairs of hypotheses and the relative content of their MEI sets. Several obstacles lie in the way of this task. First of all, comparing the content of the MEI sets of hypotheses is not merely a question of ordering them in terms of logical strength. A quick look down the list of hypotheses (21) to (29) will show that some MEIs do not imply some others. Secondly, some MEI sets contain more than one member, and we have yet to describe how to compare the content of such sets.

In identifying a question with the set of its alternative answers, we stipulated that all members of the question set are equally good in terms of fulfiling the request for information implicit in the question. For example, the question 'Is P true?' may be represented as $(P, \sim P)$, since the answers 'yes' and 'no' equally satisfy this demand. Because members of the question set often reappear in the MEI set, we will have to rephrase this

---

[13] 'Content' is a technical term for us which will apply both to MEI sets and to individual sentences. It is to be distinguished from informativeness, which is the property of hypotheses that we have been investigating, and from logical strength. Saying that X is logically stronger than Y just means that X implies Y but not conversely.

equivalency of the content of alternative answers in terms of the content of sentences. Suppose that question Q contains A_i and A_j as two of its alternative answers. We may state our *principle of answer equivalence* as follows:

Relative to Q, $X \overset{\&}{\underset{\lor}{}} A_i =_c X \overset{\&}{\underset{\lor}{}} A_j$, where X and A_i are logically independent and X and A_j are logically independent.

Here, '$=_c$' means 'is equal in content to'.[14]

In addition, we will say that if A logically implies B, then A is greater than or equal in content to B. This idea of logical strength together with the principle of answer equivalence is all we need to characterize the relative content of sentences. We can now define the notion of relative content between sets of sentences as follows:

If each member of set S is greater than or equal in content to a member of set S', but not conversely, then S is greater in content than S'.

The content relation between sets has the following consequences:

$$(A) =_c \begin{pmatrix} A \\ A \end{pmatrix} \qquad \begin{pmatrix} A \\ A \end{pmatrix} >_c (A \lor \sim A)$$

$$(A) >_c \begin{pmatrix} A \\ B \end{pmatrix} \qquad \begin{pmatrix} A \\ B \end{pmatrix} >_c (A \lor B)$$

$$\begin{pmatrix} A \,\&\, B \\ C \,\&\, D \end{pmatrix} >_c \begin{pmatrix} A \\ C \end{pmatrix} \qquad \begin{pmatrix} A \\ B \,\&\, C \end{pmatrix} >_c \begin{pmatrix} A \\ B \\ C \end{pmatrix}$$

$$(A \,\&\, B) >_c \begin{pmatrix} A \\ B \end{pmatrix}$$

With this machinery, we can make precise the inverse relationship between the informativeness of a hypothesis and the content of its MEI set relative to a question. A hypothesis H is more informative than a hypothesis H' relative to a question Q

---

[14] $X \overset{\&}{\underset{\lor}{}} A_i$ is a schema for two forms: For all occurrences of $X \overset{\&}{\underset{\lor}{}} A_i$ in a given context, one either should delete every occurrence of '&' or every occurrence of '$\lor$'.

just in case the MEI set I' of H' is higher in content than the MEI set I of H. Thus,

(37) $H >_i H'$ relative to Q iff $I' >_c I$ relative to Q,

where '$>_i$' means 'more informative than'.

This definition of informativeness now allows us to define the notion of epistemic relevance which arose in Section 1.2. In the example given there, the classical law of gravitation H was epistemically relevant to a question Q about temperature because there existed another hypothesis H' (namely, an equation relating temperature and gravitational force), and H in some sense helped H' to answer Q. According to our theory, this intuition is represented as follows: H is epistemically relevant to Q (relative to a body of beliefs B) iff there is a hypothesis H' in B such that H' is the most informative member of B in answering Q, and $H \& H' >_i H$ relative to Q. A hypothesis is epistemically relevant to a question if it genuinely increases the informativeness of the body of beliefs in which it is embedded.

To give the reader a feel for how to compare the contents of different MEI sets, we will rank hypotheses (21), (22), (25), (26), and (29) in Table 2. As before, the hypotheses will be considered relative to the question $(Fa, \sim Fa)$. The MEIs in (21) and (22) have less content than any of the other MEIs we are considering, because each of the members of the other MEI sets implies, but is not implied by, a tautology.

Now let us compare the MEIs in (25), (26), and (29). The set $(Ga \vee Fa)$ is greater in content than the set $\begin{pmatrix} Fa \vee Ga \\ \sim Fa \vee \sim Ga \end{pmatrix}$, since they have the form (A) and $\begin{pmatrix} A \\ B \end{pmatrix}$, respectively. The MEI in (29) is greater in content than the MEI in (25), because, by the principle of answer equivalence, $((Ga \& Ha) \vee \sim Fa)$ is equal in content to $((Ga \& Ha) \vee Fa)$, which in turn is greater in content than $(Ga \vee Fa)$. These results permit us to order the MEIs as follows:

$$\text{MEI}(29) >_c \text{MEI}(25) >_c \text{MEI}(26) >_c \text{MEI}(22) =_c \text{MEI}(21).$$

Because the content of the MEI set is inversely related to the informativeness of the hypothesis itself, the ordering of the hypotheses in terms of informativeness goes in the other direction:

$$H(21) =_i H(22) >_i H(26) >_i H(25) >_i H(29).$$

The comparison of MEI sets for hypotheses containing existential and mixed quantifications would proceed in the same manner. The rules also apply to the MEIs of mathematical equations with one minor variation. The MEIs of equations are sets of schemata, just like the questions that go into their construction. To compare the content of different MEIs, treat the dummy constants as real constants, and proceed as before.

After all this groundwork, our conjecture about simplicity comes to this: H is more informative than H' in the sense just defined just in case H is simpler than H'. Thus,

(38) $H >_s H'$ (relative to Q) iff $H >_i H'$ (relative to Q),

where '$>_s$' means 'simpler than'. If we combine (37) and (38), our conjecture takes the form

$H >_s H'$ (relative to Q) iff $I' >_c I$ (relative to Q).

At this point in the argument, the reader has no particular reason to suppose that '$>_s$' is an adequate explication of simplicity, although I hope that he has been persuaded that it is an adequate explication of the kind of informativeness lately discussed. To show that simplicity is informativeness, it must be shown that the proposed explication fits our intuitions to a high degree and systematizes these intuitions by exhibiting their common structure. That is, the theory must fit our pre-formal ideas about which hypotheses are simpler than which others well enough to justify calling it a 'theory of simplicity'. However, beyond merely fitting the facts, which might be accomplished trivially by an *ad hoc* recounting of disparate details, the theory also must illuminate and give a systematic account of diverse phenomena. This is merely to say that the theory of simplicity is a theory like any other. These twin constraints of fitting the facts and systematizing them are represented within our theory of hypothesis choice (see Section 1.9) by the twin desiderata of support and simplicity. In Chapter 5, the theory of simplicity will be evaluated relative to these canons of hypothesis choice.

Despite the constraint of fitting the facts, the monotony of prosaic usage (how we use the word 'simple') does not impose a stranglehold on the adequacy of our theory. At times, the theory will lead us to violate customary usage and will enjoin us to reform and educate our intuitions. Ultimately, the constraint imposed by our presystematic intuitions dictates that we can call '$>_s$' a simplicity relation only if it coincides with our intuitions to some significant degree. It might turn out that the informativeness of hypotheses as described so far is an important component of our inferential behaviour but does nothing to help us understand what simplicity is. In what follows, I will try to show that the theory does capture the overwhelming majority of our presystematic intuitions about what is simple. In this sense, I will claim that the theory deserves to be called a 'theory of simplicity'. Furthermore, simplicity will be seen to be an important quality for hypotheses to have, because informativeness is a desideratum of knowledge claims, and simplicity is informativeness. From this basis I will argue that the theory provides both an explication and a justification of the use of simplicity in hypothesis choice.[15]

1.7 Questions as Sets of Natural Predicates

I have conjectured that simplicity is a kind of question-relative informativeness. Given question Q, hypothesis H is simpler than hypothesis H' (relative to Q) just in case H is more informative than H' in answering Q. That simplicity is a question-relative notion on this account appears to be problematic. Suppose we want to compare the simplicity of two hypotheses. According to our theory, we can do this only if we first select a question as the standard against which to assess their relative informativeness. How are we to make our selection?

The theory provides us with a partial criterion for selecting Q. If we want to compare the simplicity of H and H', we must

---

[15] See Chapter 5 for a discussion of the idea of justification in general and its particular application to the role of simplicity in hypothesis choice.

find a question Q such that the MEI of H and the MEI of H' are both defined relative to Q, because unless Q is formally relevant to both H and H', the MEI of at least one of these hypotheses will not be defined and the simplicity of the two hypotheses will be incommensurable.

This condition on the selection of Q still leaves many different questions to choose from, and these remaining questions may be far from unanimous in their verdicts as to the relative simplicity of H and H'. That is, we may fix on one question and discover that relative to it H is simpler than H', but that relative to a different question, the simplicity ordering is reversed. Thus, at first glance, our simplicity criterion seems to be vitiated by a hopeless relativism.

To clarify this problem, we will look at an example of a pair of hypotheses due to Goodman:[16]

(39a) $(x)(\text{Emerald } x \supset \text{Green } x)$
(40a) $(x)\{\text{Emerald } x \supset$
    $[(\text{Green } x \,\&\, T(x) < t) \vee (\text{Blue } x \,\&\, T(x) \geqslant t)]\}$.

The quantifiers in (39a) and (40a) range over time-slices of physical objects. An enduring physical object that is an emerald changes colour at time t, according to (40a). The constant t is stipulated to be some time in the future, say, the year 2000. Both (39a) and (40a) are defined relative to the question

(41) $(\text{Green } a, \text{Blue } a, \ldots)$.

The MEI of (39a) relative to question (41) is the set

(42) $(\text{Emerald } a \vee \text{Green } a)$,

while the MEI of (40a) relative to question (41) is the set

(43) $\left(\begin{array}{l}[\text{Emerald } a \,\&\, T(a) < t] \vee \text{Green } a \\ [\text{Emerald } a \,\&\, T(a) \geqslant t] \vee \text{Blue } a\end{array}\right)$.

MEI (43) is higher in content than MEI (42), so hypothesis (39a) is simpler than hypothesis (40a) relative to question (41).

Now let us define the predicate 'grue':

Grue x iff $[(\text{Green } x \,\&\, T(x) < t) \vee (\text{Blue } x \,\&\, T(x) \geqslant t)]$.

---

[16] See Goodman, *Fact, Fiction, and Forecast*, Chap. 3. Our formulation of (40) is not the one used by Goodman in that (40) does not involve the notion of 'being examined'. This variant is used by Barker and Achinstein, 'On the New Riddle of Induction'; Blackburn, 'Goodman's Paradox'; and Hesse, 'Ramifications of "Grue"'.

The predicate 'bleen' may be defined in tandem: blue before, or green after. We can use these two predicates to reformulate (39a) and (40a), respectively, as

(39b) $(x)\{$Emerald $x \supset [($Grue x & $T(x) < t)$
$$\vee (\text{Bleen } x \text{ \& } T(x) \geqslant t)]\}$$

and

(40b) $(x)($Emerald $x \supset$ Grue $x).$

These two hypotheses are defined relative to the question

(44) (Grue a, Bleen a, . . .).

The MEI of (39b) relative to this question is the set

(45) $\begin{pmatrix} [\text{Emerald } a \text{ \& } T(a) < t] \vee \text{Grue } a \\ [\text{Emerald } a \text{ \& } T(a) \geqslant t] \vee \text{Bleen } a \end{pmatrix},$

while the MEI of (40b) relative to question (44) is the set

(46) (Emerald $a \vee$ Grue a).

MEI (46) is lower in content than MEI (45), so hypothesis (40b) is simpler than hypothesis (39b) relative to question (44). Thus, relative to a question about colours, (39) is simpler than (40); relative to a question about *grulers*, the ordering is reversed.

For us, the set of grue individuals does not possess the unity and commonality of salient properties that we associate with members of the same kind. In contrast, the set of green things seems to cohere in virtue of some important common property. Even though our language permits us to delimit both of these sets, our talk of grue things seems to be a mere artefact of our ability to lump together unrelated elements; our talk of green things seems to be motivated by a law-like feature of the world. This example suggests a new interpretation of the notion of a question and the beginning of a solution to the problem of question-relativity: *A question is a set of predicates designated as natural.*

The predicates which serve as the frame of reference against which our simplicity judgements are made are the predicates that we regard as natural. We noticed before that the simplicity ordering of (39) and (40) depends on which predicate family we designate as natural. Regarding colours as more natural than grulers and (39) as simpler than (40) go hand in hand. In contrast, we can imagine a person who has the opposite intuition about which predicates are natural, and we would expect him to see (40) as simpler than (39). The predicates we designate as natural affect our simplicity judgements, and a decision to regard one hypothesis as simpler than another constrains which predicates may be regarded as natural.[17]

In *A System of Logic*, Mill uses 'natural kind' to refer to sets that are especially rich in nomological significance. Although 'man' and 'snub-nosed' are both true of Socrates, the former but not the latter picks out a natural kind (p. 99). Being a man is an index to an indefinite number of other peculiarities that are not logically deducible from being a man. On the other hand, snub-nosed men have no common properties beyond what men have in common and beyond what is implied by their being snub-nosed.[18] Mill seems correct in viewing this difference as extremely significant. However, making the difference precise is difficult, since to do so, one would have to be able to say when a predicate determines a property and when two predicates determine different properties. Mill's idea of a natural kind is narrower than the notion of naturalness we have in mind.[19] For Mill, concepts like bachelorhood and greenness are not natural kinds, whereas for us they can be natural. We will therefore reserve 'natural kind' for Mill's notion, and we will use 'natural predicate', 'natural set', and 'natural property' to pick out our more inclusive notion.[20]

---

[17] One's set of natural predicates need not be unchangeably given. One may revise which predicates are taken to be natural. Often, the motive for doing this derives from one's acceptance of a particular set of laws. Given that we believe a set of laws, we tend to regard the predicates used in some perspicuous representation of those laws as the natural, important ones. We will see an example of this process of adjusting one's simplicity judgements and one's choice of natural predicates in Chapter 3.

[18] Mill's idea that natural kind properties are indices for individuals having other properties is very close to the idea I develop in Section 1.8 that natural predicates constitute natural sufficient conditions or tests for whether an individual falls into a given set. Mill's reason for thinking that the snub-nosed men do not make up a natural kind within the class of men seems closely related to an idea developed by Salmon that I discuss in Section 2.4; that is, partitioning the class of men into those that are snub-nosed and those that are not is statistically irrelevant.

[19] In the terminology of Putnam's 'The Analytic and the Synthetic', it seems as if all natural kind concepts are cluster concepts (i.e., not single-criterion concepts, like being a bachelor). In 'The Meaning of "Meaning"', he offers a new explication of what determines the meaning of natural kind terms.

[20] More recent discussions of the notion of naturalness have included Carnap's

By interpreting questions as sets of natural predicates, we can regard the universal generalizations in a person's belief set as inferential links between the members of different families of natural predicates. For example, the hypothesis $(x)(Fx \supset Gx)$ might be interpreted as a link from Fa to Ga where a is any individual. Our desire for simple theories turns out (at least in part) to be a desire for 'efficient' deductive networks between the members of different families of natural predicates. We want any given link to have logically minimal input conditions while at the same time yielding outputs of great logical strength; we want to be able to say a great deal about the properties of any individual in our world without first having to find out very much about its special features. The degree to which this goal is attained is a measure of how well we have succeeded in rendering particular experience redundant.

We have seen that to use our simplicity criterion, we must calculate the simplicity of hypotheses relative to those predicate families that we take to be natural. A further problem persists, however. Suppose P is the set of all our natural predicate families. In comparing the simplicity of two hypotheses, how do we go about choosing from P the appropriate question(s) to use as a standard? We can dispose of this problem once and for all by turning to a familiar problem that besets any application of probability as an explication of our informal notion of support. By tracing the analogy between simplicity and support, we will pave the way for the concluding section (1.9), which outlines the interaction of these two desiderata in our inferential policies.

'On the Application of Inductive Logic' and Reichenbach's *Nomological Statements and Admissible Operations*. Both Carnap and Reichenbach thought that natural predicates do not make explicit reference to particular places or times. Thus, 'is 200 miles from Paris' and 'is examined before the year 2000' would not be natural. Carnap hoped to use this intuition as a solution of Goodman's new riddle of induction, although Goodman convincingly argued that this would not work. In discussing the new riddle in *Fact, Fiction, and Forecast*, Goodman mentions the distinction between artificial and genuine kinds (p. 121). In fact, Goodman's theory of entrenchment may be viewed as an attempt to explicate this difference. Quine's notion of a natural kind and his closely related idea of a quality space are discussed in 'The Scope and Language of Science', p. 218; *Word and Object*, pp. 82–5; and 'Natural Kinds'.

1.8 Simplicity, Support, and the Weighting Problem

Carnap and Hempel observed that any use of probability theory to explicate our informal notion of support must obey a requirement of total evidence if radically counterintuitive results are to be avoided.[21] That is, suppose that the probability of H relative to each piece of evidence $e_1, e_2, \ldots, e_n$ is known. Which of these probability statements corresponds to our intuitive idea of the degree of support of H on the evidence? The requirement of total evidence says that the appropriate evidential standard to be used is *all* of the evidence available.

Now suppose that we want to compare the support of two hypotheses H and H' and that we know the probability of each of them relative to each piece of evidence $e_1, e_2, \ldots, e_n$. What is the relative support of H and H' with respect to the total evidence E? There is a special case in which the answer to this question is easy. If H is more strongly supported than H' relative to each piece of evidence e_i, then H is more strongly supported than H' relative to the total evidence E. But suppose that $e_1, e_2, \ldots, e_n$ are not unanimous with respect to the relative support of H and H'; that is, some e_i say that H is more probable than H', while other e_i say the reverse. What are we to do here? Clearly, we must *weight* the importance, relevance, or appropriateness of the different pieces of evidence. By deciding that some pieces of evidence matter more to the relative support of H and H' than others, we can calculate the total support as a function of the support of H and H' with respect to each e_i and the weighting of each e_i.[22]

Similarly, the theory of simplicity defines the relative simplicity of H and H' relative to many different predicate families. The first step in singling out the appropriate predicate family or families with which to assess their relative simplicity is the distinction between those predicate families that are in our P-system and those that are not. We calculate the simplicity of a hypothesis relative to the predicate families that are in the P-system and ignore the dictates of those that are outside

---

[21] See, for example, Carnap's 'On the Application of Inductive Logic' and his *Logical Foundations of Probability*, p. 211. Hempel states this requirement in 'Inductive Inconsistencies' in *Aspects of Scientific Explanation*, pp. 64–7. Carnap stresses that this requirement is part of the application rather than the pure theory of inductive probability.

[22] See Nagel, *The Structure of Science*, pp. 591–2, for a discussion of this problem.

the *P*-system. This corresponds to the first step of an application of probability as an explication of degree of support. One considers the probability of *H* relative to sentences that are in the belief set, and those sentences that we do not believe are viewed as having no bearing on our calculation. In both simplicity and support, we have an intuitive feel for which predicate families or sentences belong in the *P*-system or in the belief set. Just as a sentence is in our belief set if we believe it, so a predicate family is in our *P*-system if we regard it as natural.

This is only the first step, however. The *P*-system contains many different predicate families. Which of these are the appropriate ones to use in determining the relative simplicity of *H* and *H'*? Again, we parallel our discussion of probability by requiring that the simplicity of a hypothesis be calculated relative to the total *P*-system. This is the analogue of Carnap and Hempel's requirement of total evidence.

Just as there is a gap between the support of a hypothesis relative to individual pieces of evidence and its support relative to the total evidence, so now we are faced with the following problem: How are we to calculate the simplicity ordering of *H* and *H'* with respect to the total *P*-system when all we know initially is the relative simplicity of *H* and *H'* with respect to the different individual predicate families in *P*? This problem is as serious for simplicity as it is for support, and like the support problem, there is a special case for which the solution is obvious. When every predicate family in *P* is such that *H* is simpler than *H'*, it should turn out that *H* is simpler than *H'* relative to the entire *P*-system.[23] When the different predicate families in *P* are not thus unanimous, we must weight them to reflect our intuitions about which of them are the most appropriate standards to use in assessing the simplicity of the hypotheses considered. Unfortunately, I can offer no general criterion that dictates what the weighting must be. As in the probability case, we have only our informal beliefs about what matters.

[23] If the simplicity (support) of a hypothesis is not defined relative to some predicates (pieces of evidence), then the special case described above will be said to obtain when all predicates (pieces of evidence) relative to which the simplicity (support) is defined are unanimous. In Carnap's inductive logic, the support of every hypothesis is defined for every piece of evidence, although in our theory, there are pairs of hypotheses which are incommensurable.

In Chapter 2, we will examine a great many pairs of hypotheses whose simplicity is question-invariant. That is, no matter which of a range of equally natural-sounding questions is used to evaluate their relative simplicity, the same result is obtained. Situations like this correspond to the special case just discussed. Given the virtual unanimity of predicate families on the relative simplicity of a pair of hypotheses, it is easy to see how the simplicity of these hypotheses relative to the total P-system is a function of their simplicity relative to each predicate family in the P-system. On the other hand, we will encounter a few examples where the different predicate families, each of them intuitively natural members of our P-system, yield contrary readings of the simplicity of a pair of hypotheses. In such cases, the weighting problem will become especially significant. Interestingly enough, examples of this kind will enable us to explain how it is possible to trade off a gain in simplicity in one part of a theory against a loss of simplicity in another.

In Section 1.7, we urged that the questions used in the simplicity comparisons made within the theory be reinterpreted in terms of the intuitive notion of naturalness. We can now return to this and use our theory of simplicity to give a clearer characterization of what a natural predicate is. We have seen that the simplicity (support) of a hypothesis is to be calculated relative to the total P-system (total evidence) and is defined as a weighted composition of the testimony of individual predicate families (pieces of evidence). Given this, we can define the notion of *typicalness* as follows:

> p is typical of P on h, h' iff $h >_s h'$ relative to p and $h >_s h'$ relative to P
>
> e is typical of E on h, h' iff $h >_{st} h'$ relative to e and $h >_{st} h'$ relative to E.

'$>_{st}$' means 'is more supported than', p is an individual predicate family, P is a total P-system, e is an individual piece of evidence, and E is a total evidence set. If we had a quantitative notion of support and simplicity, typicalness could be expressed as

> p is typical of P on h iff Simp $(h/p) = n$ and Simp $(h/P) = n$
>
> e is typical of E on h iff Supp $(h/e) = n$ and Supp $(h/E) = n$.

Thus, a predicate family or piece of evidence is typical of the P-system or total evidence it belongs to if its testimony is representative of the total (weighted) testimony.[24]

In the example lately discussed of colours and grulers, we concluded that colours are typical of our P-system and that grulers are not. This gave us a way of understanding why colours but not grulers are natural properties for us. We could pursue this sort of investigation and gradually reconstruct our total P-system by taking hypotheses about whose relative simplicity we have fairly strong intuitions and then trying to find predicate families which mirror these judgements within our theory.

Grulers turned out to be atypical of our intuitions about (39) and (40); we can imagine other hypotheses about which grulers would be typical. For example, compare (40) to

(47)　Emeralds are yellow before the year 1000, green between the years 1000 and 2000, blue between the years 2000 and 3000, and orange thereafter.

Grulers are typical of our intuitions about this pair of hypotheses in that relative to question (44), (40) is simpler than (47). The point is that colours are typical of this example as well. We do not count grulers as unnatural because they are never typical but because in every example they are either atypical or redundant. We need not include grulers in our P-system to substantiate our judgement on hypotheses (40) and (47), since we already have colours around to do the job.

Now suppose that we have constructed a smallest set P such that each member of P is typical of at least one of our simplicity judgements, and for every intuitive simplicity judgement there is at least one member of P that is typical of it. We can now say that p is a natural predicate just in case $p \in P$. If the smallest P-system is not uniquely determined by the criterion above, then the criterion seems not to fully determine our notion

---

[24] e is typical of E on h just in case the complement of e in E is inductively irrelevant in Hempel's sense. See 'Inductive Inconsistencies', p. 64. The definition of typicalness for comparative simplicity and support is incomplete; it needs to be filled out for the cases where $h =_s h'$ and $h =_{st} h'$.

of naturalness. But perhaps determinacy can be achieved if we appeal to other constraints.[25] In this case, it is more correct to say that a person's simplicity judgements provide evidence for (but do not logically determine) what his P-system is. Note that the method of reconstructing a person's P-system that I am proposing itself obeys a simplicity constraint, in that we do not attribute more natural predicates to a person than are necessary to explain his simplicity judgements.

Since this procedure helps delimit a person's initial fund of natural predicates, we can ask what truth-functions of natural predicates are themselves natural. For our answer, we must distinguish between a predicate being natural in virtue of its delimiting a natural set and being natural in virtue of its determining a natural property. All of the predicates in the initial stock are natural in both senses. Moreover, all conjunctions of natural predicates determine natural sets and natural properties. Since natural kinds serve as indices for properties beyond themselves, conjunctions of natural kinds are always natural kinds: $A \& B$ is an index for every property indexed by either A or B.

The case of disjunctions of predicates drawn from the initial stock is more interesting, and it is here that the distinction between set and property finds its application. We will say that a disjunction (or any truth-function) of natural predicates determines a natural set if it is materially equivalent to some conjunction of predicates from the initial stock. If the disjunction (or truth-function) is nomologically equivalent to some conjunction (i.e., the equivalence is a natural law), we will say that it determines a natural property. Notice that a disjunctive set is natural if the use of the disjunction in its formulation is *dispensable*. The link between the naturalness of a set and the dispensability of its disjunctive characterization will recur in the discussion of transformational grammar in Section 3.6.

The distinction between natural sets and natural properties

[25] Doubtless there is more evidence relevant to determining a person's natural predicates than the one test proposed here. See, for example, Rosch's methodology in 'Natural Categories', where she offers experimental evidence that some ways of segmenting the colour spectrum are cross-culturally more natural than others. For Rosch, the naturalness of a category is linked to the ease with which the category is learned. See Section 4.6.

allows us to explain how a set can be natural in one theory and artificial in another when the two theories are jointly and reasonably believed. This can happen when A is materially equivalent to $X \lor Y$ and A is a natural predicate in the theory it occurs in, while X and Y (but not their disjunction) are each natural in the theory in which they occur. In the following examples, we will consider the naturalness of predicates relative to the specific theories in which they occur and relative to the totality of theories we hold.[26]

In the nineteenth century, Alexis Damour discovered that there are two kinds of jade: jadeite and nephrite. Jadeite is a silicate of sodium and aluminium and is a pyroxene; nephrite is a silicate of calcium and magnesium and is in the amphibole group of minerals. Jadeite and nephrite have different ranks on Moh's scale of hardness, different specific gravities, and different refractive indices. Yet jadeite and nephrite are jade; each is used in making jade carvings, for example. Notice that at the level of art history, the set of jade things can be a natural kind, while at the level of crystallography, the same set is artificial and disjunctive. Now that we have determined the naturalness of 'jade' and 'jadeite or nephrite' relative to two specific theories, what can we say of the naturalness of these two predicates relative to our total body of theory? 'Jade' is a natural predicate relative to the totality of our theories because it is natural relative to one of our theories; 'jadeite or nephrite' will be natural if it is nomologically coextensive with 'jade'. Because it seems clear that nothing *could be* jade unless it were jadeite or nephrite, the equivalence in question is no mere accident. Hence the two predicates are both natural relative to our total body of belief.

Another example is the continuing debate in colour theory over the way physical parameters, such as wave length, are related to colour perception. The view that colour is just wave length currently seems highly suspect; it now seems likely that

---

[26] These examples were called to my attention by Hilary Putnam. In these examples, scientific progress consists in the discovery that a 'macro' natural class is disjunctive and artificial at some more 'micro' level of theory. For some examples of how science has moved in the opposite direction, see Section 3.6. The concept of nomological equivalence that I am using owes an obvious debt to the view of necessity advocated by Kripke in 'Naming and Necessity' and by Putnam in 'The Meaning of "Meaning" '.

the class of situations in which we perceive brown, for example, is a disparate and heterogeneous collection of otherwise unrelated physical parameters.[27] That is, the class of brown things is natural at the level of our commonsense talk about the colour of objects, but is artificial at the level of a taxonomy of physical conditions.[28] Moreover, if an object's being brown nomologically guarantees that it has one of the physical properties specified, then both 'brown' and the disjunction of physical predicates that is nomologically coextensive with 'brown' will pick out natural properties.

The above characterization of when truth-functions of natural predicates are natural helps explain why the complements of natural sets are rarely, if ever, natural.[29] Predicates like 'not green' are neither materially nor nomologically equivalent to any conjunction of natural predicates; at best, they are materially equivalent to an elaborate disjunction of natural predicates. Furthermore, since all natural kind predicates are natural predicates, complements of natural kind predicates are rarely natural kind predicates. This seems reasonable, since no matter how little being green serves as an index for further properties, being not green is even less an indication of any property beyond itself.

Mill's insight that predicates are natural in virtue of their connection with other predicates within the inferential nexus of our beliefs is closely related to the following asymmetry between natural and nonnatural predicates. To discover whether an individual falls under a predicate M, one tries to

---

[27] In *Eye and Brain*, p. 125, Gregory takes this to be a lesson of Land's work on colour vision.

[28] The reductionist programme of identifying each mental property with a physical property would be confounded by the discovery that the predicates that determine natural properties at the level of psychology are artificial at the level of physics. The mind/body identity theory would be defeated by such a discovery, because if two predicates pick out the same property, their coextensiveness cannot be accidental. This statement of a necessary condition for property identity is presupposed by functionalism; without it, considering possible but nonactual cases (like whether Martians radically different in physical constitution from any known species could feel pain) would be entirely irrelevant. Thus Putnam's functionalism and his views on necessity are of a piece. See, for example, his 'Reductionism and the Nature of Psychology' for a discussion of how the lack of alignment between mental and physical properties guarantees a degree of autonomy to the different levels of our total theory.

[29] In 'Natural Kinds', Quine expresses this idea.

find a natural predicate T such that T is a sufficient condition for M:

$$(x)(Tx \supset Mx).$$

Any such T is a test for falling under M. Now consider a disjunctive predicate $A \lor B$ that does not determine a natural set. It often will happen that all natural sufficient conditions for membership in $A \lor B$ also will be tests for membership in A or tests for membership in B. But where $A \lor B$ is natural, there will be tests for membership in $A \lor B$ that are not also tests for membership in A or tests for membership in B. In fact, where A and B each determine nonempty sets, there must be such a test for membership in $A \lor B$, since if $A \lor B$ determines a natural set, it must be materially equivalent to some natural predicate that is not materially equivalent to either A or B. Thus, we can know that a particular painting is Impressionist without having to know which Impressionist artist painted it. On the other hand, it seems that we can only place an individual in the set consisting of automobiles and prime numbers by first knowing that it is a car or knowing that it is a prime number.[30] This difference helps explain what it is for natural sets to be unified and why nonnatural sets appear to be unsystematic collections. If $A \lor B$ is nonnatural, the subsets determined by A and B retain their separate identities and their separate tests for membership. However, if $A \lor B$ is natural, the subsets shed their separate identities to some degree, and the larger set $A \lor B$ itself has membership conditions that are not also conditions for the constituent subsets.

At the start of our discussion of naturalness, we recognized that although colours are natural for us, grulers might be natural in some other P-system. With this intuition comes the suspicion that the two predicate families do not mix; it might seem that they cannot both be natural. Our previous characterization of typicalness allows us to explain what is true in this idea. We will say that a P-system is *incoherent* just when two predicate families in it are each typical of P with respect to

[30] In *A Study of Thinking*, p. 158, Bruner, Goodnow, and Austin point to much the same asymmetry between disjunctive and nondisjunctive categories within the context of their experiments on concept attainment. For a geographical example of this asymmetry, see Section 4.4.

hypotheses h and h' and yield contrary readings of the relative simplicity of h and h'. A similar notion of incoherence applies to evidential support, and the notion of incoherence applied to either concept can be given a quantitative as well as a comparative formulation. This explains why viewing colours as natural seems to preclude our viewing grulers in the same way, since if both were viewed as typical of our intuition of the simplicity of (39) and (40), our P-system would be incoherent. Notice, however, that there is nothing in the logical nature of 'green' and 'grue' that prevents both from being members of a single, coherent P-system.[31]

A further, deeper kind of incoherence is also possible. When a body of evidence is self-contradictory, every hypothesis is maximally supported. Thus, for any hypothesis h, e_i will be typical of E on h just when h is maximally supported relative to e_i (when e_i implies h). Similarly, we will say that a P-system is *deeply incoherent* when every hypothesis is maximally simple. This occurs when for any hypothesis h, a predicate family p is typical of P on h just when h is maximally simple relative to p (when h implies an answer to p without any outside help). When an evidential class is self-contradictory, a contradiction is typical of E on every hypothesis, since a contradiction will imply every hypothesis. When a P-system is deeply incoherent, the question 'What is the case?' is typical of P on every hypothesis, since every hypothesis implies an answer to this question without any extra information.

In summary, a person's initial stock of predicates is reconstructed by applying the simplicity criterion to sample pairs of hypotheses. A truth-function of predicates determines a natural set just when it is materially equivalent to some conjunction of predicates from the initial stock, and it determines a natural property just when it is nomologically equivalent to some conjunction of predicates from the initial stock. Thus, a sufficient condition for two coextensive predicates to determine different properties is that one predicate be natural and the other artificial according to our simplicity criterion.

---

[31] The three natural predicates 'child', 'adult', and 'human' are logically related to each other in roughly the same way that 'green', 'blue', and 'grue' are related to each other.

1.9 Simplicity in the Context of Hypothesis Choice

In developing the machinery for comparing the simplicity of hypotheses, we set the contents of the alternative answers to a question on a logical par. The strategy seemed reasonable, since any answer is as good as any other in the sense that each satisfies the question's demand for information. But from another point of view—that of truth—this policy hardly seems appropriate. Surely a true answer is to be preferred to a false one.

In this world of incomplete and uncertain evidence, our desire for truth takes the form of a desire for sufficiently supported hypotheses. 'Support' is used to express the informal idea that some of our beliefs give us evidence for others. Since support comes in degrees, one piece of evidence can support two incompatible hypotheses. Further, we will assume that if H implies H', then H' is greater than or equal in support to H. This stipulation mirrors the intuition that the safer a hypothesis, the higher its support.[32]

The twin goals of informativeness and support are related by a fundamental tension. If we were to choose hypotheses solely on the basis of their support, the safest course would be merely to reaffirm the evidence and its consequences. If, on the other hand, we were to abandon support and seek only to make the most informative statements possible, our otherwise reasonable statements would be swollen with fantastic prophesies. By following the stricture of maximum support alone, we would say little that is interesting; by pursuing informativeness alone, we would say little that is true.[33] Thus, those instances of our inferential behaviour that we would call 'reasonable' are simultaneously risky and prudent: We do stick our necks out and go beyond the evidence at times, but we do not do so to the nth degree. This policy is represented in the following rules for choosing between competing hypotheses H and H'.

[32] This requirement on our notion of support is compatible with a probabilistic explication of support. Our assumption implies that equivalent hypotheses are equally supported on any evidence; our explication of simplicity also satisfies this equivalence condition.

[33] This does not mean that simplicity or informativeness (as we have described them) is low probability, as Popper claims (see *The Logic of Scientific Discovery*, Chap. 7). For the moment, we are merely contrasting two very extreme policies of hypothesis choice.

Let Supp (H/E) be a real-valued function that correlates the support of a hypothesis H given evidence E with a real number n, where $0 \leqslant n \leqslant 1$. Simplicity will be represented by the relations '$>_s$', '$=_s$', etc. We also need a constant k, such that $0 \leqslant k < 1$. In conformity with our discussion in the previous section, we will require that the evidence considered be the total evidence available, and that the simplicity of hypotheses be assessed relative to the total P-system. In both cases, the relativity to total evidence or total P-system will be left tacit.

> Rule 1: If Supp $(H) \leqslant k$ and Supp $(H') \leqslant k$, then choose neither.
>
> Rule 2: If Supp $(H) > k \geqslant$ Supp (H'), then choose H.
>
> Rule 3: If Supp $(H) > k$ and Supp $(H') > k$, then choose the simpler.
>
> Rule 4: If $H =_s H'$ and Supp $(H) >$ Supp $(H') > k$, then choose H.

The constant k may be thought of as representing the caution threshold we bring to bear in a particular situation of hypothesis choice.[34] In some situations, the rewards and punishments may be such that we are unwilling to go beyond the evidence. Here we would set k very close to 1, and as a consequence, we would exclude all of the competing hypotheses save the safest one. In cases where we are more willing to gamble, however, k would be given a somewhat lower value; and we would choose on the basis of simplicity between those hypotheses with more than minimal support. The value of k changes from situation to situation and may be different for different people. Determining what factors influence our choice of k is a fascinating epistemological problem but is beyond the scope of this work.

One of the problems facing this outline of a theory of hypothesis choice is explicating the informal concept of support.

---

[34] This is similar to the constant q used in Levi's *Gambling with Truth* and also has affinities with the λ parameter of Carnap's *Continuum of Inductive Methods*. Both authors envisage a trade-off between the requirements of high probability and a kind of informativeness.

Levi's book stresses that hypothesis choice is a goal-directed activity with goals that go beyond the desire for truth. Moreover, Levi's concept of an ultimate partition is an obvious analogue of my concept of a question.

Probability looms large as a candidate for the job, but well-known obstacles confront the use of probability theory in this way. I know of no general solution to those problems, and so the notion of support will have to remain on a fairly informal level. However, in some circumstances, a well-defined explication of support is available and acceptable. For example, in the curve-fitting problem (Section 2.6), certain goodness-of-fit measures seem to be acceptable. In such cases, we will assume that our notion of support is to be interpreted in terms of commonly accepted theory.

Our rules are meant to capture the idea that a criterion of simplicity often is invoked in a 'situation of indifference'. When evidence supports two or more competing hypotheses to the extent that each is a reasonable alternative, one chooses the simplest. Rule 3 ensures that the evidence bestows on the hypotheses some greater-than-minimal degree of support before simplicity is called upon to decide between them. Thus, in cases where a 'crucial experiment' renders H' very unlikely (i.e., where its support plunges) and we choose H in preference to it, no simplicity criterion is applicable. Here the support of H is greater than k, while the support of H' is not greater than k; by Rule 2, we opt for H. On the other hand, if the rival hypotheses are equal in simplicity (and each is more than minimally supported), then we choose the hypothesis that is best supported. The examples discussed in the next chapter will show in greater detail how these rules work.

Notice that the rules do not tell us what to do if H and H' are equally simple and equally supported (to some more-than-minimal degree). In such a situation, we may have to postpone choice until further experiments can be performed; after that a decision on grounds of support may be possible. Similarly, we may be able to choose between H and H' by considering the simplicity of the more inclusive theories in which they are respectively embedded. It may be that the theory that H is part of is simpler than the theory that H' is part of, and this fact might then give us a reason for choosing H in preference to H'. Of course, it is also possible that we may not have to postpone choosing between H and H' until further experiments or further considerations of simplicity can be brought to bear. Presumably if there were some desideratum of hypotheses that cannot be represented in terms of simplicity and support, it might be invoked to make the choice. In Chapter 2, I try to show that many virtues of hypotheses that seem to be different from simplicity in fact can be reduced to this concept as it is explicated in our theory. Thus, I regard it as an open question whether there is such a desideratum that can be invoked to choose between H and H' when they are equally simple and equally supported (to a degree greater than k).

The rules for hypothesis choice are prefaced by the requirement that H and H' are competing hypotheses. When are two hypotheses competitors? Clearly, if H and H' are incompatible with one another, they are competitors. But suppose that H merely restates the evidence, while H' is a conjecture that encompasses the evidence and goes beyond it. Here H and H' are compatible; in fact, H' implies H. We want to say that in this situation H and H' are competitors. These two cases make it reasonable to say that two hypotheses are competitors just in case they are logically dependent; that is, the truth or falsity of one implies the truth or falsity of the other.[35]

This explication of hypothesis choice, in so far as it proves to be illuminating, should lead us to revise our notion of what a theory is. It is customary to characterize theories as composed of two different sets of sentences, both taken to be closed under implication. The first is the set of relatively general hypotheses; the second is the set of evidential statements (which paradigmatically includes particular judgements about the properties of individuals). This picture of a theory as an ordered pair $\langle H, E \rangle$ makes it plausible to think of theory goodness as explicable solely in terms of a relation of support that exists between H and E. Where H is assumed to be general and E is assumed to be particular, support tends to be explicated in terms of instance confirmation. However, in the view I am advancing, theories are ordered triplets $\langle H, E, P \rangle$ where H and E together comprise the set of all accepted statements and P is the set of all predicate families that are regarded as natural within the theory. Hypotheses and evidence are not

[35] Hypotheses taken in isolation can be competitors or they can be competitors in the light of some further assumptions. Thus, hypotheses (39) and (40) are logically independent, but with the assumption that there will be an emerald after time t, the two are seen to be competitors by our standards.

distinguished by any logical property. Rather, within a given situation of hypothesis choice, some hypotheses will be assumed and others will be evaluated in the light of these assumptions (or not considered at all). The assumed hypotheses will be called the evidence and may include theories and observations, generalities and particularities. Which beliefs count as assumed evidence and which as scrutinized hypotheses may vary from situation to situation. This way of looking at theories makes it reasonable to explicate theory goodness in terms of the inter-action of two considerations: support, which is a relation between H and E, and simplicity, which is a relation between H and P.

The rules presented above do not constitute an explanation of our inferential behaviour, since support remains unexpli-cated. Nevertheless, these rules should give the reader some feel for the dynamics of the situation. Two or more hypotheses are more than minimally supported by the set of data that comprises our beliefs. We cannot choose between the com-petitors by appealing to some fact that makes one of them significantly more supported than the others. At this point, we must appeal to a criterion quite distinct from support. Our task now is to show that simplicity as informativeness explains this further criterion.

2

General Applications of the Theory

2.1 Heterogeneity

A frequently expressed intuition about the role of simplicity in hypothesis choice is that hypotheses that predict a change in the world are less simple than hypotheses that predict no change. An allied intuition is that hypotheses which say that a given class of individuals is uniform and homogeneous are simpler than those which say that the class is nonuniform and heterogeneous. These two intuitions are closely related; change hypotheses express a special, temporal, kind of heterogeneity. Indeed, the special place in theorizing that is accorded to invariance and conservation testifies to the importance of homogeneity hypotheses.

Let us consider the general form of change and no-change hypotheses. The change hypothesis

> Any object that is Y has property P until time t, and after that it has property Q[1]

has the form

$$(1) \qquad (x)\{Yx \supset [(Px \ \& \ Tx) \lor (Gx \ \& \ {\sim}Tx)]\},$$

where T means before time t. A no-change hypothesis having the form

> Any object that is Y has property P

does not limit the application of P to any particular period of time and may be represented as

$$(2) \qquad\qquad (x)(Yx \supset Px).$$

Assume that we want to choose between hypotheses (1) and (2) and that each hypothesis fits the evidence E well enough to merit considering their relative simplicity. In terms of the rules

---

[1] We assume that P and Q are mutually exclusive. This is the logical form of Goodman's 'grue hypothesis'. See Section 1.7.

for hypothesis choice given in Section 1.9, this means that Supp $[(1)/E] > k$ and Supp $[(2)/E] > k$.

As might be expected, (2) is simpler than (1) relative to the question

(3) $\qquad\qquad (Pa, Qa, \ldots),$

because the MEI of (2) relative to question (3) is the set

(4) $\qquad\qquad (Ya \vee Pa),$

while the MEI of (1) relative to question (3) is the set

(5) $\qquad\qquad \begin{pmatrix} (Ya \ \& \ Ta) \vee Pa \\ (Ya \ \& \sim Ta) \vee Qa \end{pmatrix}.$

MEI (5) is higher in content than MEI (4), so (2) is simpler than (1). That hypothesis (1) posits only one change does not affect its being more complicated than hypothesis (2); no matter how many changes a change hypothesis posits, within our theory it still turns out to be less simple than its no-change counterpart.

The same result applies to a hypothesis which says that a given universe of discourse is heterogeneous and one which says that it is homogeneous. For example, if we give the predicate T a spatial interpretation, then (1) would be a heterogeneity hypothesis, and (2) would be its homogeneity counterpart. The simplicity ordering relative to question (3) is preserved, of course, so we may conclude that a heterogeneity hypothesis is less simple than its homogeneity counterpart.

This result is not limited in its application to homogeneity with respect to such quotidian qualities as colours. Moreover, the individuals that comprise the domain need not be physical objects. For example, the fact that hypotheses of a given *form* (e.g., differential equations or equations that use trigonometric functions) have proved successful in an area of theorizing is often a reason to think that hypotheses of the same form will suffice in a kindred area. This belief betrays a preference for simplicity; adopting it tends to maximize the homogeneity of our beliefs with respect to their logical form. The same applies to our preference for explanations that posit *underlying mechanisms* which have already proved successful elsewhere.

Like the idea of a change in position as it occurs in mechanics, the idea of a change hypothesis makes sense only relative to a frame of reference. This fact virtually guarantees that a theory of simplicity can mirror the intuition that change hypotheses are less simple than their no-change counterparts only if the theory allows for a parameter that does the work of specifying a rest frame. Within the theory I am defending, it is the P-system—the set of predicate families designated as natural—that plays the role of determining a coordinate system against which it becomes intelligible to count hypotheses as variously positing heterogeneities or homogeneities.

2.2 Existential Razors

Ockham's razor bids us not to multiply entities beyond necessity. It is an obvious instance of how our desire for simplicity is a desire for less, in this case, a desire to minimize the number and kinds of entities admitted by our theory. But what justifies this desire for less? Given that our evidence leaves logically open whether a particular entity exists or not, why then do we so often opt for the denial of the existential claim? Why not just conjecture that the entity exists, bloat our ontology, and be done with it? Alternatively, if our evidence leaves the question logically open, why don't we leave the question open in the hypotheses we make? That is, why don't we merely suspend judgement? The theory of simplicity provides a partial justification for using Ockham's razor in the sense that it shows that using the razor results in more informative hypotheses than those yielded by using the opposite policy. The theory does not, however, show why Ockham's razor should result in *true* hypotheses more often than any other policy. Whether this further justification is needed will be discussed in Chapter 5. For the moment, we will show that using Ockham's razor is justified because it leads us to adopt simpler hypotheses.

There seem to be two ways of formulating the principle of parsimony. Under an agnostic version, one asserts the existence of an entity only when doing so is indispensible to the theory. Under an atheistic formulation, one asserts the existence of an entity when it is indispensible and asserts the nonexistence of an entity when it is eliminable. The atheistic attitude is more ambitious than the agnostic when both are confronted with a superfluous existential claim—here, the agnostic remains silent while the atheist denies. Without claiming that our attributions are historically accurate, we will call the atheistic version 'Ockham's razor' and the agnostic version 'Russell's razor'. Both philosophers seem to have given agnostic formulations of the razor, but occasionally to have used the razor to atheistic effect. As we will see, the fact that an agnostic formulation often leads to atheistic consequences is no accident; it is part of the deep affinities that exist between the two policies.[2]

Ockham's razor, thus construed, bids us to accept

(6) $\sim(\exists x)(Fx)$

and to reject

(7) $(\exists x)(Fx)$

when (6) and (7) are each more than minimally supported by what we believe about the world. To see that (6) is simpler than (7), consider the question

(8) $(Fa, \sim Fa)$.

(6) is self-sufficient relative to question (8), while the MEI of (7) relative to (8) is the set

$$\begin{pmatrix} Fq \supset Fa \\ Fq \supset \sim Fa \end{pmatrix}.$$

This means that (6) is simpler than (7). Thus, using Ockham's razor leads us to adopt hypotheses that are simpler than those obtained by the opposite policy.

Russell's razor bids us accept

(9) P

in preference to

(10) $P \,\&\, (\exists x)(Fx)$,

[2] Boehner, in his Introduction to *Ockham: Philosophical Writings*, p. xx, says that Ockham formulates the razor as 'Plurality is not to be posited without necessity' and as 'What can be explained by the assumption of fewer things is vainly explained by the assumption of more things'. The familiar maxim 'entities must not be multiplied without necessity' seems not to occur in Ockham, however. These statements of the razor seem more agnostic than atheistic, as are Boehner's own formulation and the one given by Moody in 'William of Ockham', p. 307. Thorburn's 'The Myth of Ockham's Razor' gives an interesting outline of the wandering history of this principle. Russell urged the elimination of existential claims as justified by the increase in probability that accrues to the total theory. See, for example, his 'Reply to Criticisms', *The Philosophy of Betrand Russell*, p. 708; 'The Relation of Sense Data to Physics', pp. 148, 155; and *My Philosophical Development*, pp. 71, 265, 267-9.

where the existential claim in (10) is dispensable. More generally, it says that if two theories have equal explanatory power, the failure of one theory to assert an existential claim counts in that theory's favour. Russell's razor is an elimination rule that at times seems to be justified on grounds of probability; (9) is more probable than (10). But what is its connection with simplicity? For one thing, eliminating an existential hypothesis opens the door for introducing a uniformity hypothesis (i.e., for the denial of the eliminated existential claim). Here, Russell's razor is justified because it prepares the way for an application of Ockham's razor. Another way that Russell's razor is justified has nothing to do with the logical form of the hypotheses that it eliminates. Any hypothesis that plays no explanatory role—regardless of its logical form—is justifiably eliminated. In Section 2.5, I discuss this notion of explanatory irrelevance and link it with simplicity.

Thus, the two razors are intimately related by a theoretical policy that allows the eliminability of an existential claim to serve as a reason for asserting its negation. If one can show that a particular existential posit is not required in a theory, one can then go on to deny its existence (assuming that it is not required by another accepted theory). A well-known example of this transition is the fate suffered by the ether at the hands of Einstein's special theory of relativity. In his 1905 paper,[3] Einstein claims to show that his theory renders 'superfluous' the introduction of a luminiferous ether, and the success of his theory provided the justification of our belief in the nonexistence of such an entity.

Given the link noticed earlier between simplicity and homogeneity, it would seem that the simplest hypothesis we could make with respect to a predicate family is a hypothesis of the form $(x)(Fx)$. When a hypothesis positing such perfect uniformity is precluded, simplicity is often maximized by minimizing the number of exceptions to perfect homogeneity. Thus, the hypothesis

$$(\exists x)[(\sim Fx) \ \& \ (z)(\sim Fz \supset z = x)]$$

---

[3] 'On the Electrodynamics of Moving Bodies', p. 38. Chapter 10 of Hesse's *The Structure of Scientific Inference* gives a detailed account of Einstein's use of simplicity and argues that our methodological preference for economy presupposes a clustering postulate.

claims that there is just one exception, while the hypothesis

$$(\exists x)\{(\sim Fx) \ \& \ (\exists y)(\sim Fy \ \& \ x \neq y)$$
$$\& \ (z)[\sim Fz \supset (x = z \lor y = z)]\}$$

posits two exceptions to the uniformity. Notice that the former hypothesis is simpler, since

$$(\exists x)(z)(z \neq x \supset Fz)$$

is more informative than

$$(\exists x)(\exists y)(z)[(z \neq x \ \& \ z \neq y) \supset Fz],$$

relative to the question

$$(Fa, \sim Fa).$$

This argument also tends to show a way in which simplicity favours meagre existential commitments.

Returning to our analysis of Ockham's razor, an interesting consequence of the relation of hypotheses (6) and (7) to question (8) becomes more evident if we rewrite (6) and (7) as universal generalizations

(11) $$(x)(\sim Fx)$$

and

(12) $$\sim(x)(\sim Fx).$$

Imagine that these two hypotheses were framed in part on the basis of particular facts, such as

$$\sim Fa \ \& \ \sim Fb \ \& \ \sim Fc \ \& \ \ldots$$

That is, we have noticed that some of the members of the universe of discourse are not F (and have not noticed any that are F), and on this basis, we have framed (11) and (12) as rival conjectures. (11) says that the universe of discourse is uniform and homogeneous in that all of the individuals are not F. (12), together with the evidence on which it is based, says that the universe of discourse is nonuniform and heterogeneous; even though all of the members of the sample class lack F, at least one member of the total class has F. As we saw before, (6) is simpler than (7) relative to question (8). Since (11) and (12) are merely trivial rewrites of (6) and (7), the same holds for them. Note that this result reinforces that of Section 2.1, in which we saw that a heterogeneity hypothesis is less simple than its homogeneity counterpart. Here we see that a homogeneity hypothesis is simpler than its negation.

Just as the fact that (6) is simpler than (7) justifies using Ockham's razor instead of the opposite policy, the fact that (11) is simpler than (12) justifies the following policy of enumerative induction over its opposite:

> If each member of the sample class has property P, then infer that each member of the total class has P also.

This maxim looks significantly like a generalization of Reichenbach's straight rule, which deals specifically with cases in which P is the probability that a given individual will have a given property.[4] Thus, Ockham's razor, which appears to be a policy limited to existential hypotheses, and Reichenbach's rule, which bids us assume that the sample class is typical of the total class from which it is drawn, are in fact variants of the same policy—a policy, as we have seen, that works in the interests of simplicity.

Does this provide us with a justification of the straight rule? Clearly not. We have shown only that Reichenbach's straight rule leads to hypotheses that are simpler than those yielded by the opposite policy. But we have not shown that the straight rule yields simpler hypotheses than those yielded by any specific nonstraight rule. This will be our next task.

2.3 Reichenbach's Straight Rule

Suppose we want to infer the relative frequency of individuals who have property P in a total class and that we know that the relative frequency of individuals who have P in a sample class is x (where $0 \leqslant x \leqslant 1$). The straight rule[5] bids us

[4] In fact, the straight rule is phrased in terms of the relative frequencies of properties in sets, not in terms of the odds on individuals having properties. I have represented the straight rule in this way in order to display its affinities with Ockham's razor.

[5] In *The Theory of Probability*, p. 447, Reichenbach says that the straight rule has greater descriptive simplicity than any nonstraight rule. However, he does not view descriptive simplicity as having a bearing on the truth of a hypothesis. Salmon, in *The Foundations of Scientific Inference*, p. 89, seems right in criticizing Reichenbach here, since the straight and nonstraight rules are not empirically equivalent, and Reichenbach says that his notion of descriptive simplicity is grounds only for choosing between empirically equivalent hypotheses. However, Salmon does go on to say (p. 89) that the straight rule is in some sense the simplest of the asymptotic rules.

infer that the relative frequency in the total class is x as well.[6] Any nonstraight rule, on the other hand, tells us to conjecture that the relative frequency of P in the total class is $(x + y)/2$ [where $0 \leqslant (x + y)/2 \leqslant 1$]. Here, y takes values between 0 and 1 and is a function $f(\ )$ of the size C_s of the sample class and of the size C_t of the total class.

If C_t is infinite, then y tends to zero as C_s tends to infinity. But if C_t is some finite number k, then y tends to zero as C_s tends to k. Thus, when the sample class simply is the total class, y is zero; and any nonstraight rule yields a result identical with the one yielded by the straight rule. We may express this constraint on the function $f(\ )$ as follows:[7]

$$\lim_{C_s \to C_t} f(C_s, C_t) = 0.$$

The straight rule is generally discussed for the case in which C_t is infinite. In what follows, we will discuss it for the more general case in which C_t can take any value at all. Proceeding in this fashion does not affect the outcome of the analysis; whether C_t is infinite or finite, it can be shown that the straight rule yields simpler hypotheses than those yielded by any nonstraight rule.

Where s is the sample class, t the total class, and $R(\ )$ a relative frequency function taking values between 0 and 1 inclusive, we may represent the straight rule as instructing us to accept the general hypothesis

[6] Discussions of the straight rule usually characterize it as being applied over and over in a series of inferences. A sample class s_1 is taken from the total class t, and the relative frequency of the property in question in s_1 is x_1. The straight rule tells us to infer that the relative frequency in t is x_1. We then increase the size of the sample class by adding to it members that are in the total class. Call this augmented class s_2, and let the relative frequency in it be x_2. We then discard the previous inference based on s_1, apply the straight rule to s_2, and infer that the relative frequency in t is x_2. This policy is repeated again and again for successively larger s_i. The sample class grows in size until we reach an s_i which is equivalent to the total class t. At this point, the straight rule ensures that the value we infer for the relative frequency in t is the correct value.

[7] In addition to requiring that the value of the corrective factor converge, we usually require that the limit of the relative frequency of successive sample classes exist for cases where C_t is infinite; where C_t is finite, some kind of 'early convergence' is postulated. None of these special assumptions is needed for the purpose of our argument. All that we require is that the corrective factor of any nonstraight rule is zero when the sample class is the total class and nonzero for at least some cases. However, for the sake of representing usual formulations of the problem, we will assume the convergence condition to obtain.

(13) $(x)(z)\{[R(s) = x \;\; \& \;\; x = z] \supset R(t) = z\}.$

Any nonstraight rule yields this quite different conjecture:

(14) $(x)(y)(z)\{[R(s) = x \;\; \& \;\; f(C_s, C_t) = y$
           $\& \;\; z = (x + y)/2] \supset R(t) = z\}.$[8]

Now consider the question

> What is the relative frequency of property P in the total class t?

We identify this question with its answer schema

(15) $R(t) = \gamma.$

By forming the contribution that (13) and (14) each make toward answering question (15), we can construct their respective MEI sets:

(16) $([R(s) = \alpha \;\&\; \alpha = \gamma] \vee R(t) = \gamma)$

(17) $([R(s) = \alpha \;\&\; f(C_s, C_t) = \beta \;\&$
           $\gamma = (\alpha + \beta)/2] \vee R(t) = \gamma).$

Since (16) is lower in content than (17), (13) is simpler than (14).

This result mirrors our intuition that to use the straight rule to calculate relative frequencies in the total class, all we need know is the relative frequency in the sample class. To apply any nonstraight rule here, we must know the sample class relative frequency together with the sizes of the sample and total classes. Thus, the straight rule is simpler than any nonstraight rule.[9]

---

[8] We use these rather verbose representations of the straight and nonstraight rules to simplify the comparison of their MEI sets. Our acceptance of (13), for example, is of course linked in any application to a requirement of total evidence. Where s_1 and s_2 are successive sample classes of t and where $R(s_1) = x_1$ and $R(s_2) = x_2$ ($x_1 \neq x_2$), we do not infer, via (13), that $R(t) = x_1$ and $R(t) = x_2$. Via a requirement of total evidence, we infer that $R(t) = x_2$. This is spelled out in footnote 6. Note also that expressing the straight rule as a hypothesis as in (13), or alternatively as a deductive rule of inference ('If $R(s) = x$, then infer that $R(t) = x$'), may be somewhat misleading. Perhaps a more realistic formulation of the straight rule would be: if the proportion in the sample class is n, then infer that the best estimate of the relative frequency in the total class is n. This alternative formulation would not, however, affect the outcome of our argument.

[9] In 'A Conditional Vindication of the Straight Rule', Hunt shows that 'the only rule for inducing [total] population properties from sample properties, in the case of actually or potentially finite populations of unknown magnitude, which is convergent and whose success does not depend upon correct estimates of the [total] population size is the straight rule'. Hunt's result is a special case of our discussion above.

2.4 Explanations and Predictions

Until now, we have mainly focused on using simplicity to select hypotheses. We now turn to a slightly different, but vital, role of simplicity—its use in the construction of explanations. In an explanation, one assembles facts that are already believed. Simplicity is not here a partial criterion for belief so much as a partial criterion for ordering and selecting items that are already in the belief set.

Hempel's hypothetico-deductive (HD) model of explanation[10] is a good starting point for our discussion. In this model, there are two broad logical categories of explanations. In deductive-nomological explanations, the *explanandum* is explained by deducing it from a conjunction of statements of covering laws and statements of initial conditions. In inductive-statistical explanations, the *explanadum* is explained by showing that it has a high degree of probability based on a conjunction of statements of statistical laws and statements of initial conditions. Both kinds of explanations have the form of arguments—deductive or inductive; both are supposed to have true premises and obey the Principle of Total Evidence (see Section 1.8); and both are supposed to explain why an event occurred by showing that it was to be expected (either with certainty or with high probability) given the truth of the *explanans* statements. It now seems clear that Hempel's conditions are not sufficient for explanation, and we will consider later some interesting arguments that they are not necessary either. For the present, we will take the HD model as a point of departure.

Because according to the HD view explanations are arguments, we can define the simplicity of an explanation in terms of the amount of extra information needed by the explanatory laws to yield the *explanandum*. That is, 'a simple explanation of an event' should be understood as shorthand for 'an explanation of an event that uses simple laws'. When the explanation is deductive-nomological, the covering laws imply the *explanandum*

---

[10] For a brief outline of the hypothetico-deductive account of explanation, see Hempel, *Philosophy of Natural Science*, Chap. 5. Our discussion in this section, as in most of Chapter 2, focuses on the explanation of particular events; however, it seems plausible to expect some transfer from our results in this area to the simplicity of explanations of generalizations.

sentence with the help of the initial condition sentences; this is a straightforward instance of how a hypothesis answers a question with the help of its MEI. In inductive-statistical explanation, however, the application of the theory of simplicity to the model of explanation is less automatic. Statistical laws together with initial condition statements do not imply the *explanandum* statement; they give it some degree of inductive support. Given an inductive-statistical explanation like the following

$$
\begin{array}{c}
\text{Prob } (A/B) = n \\
B \\
\overline{} \; n] \\
A
\end{array}
,
$$

we will say that the statistical law explains A with the help of extra information B. As in deductive-nomological explanation, the initial condition statements correspond to the MEI that a hypothesis requires to yield an answer. How our simplicity criterion applies to inductive-statistical explanations will become clearer in what follows. That such an application is possible shows that until now we have been focusing on a special case in which hypotheses *imply* answers to questions.

Scientists often assume that the fewer the theoretical assumptions needed to explain a given event the better, but how are we to measure the number of such sentences? Clearly, we cannot just count them up, for the number of assumptions may be reduced to one by conjunction. What seems to be needed is a criterion for individuating statements. Yet even if such a criterion were available, what good would it do? Even if we could count up the number of assumptions used in an explanation, why should fewer assumptions be better than more?

The theory of simplicity furnishes answers to these questions. Suppose that the theory T_1 can explain the truth of E, and that $C_1 \,\&\, C_2$ describes the initial conditions that T_1 needs to do this. The explanation formed by combining these elements is

(18) $[(C_1 \,\&\, C_2) \,\&\, T_1] \to E.$

Now suppose that T_1 were challenged by a rival theory T_2 which is also able to explain E but has as its description of boundary conditions the sentence C_1. This yields the explanation

(19) $(C_1 \ \& \ T_2) \rightarrow E.$

Explanation (19) would be regarded as simpler, because it rests on a more meagre foundation of initial condition assumptions. The conjecture that simplicity is informativeness mirrors this intuition; consider the extra information sets that T_1 and T_2 require to yield E as a logical consequence. For T_1 to imply E, $C_1 \ \& \ C_2$ must be conjoined, but for T_2 to imply E, only C_1 need be conjoined. Thus, T_2 requires less extra information than does T_1 to imply E, and is simpler as a result. It follows that explanation (19) is simpler than explanation (18), because it is built around a simpler theory.[11]

In addition to paucity of assumptions, we also value generality and breadth of scope in theories and explanations. Suppose that we used a generalization of the form

(20) $(x)[(Gx \ \& \ Hx) \supset Fx]$

to explain the fact that

(21) $Fa.$

The minimum description of boundary conditions that (20) needs to imply (21) is

(22) $(Ga \ \& \ Ha) \vee Fa.$

(20), (21), and (22) yield the explanation

$\{[(Ga \ \& \ Ha) \vee Fa] \ \& \ (x)[(Gx \ \& \ Hx) \supset Fx]\} \rightarrow Fa.$

However, suppose that (20) could be supplanted by a more general hypothesis, for example by

(23) $(x)(Gx \supset Fx).$

For (23) to imply the *explanandum* sentence (21), the minimum description of boundary conditions is

$(Ga \vee Fa).$

Clearly, (23) requires less extra information than (20) does to imply (21). So (23) is simpler than (20), and the explanation based on the former is simpler than the one based on the latter. This shows that the scope and generality of a hypothesis are

---

[11] In this case, dictates of simplicity concur with dictates of support. By minimizing one's assumptions, one also increases the chances that they are true.

manifestations of its simplicity.[12] By extension, simple explanations use laws of greater scope and generality.

The relationship between scope and simplicity is especially evident in cases where we contract a theory to avoid refutation. Suppose we believe (23) and decide to test it in a new realm of experience (e.g., where '$\sim H$' holds true). So we find an individual a which has '$\sim H$' true of it, and we see whether (23) holds true of that individual. What do we do if we discover, to our chagrin, that a has G but lacks F? One tactic (often disdained as *ad hoc*) is to contract the theory and say that it really does not apply to such unusual situations, but only to cases which have 'H' true of them. If we then discard (23) and accept (20) instead, we are sacrificing scope (and simplicity) to keep our conjecture afloat.

Another tempting way to sidestep recalcitrant experience is to split our world view and sacrifice a univocal treatment of phenomena. Suppose in the above case that a has the property J (where 'F' and 'J' are incompatible). In the face of the challenge to (23), we might reject it and complicate our theory by conjecturing that

$$(x)\{[(Hx \text{ \& } Gx) \supset Fx] \text{ \& } [(\sim Hx \text{ \& } Gx) \supset Jx]\}.$$

However, this new proposal has the form of a heterogeneity hypothesis, and (23) is its homogeneity counterpart. Here again, the new hypothesis sacrifices simplicity in its haste to avoid refutation.[13]

Such considerations regarding paucity of assumptions and breadth of scope illuminate some flaws, discussed by Salmon,[14] in the hypothetico-deductive model of explanation. According to the HD account, both of the following would count as explanations:

(24) b melted, because it is a piece of ice in an environment where the temperature is greater than 32°F and b is shaped like a swan and all swan-shaped pieces of ice

---

[12] This does not mean that if T implies T' but not conversely, then T is simpler than T'. That our simplicity criterion does not have this property is quite significant and will be discussed in Section 2.5.

[13] Lakatos' 'Proofs and Refutations' contains a detailed examination of the dynamics of these different strategies.

[14] Wesley Salmon, 'Statistical Explanation'. Salmon's proposal and the applications he makes of it are considerably more subtle and detailed than the fragment I will discuss here.

melt in environments where the temperature is greater than 32°F.

(25) Jones probably will live to be 50 years old, because he is now 40 years old and has blue eyes and most blue-eyed 40-year-olds live to be 50 years old.

In both cases, the *explanans* contains facts that serve no explanatory function. Salmon's object is to rule out such explanations in favour of their more reasonable counterparts:[15]

(26) *b* melted, because it is a piece of ice in an environment where the temperature is greater than 32°F and all pieces of ice in such environments melt.

(27) Jones will probably live to be 50 years old, because he is now 40 years old and most 40-year-olds live to be 50 years old.

We can express the generalizations in (24) and (26) as

(28) $(x)[(x$ is a piece of ice and x is in an environment where the temperature is greater than 32°F and x is swan-shaped$) \supset x$ melts$]$

and

(29) $(x)[(x$ is a piece of ice and x is in an environment where the temperature is greater than 32°F$) \supset x$ melts$]$.

Notice that (29) is simpler than (28) relative to the question

(a melts, a does not melt).

Similarly, we can represent the generalizations in (25) and (27) as

(30) Prob (x lives to be 50 years old/x is now 40 years old and has blue eyes) $> k$

and

(31) Prob (x lives to be 50 years old/x is now 40 years old) $> k$.

Here, k is between 0 and 1, say 0·5. Notice that (31) is simpler than (30) because (31) requires less extra information than (30) to explain one of the following:

---

[15] Although Salmon wants to show that (24) and (25) are not explanations at all, the upshot of our discussion will be to show ways in which (24) and (25) are bad explanations.

(32)   (*a* lives to be 50 years old, *a* does not live to be 50 years old).

Thus, explanation (26) is simpler than explanation (24), and explanation (27) is simpler than explanation (25). Our intuitive preference is explicable on grounds of simplicity.

Just as considerations beyond simplicity are crucial in hypothesis choice in general, so considerations beyond simplicity are crucial to the choice of explanations. The following explanation is preferable to (27):

(33)   Jones probably will live to be 50 years old, because he is now 40 years old and is in excellent health and most 40-year-olds in excellent health live to be 50.

even though the hypothesis

Prob (*x* lives to be 50 years old/*x* is now 40 years old and *x* is in excellent health) > *k*

is *less* simple than hypothesis (31) relative to question (32). This means that our preference for explanation (33) over explanation (27) flies in the face of the fact that explanation (27) is simpler. It might seem that (33) is a better explanation than (27), because the *explanandum* is more probable on the *explanans* in (33) than on the *explanans* in (27). However, Salmon persuasively argues that the higher probability in this case is merely 'a pleasant byproduct' of the satisfaction of another constraint. The real reason is that (33) takes account of more relevant information than (27) does. We will return to this point later.

Salmon tries to determine what general policies are involved in these preferences by looking at a problem that has traditionally beset philosophers, like Venn and Reichenbach, who hold frequency interpretations of probability. This is the problem of assigning probabilities to single events. For a frequentist to do this, he must associate the single event in question with a reference class of events. The problem is that a given event can be described in a variety of ways, and each description may determine a different reference class. Which of these is the one to be used in assigning a probability to the single event?

As an attempt to explicate an idea of Reichenbach's, Salmon offers two constraints on this choice. First, one must choose a reference class that is homogeneous. The intuitive idea is that a reference class is homogeneous if there is no statistically relevant way to partition it. For example, partitioning the class of 40-year-olds into those with blue eyes and those without blue eyes is statistically irrelevant to whether an individual will live to be 50, since

Prob (x lives to be $50/x$ is 40) $=$
Prob (x lives to be $50/x$ is 40 and x has blue eyes) $=$
Prob (x lives to be $50/x$ is 40 and x does not have blue eyes).

However, the class of 40-year-olds is not a homogeneous reference class with respect to whether an individual will live to be 50, since partitioning the class of 40-year-olds into those individuals with excellent health and those without it is statistically relevant:

Prob (x lives to be $50/x$ is 40) $\neq$
Prob (x lives to be $50/x$ is 40 and x is in excellent health).

Thus, satisfying the requirement that the reference class be homogeneous implies that one has included in one's explanation all of the facts that are statistically relevant to the *explanandum*. It is on this basis that explanation (33) is better than explanation (27). The second constraint Salmon proposes is that the homogeneous reference class be the largest one possible. This guarantees that no irrelevant facts are thrown into the explanation. The class of 40-year-olds is larger than the class of 40-year-olds with blue eyes, so explanation (27) is better than explanation (25) because (27) relies on a larger reference class.

These two constraints suffice to reflect the intuitions we have about the relative adequacy of explanations (24)–(27) and (33). The rule of choosing the largest homogeneous reference class helps solve the frequentist's problem of selecting reference classes with which to define the probabilities of single events. But the solution is only partial; once an initial selection of a class is made, the rule defines which subclass or superclass will serve as the reference class. But the rule does not tell us which of two classes is the reference class if one does not contain the other.

A consequence of Salmon's criteria is that in cases of deductive-nomological explanation (as opposed to the inductive-statistical examples we have been discussing), generality and breadth of scope are always to be preferred. That is, an explanation of the fact that an individual has B which uses

$$(34) \qquad\qquad (x)(Ax \supset Bx)$$

as the explanatory hypothesis is better than one which uses

$$(x)[(Ax \,\&\, Cx) \supset Bx],$$

since partitioning the class of things that are A's in terms of those that have C and those that lack C is statistically irrelevant:

$$\text{Prob } (B/A) = \text{Prob } (B/A \,\&\, C) = 1.$$

Similarly, an explanation which uses

$$(35) \qquad\qquad (x)[(Ax \lor Cx) \supset Bx]$$

as the explanatory hypothesis is better than one which uses (34). The superiority of (35) over (34) is a consequence of Salmon's theory, and according to our theory (35) is simpler than (34).[16]

However, this result may cause problems for Salmon's proposal. Even though (35) is simpler than (34), it is not at all clear that explanations which use (35) as a covering law will always be better than ones which use (34). For example, compare explanation (26) with the following:

> b melted, because b is either ice or X and anything that is either ice or X melts when placed in an environment where the temperature is greater than $32°F$.

Let us assume that X is some substance completely unrelated to water, except that it melts at $32°F$. This explanation places b in a homogeneous reference class larger than the one used in (26). Accordingly, the explanation should be better than (26), but it isn't. Although the set determined by this explanation is homogeneous, it is not natural; the predicate 'ice or X' does not determine a natural property or a natural set (see Section 1.8). Since ice and X have nothing in common structurally except that both melt at $32°F$, placing b in this artificial set does not help us at all to pinpoint the mechanism that causes melting at $32°F$. This harks back to Mill's idea that natural kinds are

---

[16] This consequence goes counter to the intuition expressed in Goodman's 'Safety, Strength, Simplicity', in which it is argued that an adequate theory of simplicity must show that in at least some cases a hypothesis of the form $(x)(Fx \supset Hx)$ is simpler than both a hypothesis of the form $(x)[(Fx \,\&\, Gx) \supset Hx]$ and one of the form $(x)[(Fx \lor Gx) \supset Hx]$. This apparently counterintuitive consequence of our theory is discussed in Section 3.6.

indices to individuals having properties. Presumably, explaining why b melts involves placing b in a natural kind that serves as an index for melting at 32°F.[17]

This brings out one difference between selecting hypotheses for inclusion in the belief set and selecting hypotheses from the belief set for use in an explanation. It seems reasonable that we should accept.(35) in preference to (34) where both are more than minimally supported, and this intuition is mirrored within the rules for hypothesis choice as a preference for simplicity. Yet the choice of (35) over (34) for inclusion in the belief set does not imply that if both happen to be believed, an explanation using (35) will be better than one using (34). In fact, the desideratum of naturalness can dictate just the opposite.

The difference between the constraints on believing a hypothesis and those on constructing explanations goes even deeper. In choosing hypotheses for inclusion in our belief set, we require that they be more than minimally supported. However, when we select hypotheses from our belief set to use in explanations, we do not select them with the aim of rendering the *explanandum* more than minimally probable. Salmon, in 'Statistical Explanation', and Jeffrey, in 'Statistical Explanation vs. Statistical Inference', argue that if we insist on explanations conferring a very high (or even a more-than-minimal) probability on *explananda*, we are committed to the *a priori* view that either there are no events that happen to be less probable than the requisite minimum or such events must be inherently inexplicable. One reason to think both alternatives unpalatable is that quantum mechanics countenances the existence of inherently improbable events and offers an explanation of why they take place. Just as we reject the determinist requirement that every explanation must confer a probability of 1 on its *explanandum*, we also should reject the more modest but no less incorrect requirement that every explanation must confer a high probability on its *explanandum*. A consequence of Salmon's and Jeffrey's critiques is that an explanation of an event assigns to the event a probability relative to the *explanans* and thereby shows that the event was the result—however improbable and

---

[17] In fairness to Salmon, I should mention that he recognizes the need for a constraint on the reference class which will bring out the role of causal factors in statistical explanation (p. 81).

unexpected—of the stochastic processes and initial conditions described in the *explanans* sentences.

The statistical relevance view thus asserts that an event can be explained even when it is extremely improbable and unexpected on the totality of evidence. Because most events are more probable than not, the oddity of this consequence does not often intrude, and Hempel's link between explaining and conferring high probability attains its initial plausibility. In those cases where the *explanandum* is improbable, a holistic approach to explanation somewhat lessens the oddity of the statistical relevance view. In his 'Explanation and Information', Greeno has suggested that the adequacy of an explanation of a single event is to be partially determined by seeing how well the theory it uses explains other events. Most explanations will confer some more than minimal probability on the *explanandum*. The fact that the statistical relevance model allows for some explanations having an improbable *explanandum* need not lead to the absurdity that every explanation can have an improbable *explanandum*. Rather, the statistical relevance view admits, but the Hempelian account precludes, the possibility that the improbable can be rendered intelligible within the total fabric of our explanations.

If we agree that some explanations can confer very low probabilities on their *explananda* and accept our constraint on acceptance which says that acceptable hypotheses must be more than minimally probable on the evidence, then we begin to see how acceptance and explanation part ways. That is, it is possible that a given hypothesis should explain a body of evidence and yet be unacceptable relative to that body of evidence. This can come about where Prob (h/e) is less than k, and Bayes' theorem allows the inference that Prob (e/h) is also less than k. The former probability precludes accepting h on the basis of e, but the latter does not preclude h's explaining e.

So far we have given two arguments to show that the constraints on acceptance and explanation are not the same. A third argument can be made. At times two hypotheses are unequally acceptable on a body of evidence and yet equally explanatory of that body of evidence. For example, suppose that we want to accept a hypothesis about the result of the next coin toss. Our evidence is that the coin tossing device is biased towards heads. This allows us to choose the hypothesis 'Heads will come up next' in preference to 'Tails will come up next'. Yet neither hypothesis in the slightest way explains why the coin tossing device is biased towards heads. This is a familiar point, much like those used to show the differences between explanation and prediction. I bring it up here to further undermine the view which claims that the logic of acceptance *is* the logic of inference to the best explanation. In general, each of the three arguments just presented denies that '*h* is more acceptable than *h'*, relative to *e*' implies or is implied by '*h* is a better explanation than *h'* of *e*'. This point will have important consequences for our discussion of linguistic theory in Chapter 3.

We may summarize our discussion of the statistical relevance view as follows. Salmon's requirement that the reference class be the largest (homogeneous) one is in fact a simplicity constraint. However, in our view, the reference class must be natural as well as the largest homogeneous class, and naturalness and largeness can at times be at odds with each other. Furthermore, we found that hypothesis choice and explanation construction are subject to somewhat different constraints: Choosing beliefs involves constraints of more than minimal support and simplicity, while constructing explanations from the stock of beliefs involves constraints on the reference class of homogeneity, simplicity, and naturalness.

Now let us look at a rather different aspect of our simplicity judgements, one involving mathematical equations. Suppose that we want to explain why a given variable has a certain value in situation *a*. That is, we want to explain the truth of

$$(36) \qquad\qquad y(a) = c'$$

where c' is a constant. To explain (36), we might use the general law

$$(37) \qquad\qquad v = f(v_1, v_2, \ldots, v_n).$$

The description of initial conditions needed for (37) to explain (36) is

$$38) \quad [y(a) = c'] \vee$$
$$[v_1(a) = c_1 \ \ \& \ \ v_2(a) = c_2 \ \ \& \ \ \ldots \ \ \& \ \ v_n(a) = c_n],$$

where $c_1, c_2, \ldots, c_n$ are constants.

Now consider an explanation built around a different general law, one involving fewer variables:

$$(39) \qquad y = f'(v_1, v_2, \ldots, v_{n-1}).$$

For (39) to yield an explanation of (36), the following description of initial conditions must be conjoined with it:

$$(40) \qquad [y(a) = c'] \vee$$
$$[v_1(a) = c_1 \quad \& \quad v_2(a) = c_2 \quad \& \quad \ldots \quad \& \quad v_{n-1}(a) = c_{n-1}].$$

(40) has less content than (38), so equation (39) is more informative than equation (37). We therefore conclude that (39) is simpler than (37). In general, this shows that the fewer variables in an equation the simpler it is.

Both the link between simplicity and generality and the one between simplicity and the number of variables in an equation manifest themselves in our belief that invariance is a mark of simplicity.[18] In believing that a property P is invariant with respect to a property Q, we believe that an equation relating the value of P to other variables need not include a parameter representing the value of Q. Similarly, such an equation is fully general in that it applies to any situation regardless of the value of Q in that situation.

The result above concerning the number of variables in an equation enables us to mirror the related fact that in an explication the fewer the number of places in the *explicans* predicate, the simpler it is. Consider two competing explications of the predicate Rx:

$$(41a) \qquad (x)(y)(Pxy \text{ iff } Rx)$$

$$(42a) \qquad (x)(y)(z)(Qxyz \text{ iff } Rx).[19]$$

Each of the *explicans* predicates is linked with its characteristic function in the usual way:

$$(x)(y)[Pxy \text{ iff } F(x, y) = 0]$$
$$(x)(y)(z)[Qxyz \text{ iff } G(x, y, z) = 0].$$

---

[18] Post, in 'Simplicity and Scientific Theories', emphasizes the importance of invariance as a mark of simplicity.

[19] We assume that the ranges of the quantifiers 'x', 'y', and 'z' are specified elsewhere in the proposed explications. In our example, the *explicans* predicates have more places than the *explicandum* predicate. This is quite usual (witness our own theory of simplicity) and is the result of making explicit what was only tacit in the area being explicated.

So we can rewrite (41a) and (42a) equivalently as

(41b) $(x)(y)[F(x,y) = 0 \text{ iff } Rx]$

(42b) $(x)(y)(z)[G(x,y,z) = 0 \text{ iff } Rx]$.

(41b) will require less extra information than (42b) to answer the question

$$(Ra, \sim Ra),$$

so (41a) is a simpler explication than (42a). Thus, the fewer the number of places in an *explicans* predicate, the simpler the explication.

Our recent reflections on the simplicity of explanations and theories carry over into the realm of predictions. For our present purposes, we can assume that predictions are arguments in which the 'answer to the question' is not known in advance. In a prediction, we want to know whether or not a certain sentence P is true. To find out, we try to make use of laws and other information that we believe and to deduce P or deduce $\sim P$ from these other statements.

Suppose that we want to know whether P is true, and that theoretical statement T_1, together with boundary description C_1, answers this question:

(43) $(C_1 \& T_1) \rightarrow \pm P,$

where both C_1 and T_1 are members of our belief set.[20] Now suppose that this prediction is reinforced by another theory T_2 together with its own description of boundary conditions C_2:

(44) $(C_2 \& T_2) \rightarrow \pm P,$

where we believe C_2 and T_2 as well. (43) and (44) may be combined into a single inference, which *triangulates*[21] the prediction of $\pm P$:

(45) $[(C_1 \& T_1) \vee (C_2 \& T_2)] \rightarrow \pm P.$

(45) triangulates the prediction of $\pm P$, since T_1 and T_2 both lead to this common conclusion. We value predictions that do this, and sometimes even find them more persuasive than predictions that do not. The preference for triangulated

[20] '$\pm P$' is a schema for two forms: For all occurrences of '$\pm P$' in a given context, one either should delete every occurrence of '$\pm$' or every occurrence of '$+$'.

[21] A prediction is triangulated when it is implied by each of several different pairs $\langle T_i, C_i \rangle$, where T_i is a theory and C_i is its description of initial conditions.

predictions over untriangulated ones is mirrored in our theory. For T_1 to imply $\pm P$, C_1 must be conjoined to it; but for T_1 & T_2 to imply $\pm P$, $C_1 \vee C_2$ must be conjoined. Hence, triangulated predictions depend on less extra information than their untriangulated counterparts, and as a result they are simpler.

2.5 The Problem of Logical Strength

Logical strength seems to play an important part in our choice of hypotheses. Given two hypotheses H and H' such that H implies H' (but not conversely), we sometimes seem to prefer H over H' because H is logically stronger; but the precise significance of logical strength is difficult to pinpoint. Sometimes the fact that H implies H' counts as an asset of H; other times it counts as a liability. To solve the problem of logical strength, we must determine what underlies this difference.[22]

In an inductive logic where logical strength and consistency with the evidence are the only two criteria of choice, greater strength is always to be preferred. On the other hand, in an inductive logic where high probability is the only criterion of choice, greater strength is never to be preferred; one always opts for the weaker hypothesis. I have argued in Section 1.9 that both of these policies are manifestly unrealistic. Our inferential behaviour seems to be a mixture of prudence and audacity; any policy which says either that prudence is all or that audacity is all must be rejected as fundamentally inadequate.

Once we recognize the tension between safety and risk, it becomes tempting to set up a system of rules which leads to a compromise between these opposing attractions. We might require that each competing hypothesis be more than minimally probable but that we choose the strongest hypothesis from the group. That is, we choose the most improbable of the more-than-minimally probable. However, this model is fatally flawed. Imagine a choice situation in which hypothesis H is supported to a degree h greater than the minimum degree k. We can trivially construct a competitor H' out of H as follows. Let H' be H & A, where A is a hypothesis about the outcome of a coin toss. Fix A so that the degree of support h' of H' is such

---

[22] This problem is sometimes posed as a criticism of Popper's theory of simplicity. See, for example, Hempel's *Philosophy of Natural Science*, pp. 44, 45.

that $h > h' > k$. In this case, the above rules tell us to choose H' over H, since both are more than minimally supported, and H' is logically stronger than H.

This particular model seems to be incorrect, because it fails to distinguish between good and bad logical strength. If we want a law of refraction, we prefer Snell's Law over Snell's Law conjoined with coin-toss hypothesis. On the other hand, wanting a law of refraction will lead us to prefer Fermat's Law to Snell's Law. In the former case, the extra strength of the stronger hypothesis is bad; in the latter case, the extra strength of the stronger hypothesis is good. Our compromise model of 'support + logical strength' is as incapable of mirroring this aspect of our inferential behaviour as were each of the one-dimensional models mentioned above. The problem remains unsolved.

Our measure of simplicity is not equivalent to a measure of logical strength. As we have seen, incompatible hypotheses are comparable on grounds of simplicity; they would not be comparable if simplicity were merely logical strength. Moreover, it is possible to exhibit pairs of hypotheses H and H' where H implies H' (but not conversely) and yet H and H' are equally simple. Thus, even within the restricted domain of hypotheses that are related by '$\rightarrow$', a simplicity ordering is not always the same as an ordering in terms of logical strength.[23]

This difference between simplicity and logical strength provides a solution to the problem we have been considering. Given any two hypotheses H and H' where H implies H' (but not conversely), the strength that H has over and above that possessed by H' we will call its *extra strength*. Our simplicity criterion has the following property. If the extra strength that H has over H' is good, then H will be simpler than H'; but if the extra strength that H has over H' is bad, then H and H' will be equally simple. In the former case, if H and H' are each more than minimally supported, our rules tell us to choose H. In the latter case, if H and H' are each more than minimally supported, our rules tell us to choose H' (since it is better

[23] This property of the theory of simplicity distinguishes the notion of informativeness I develop from the idea of semantic information that motivates Bar-Hillel and Carnap's 'Outline of a Theory of Semantic Information', Putnam's 'Formalization of the Concept of "About" ', and Hintikka's 'On Semantic Information'. The moving idea of these proposals is the Popperian one that the more possibilities a sentence rules out, the more informative it is.

supported). Thus, given that both hypotheses are more than minimally supported, our rules tell us to choose H just in case the extra strength in H is good, but to choose H' just in case the extra strength in H is bad. This outcome seems to be highly realistic.

I can offer no general proof that the simplicity criterion has this property, since our distinction between good and bad strength is presystematic and informal. The absence of a general proof is a characteristic of any explication and is not a special failing of the simplicity criterion. In the remainder of this section, I apply the simplicity criterion to several rather interesting cases and show that it yields satisfactory results.

Snell's Law and Fermat's Law are well-known examples of a pair of hypotheses H and H' where H implies H' (but not conversely) and where the extra strength in H is good. Consider the path of a ray of light as it passes from one medium into another. Snell's Law is given by

$$(46) \qquad \frac{\sin \alpha}{\sin \beta} = \mu,$$

where μ is the characteristic refraction index of the two media (see Figure 1). Fermat's Law, the famous 'Law of Least Time',

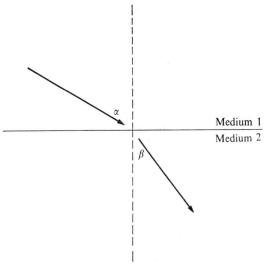

Fig. 1. The path of a ray of light as it passes from one medium into another

implies Snell's Law (but not conversely). Deducible from Fermat's Law is the equation

$$(47) \qquad \frac{\sin \alpha}{\sin \beta} = \frac{v_1}{v_2} = \mu$$

where v_1 and v_2 are the characteristic velocities of light through the media in question.

Now let us compare the simplicity of (46) and (47) relative to the question

(48) What is the value of the variable _____ in situation s?,

where the blank may be filled in with 'α', 'β', or 'μ'. It makes no difference which one we choose. Let's take 'α'. For (46) to answer this question, we must conjoin a disjunction to it: the value of α, or the value of β and the value of μ. That is, the MEI of (46) relative to question (48) is the set

$$(49) \qquad ([\alpha = k_1] \vee [\beta = k_2 \,\&\, \mu = k_3]),$$

where k_1, k_2, and k_3 are constants. For (47) to answer question (48), we must conjoin to it a disjunction: the value of α, or the values of β and μ, or the values of β, v_1, and v_2. The MEI of (47) relative to (48) is the set

$$(50 \qquad ([\alpha = k_1] \vee [\beta = k_2 \,\&\, \mu = k_3]$$
$$\vee [\beta = k_3 \,\&\, v_1 = k_4 \,\&\, v_2 = k_5]),$$

where k_4 and k_5 are also constants. Applying the rule for comparing the MEIs, we find that MEI (50) is lower in content than MEI (49). Hence, Fermat's Law is simpler than Snell's Law.[24]

In contrast, let us compare Snell's Law, (46), to the hypothesis

$$(51) \qquad \frac{\sin \alpha}{\sin \beta} = \mu \,\&\, \text{snow is white}.$$

According to the simplicity criterion, (46) and (51) are equally simple, because they can be compared only relative to questions about the value of variables that essentially occur in both of them. (46) and (51) are equally informative relative to questions about the values of α, β, and μ.

---

[24] Strictly speaking, we have shown that a consequence of Fermat's Law is simpler than Snell's Law. However, since in our theory a consequence of a hypothesis is never simpler than the hypothesis itself, it follows that Fermat's Law is simpler than Snell's Law.

Now suppose that Snell's Law and (51) are both more than minimally supported in some choice situation. They are equally simple, so no choice is possible on that basis. In this case, our rules tell us to choose the better supported hypothesis, Snell's Law. Notice that we do not opt for greater logical strength, because it brings us no gain in simplicity. On the other hand, if we suppose that Snell's Law and Fermat's Law are both more than minimally supported in some choice situation, our rules bid us choose Fermat's Law over Snell's on grounds of simplicity. Here we do opt for greater logical strength, because it brings us gains in simplicity.

Since both Fermat's Law and (51) imply Snell's Law, both have the form

(52)   Snell's Law & X.

We just saw that when X is filled in to turn (52) into Fermat's Law, the resulting instance of (52) is simpler than Snell's Law. Yet, when X is filled in with 'snow is white', the resulting instance of (52) and Snell's Law are equally simple. What is going on in the theory of simplicity that determines this difference? (52) can be turned into Fermat's Law in a variety of ways, depending on what sentence is substituted for X. But no matter which sentence is substituted, it will contain an essentially occurring predicate which also essentially occurs in Snell's Law. On the other hand, if (52) is turned into (51), this no longer holds. That is, there is at least one substitute for X (namely 'snow is white') which contains no essentially occurring predicate that also essentially occurs in Snell's Law. This difference is the source of our initial intuition that the extra strength that (51) has over Snell's Law is somehow irrelevant and useless, while the extra strength of Fermat's Law over Snell's Law is relevant to the subject matter already dealt with in Snell's Law.

At this juncture, we can give a general characterization of the notion of good extra strength by using the idea of epistemic relevance defined in Section 1.6. Consider a case where H implies H' (but not conversely) and where Q is a question that is an appropriate (typical) standard against which to assess the simplicity of H'. Imagine any rewrite of H in the form H' & X. H will have good extra strength over H' just in case X is epistemically relevant to Q in that it helps H' answer Q. This is another way of saying that H has good extra strength over H' when $H >_s H'$ relative to Q. As noted above, a necessary condition for H to have good extra strength over H' is that H' and every substitution instance of X share an essentially occurring predicate.

In situations of hypothesis choice, we are willing to run the risk of accepting a hypothesis having greater logical strength over one having less only if we gain in simplicity. Thus, in the tension between prudence and risk, we take risks only in those cases where the risks bring gains in simplicity. This is quite different from obeying an inferential policy which bids us say as much as possible no matter how our beliefs are complicated in the process.

In Section 2.2, I discussed the simplicity of Ockham's and Russell's razors. We saw that both an agnostic and an atheistic attitude towards superfluous entities are vindicated by our theory, and that deep affinities in fact exist between the two policies. I now want to show that our discussion of logical strength throws further light on the virtues of Russell's razor. According to Russell's razor, superfluous entities are to be eliminated when they are theoretically dispensable. The razor bids us choose

(53) P

over

(54) $P \ \& \ (\exists x)(Fx)$

when $(\exists x)(Fx)$ is irrelevant to P. The existential claim is irrelevant when it does not help P to explain or predict anything that is part of the subject matter of P. Put within our theory, this will be the case when there is no question Q that is typical of P relative to which (54) is simpler than (53). If $(\exists x)(Fx)$ is irrelevant to P in this sense, then (54) will have bad extra strength over (53). We therefore choose (53) over (54), and the grounds for eliminating the existential claim are explained by our theory of simplicity.[25]

---

[25] Note that good extra strength, like our initial explication of simplicity, is a question-relative concept. Thus, in determining whether adding a statement to a theory would be a gain in simplicity, we must first determine what the appropriate questions are in assessing the theory's simplicity.

The *accuracy* of one hypothesis over another provides another case of good extra strength. Consider two hypotheses that are compatible but differ as to their degree of accuracy:

(55) $3 \leqslant y \leqslant 8$
(56) $7 \leqslant y \leqslant 8,$

where (55) and (56) both give a value of a variable y in some particular situation. (55) is less accurate than (56). We may rewrite (56) as a conjunction of (55) and some other hypothesis. (56) is equivalent to

$$(3 \leqslant y \leqslant 8) \ \& \ \sim(3 \leqslant y < 7).$$

Notice that this rewrite of (56) as a conjunction of (55) and some other hypothesis X is such that X and (55) have an essentially occurring variable (i.e., 'y') in common, and any such rewrite would have this property as well. We conclude that the extra strength of (56) is good, and so (56) is simpler than (55).

Linking simplicity and accuracy runs counter to the general point of view which links simplicity and high probability.[26] Admittedly, a hypothesis such as '$y = 6\cdot7$' looks simpler in some preformal sense than the hypothesis '$y = 6\cdot694$',[27] but the apparent counterintuitiveness of our theory in this case may be dispelled by considering the role of simplicity within hypothesis choice in general. Given two hypotheses that are compatible but differ in accuracy, we can invoke simplicity as a grounds for choice only if they are each more than minimally supported. If, for example, our measurements are not accurate enough to yield a value for y that is accurate to three decimal places, we then dismiss '$y = 6\cdot694$' not because of simplicity, but because it imputes more accuracy to the data than the data can sustain. Simplicity comes to bear when the data are precise enough to warrant either hypothesis. In this case, it seems that we should opt for the more accurate one in conformity with the scientific practice of giving as accurate an account as the data permit. However, in cases where the data do not sustain both hypotheses, no choice on grounds of simplicity is

---

[26] See, for example, Jeffreys' *Scientific Inference*, Kemeny's 'The Use of Simplicity in Induction', and Quine's 'Simple Theories of a Complex World'.

[27] The sense in which '$y = 6\cdot7$' is a simpler *inscription* than '$y = 6\cdot694$' can be mirrored in our theory. See Section 4.4.

required. We dismiss over-ambitious hypotheses because their support falls below the requisite minimum.

If our explication of good extra strength is adequate, I think that we may conclude that it is misleading to say that logical strength *per se* is a desideratum in our inferential behaviour. There are times when we reject hypotheses having greater strength in favour of safer alternatives; when we do in fact choose hypotheses that happen to have greater strength than the alternatives, we do so because greater strength happens to coincide with greater simplicity.

2.6 More on Mathematical Equations

So far, we have measured the simplicity of hypotheses represented as mathematical equations by considering how well they answer questions about the values of variables. Although this technique seems to capture fairly well the informativeness of logical formulae, it is fundamentally inadequate when we come to assess the informativeness of mathematical equations. Mathematical equations do not merely enable us to calculate the value of one variable given the values of the others. They also characterize the relationships between variables and enable us to compute how any variable changes relative to the others. This means that in considering the informativeness of an equation we must attend to how informative it is about the derivatives of the variables as well as about the values of the variables themselves. Thus, we will use the following question form to compare the informativeness of continuous and discontinuous polynomials:

(57)   What is the nth derivative of y at $x = a$?

Here n may be replaced by 0, 1, or any integer. If it is replaced by 0, (57) is to be construed as asking for the value of y at $x = a$. Introducing this new question is not a major departure from our previous policy, in so far as our apparatus for comparing the simplicity of hypotheses still holds sway. What is new is that we have acknowledged that any P-system which is rich enough to sustain comparisons of the simplicity of mathematical equations (even of the elementary sort we will deal with in what follows) must include natural predicates other than those concerning the value of variables.

Before considering the relative simplicity of actual equations, let us consider the relative simplicity of conjectures about the *form* that an equation takes. Popper's theory of simplicity is able to account for the relative simplicity of the following two hypotheses by appealing to his general doctrine of falsification:

(58)   The equation relating x and y is linear

(59)   The equation relating x and y is circular.

Popper points out that (58) requires two data points and that (59) requires three data points to answer the question:

What is the equation relating x and v?

Another way of saying this is that hypothesis (58) is falsifiable by three data points while hypothesis (59) requires four data points to falsify it.[28] I entirely agree with this analysis, and Popper's account obviously fits into the general dictates of our theory. But Popper's falsificationist views cannot account for the simplicity of

$$y = 3x + 6$$

over that of

$$y = 5x^4 + 4x^2 - 75x + 168.$$

Each of these equations is falsifiable by one point, since that point may not lie on the unique curve that each defines. Popper's theory, although it can handle some conjectures about the general form that an equation will take, cannot handle equations themselves.

We saw in Section 2.1 that a change hypothesis is less simple than its no-change counterpart. This conclusion obtains for mathematical equations as well. Consider the no-change hypothesis

(60) $y = c$

and the change hypothesis

(61) $y = c$ iff $x \leqslant b$
                        $v = c'$ iff $x > b$.

Here c and c' are constants whose values are given. Now consider (60) and (61) relative to the question

(62)   What is the value of y at $x = a$?

---

[28] Kneale's *Probability and Induction*, pp. 228–30, offers the same explanation for the greater simplicity of (58) over (59). For Popper's theory, see his *Logic of Scientific Discovery*, particularly Chap. 7.

(60) needs no additional information to answer this question. However, for (61) to answer question (62), we must first know whether or not a is greater than b. So (60) is more informative, and hence simpler, than (61).[29]

This result precisely parallels our discussion of homogeneity/heterogeneity hypotheses in Section 2.1. Indeed, if the variable x represents time, then (61) is a change hypothesis and (60) is

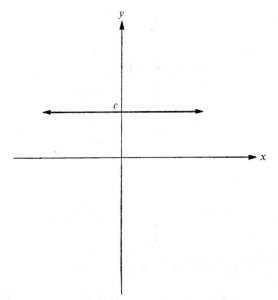

Fig. 2. A perspicuous representation of the equation '$y = c$', where x and y are natural properties

its no-change counterpart. In fact, if we also let the y variable represent emerald colour and the point b denote the year 2000, equations (60) and (61), respectively, represent the hypotheses 'All emeralds are green' and 'All emeralds are grue'.

How would we choose a coordinate system to represent the two equations graphically? A completely natural method is to let the x-axis represent time and the y-axis represent emerald colours. Equation (60) would be represented as Figure 2 and

[29] Notice that this simplicity ordering is preserved if we consider (60) and (61) relative to questions about the derivatives of y with respect to x.

equation (61) as Figure 3. However, there are other ways of representing the hypotheses. For example, if we let the *x*-axis represent time and the *y*-axis represent emerald *grulers*, (60) would be represented by Figure 3 and equation (61) by Figure 2.

The first method of representation is undoubtedly the more

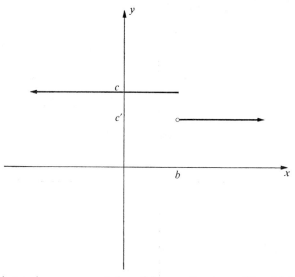

Fig. 3. A perspicuous representation of the equation '$y = c$ iff $x \leqslant b$ & $y = c'$ iff $x > b$', where x and y are natural properties

natural one, and the fact that we prefer it reveals an important aspect of our penchant for *perspicuous notation*. We select coordinate systems so that 'deep' properties, such as the simplicity of hypotheses, are manifested in 'surface' properties, such as whether a line is broken or not. This technique of representation seems so obvious as to be unworthy of mention, until we notice that from our intuitions about the simplicity of equations or hypotheses it is a further step to deciding what coordinate system or choice of notation to use in their representation. We will discuss this phenomenon again in Sections 3.5 and 4.5.

Now let us consider another pair of straight-line equations that are related in the same way as are (60) and (61):

(63) $y = mx + d$

(64)
$$y = mx + d \text{ iff } x \leqslant b$$
$$v = m'x + d' \text{ iff } x > b.$$

Here m, d, m', d', and b are constants whose values are given. By our policy of choosing perspicuous representations, equations (63) and (64) are respectively represented in Figures 4 and 5.

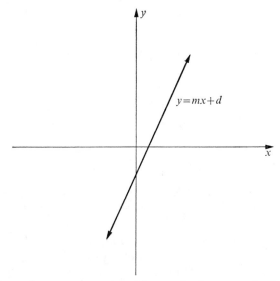

Fig. 4. A perspicuous representation of the equation '$y = mx + d$', where x and are natural properties

Notice that (63) and (64) are equally informative relative to a question about the value of y, because for either hypothesis to imply an answer, the value of x at the point in question must be conjoined with it. However, this parity breaks down once we begin considering questions about the derivatives of y. The first derivative of y in equation (63) is a constant, while the first derivative of y in (64) is not defined at point b, and has one value for points x such that $x < b$ and another value for points x such that $x > b$. Thus, relative to a question about the first derivative of y at an arbitrary point $x = a$, (63) is more informative than (64). The verdict favouring (63) over (64) holds for all further questions about the value of the nth derivative of y at $x = a$. (63) can answer a question about any derivative

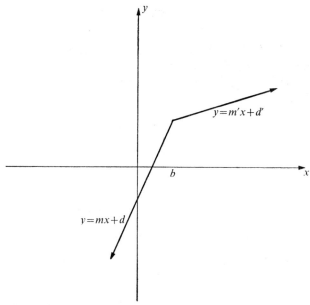

Fig. 5. A perspicuous representation of the equation '$y = mx + d$ iff $x \leqslant b$ & $= m'x + d'$ iff $x > b$', where x and y are natural properties

of y without needing any extra information, while (64) will always require extra information to yield an answer. We conclude that (63) is simpler than (64).

This result obtains for any continuous polynomial C and its discontinous counterpart D, for the derivatives of y in equation C eventually go to zero while the derivatives of y in equation D never become uniformly constant. This means that there is at best a finite number of questions such that $C =_s D$ and an infinite number of questions such that $C >_s D$. Therefore, C must be simpler than D, no matter what the order of the polynomials.[30] Similar results could be obtained for equations other than polynomials, so we may conclude that a continous curve is simpler than its discontinuous counterpart. This does not mean, however, that we are never justified in accepting a discontinuous hypothesis over its continuous counterpart. A

---

[30] An argument similar to this one would also show that where n is an integer and m is not, '$y = x^n$' is simpler than '$y = x^m$', relative to a battery of questions about the derivatives of y.

scientist may be justified in adopting the point of view that certain phenomena have discontinuous properties by the quite separate criterion of support or by simplicity considerations arising out of a broader theoretical context.

Now let us consider any two continuous polynomials N and M of order n and m, respectively. Assuming that $n > m$, we proceed to compare N and M relative to a series of questions, first about the value of y, then about the first derivative of y, then about the second derivative of y, and so on. For N, the first n questions will be such that the value of x at $x = a$ must be conjoined to N for it to yield an answer. N will be able to answer all of the subsequent questions without any outside help, since the nth and greater derivatives of y are constants. For M, the first m questions will be such that the value of x at $x = a$ must be plugged into M for it to imply an answer. Relative to the rest of the questions considered, M will be self-sufficient.

Since $n > m$, there will be some questions such that M is self-sufficient relative to them, but N is not. In fact, there will be $n - m$ questions relative to which M is more informative than N, but no question such that N is more informative than M. According to our theory of simplicity, then, M is simpler than N. Hence, the lower the order of a continuous polynomial, the simpler it is.[31]

Another intuition about the simplicity of equations that is amenable to our treatment is that circles are supposed to be simpler than ellipses. Consider how a specific circle hypothesis C and a specific ellipse hypothesis E would fare relative to either of the following questions:

What is the distance from the centre to point a on the curve?
What is the curvature of the curve at point a?

C requires no extra information to answer either question. For E to yield an answer, some extra information is needed—we

---

[31] As an example, let N be '$x^4 - 3x^3 + 32$' and let M be '$x^2 + 24x - 5$'. According to what we have just said, there should be $n - m$, or two, questions such that M is more informative than N, but no question for which this ordering is reversed. For N and M to answer questions about the oth and 1st derivatives, both require that the value of x at $x = a$ be conjoined. For the 2nd and 3rd derivatives, M requires no extra information to yield an answer, but N does. For all subsequent derivatives, neither hypothesis requires any extra information.

must know the coordinates of a. It follows that C is simpler than E relative to either question.[32]

The two questions above, in the way they are presently formulated, depart somewhat from the kinds of questions considered previously. They are not about the value of the variables that occur in the equations C and E, nor are they about the value of a derivative of these variables. This shows that a P-system consisting only of questions about the values and derivatives of variables cannot sustain comparisons between the simplicity of ellipse and circle hypotheses, while a P-system including either of the above two questions can. Finding out which properties are regarded as natural is just as much a job for the theory of simplicity as is discovering which hypotheses are simpler than others. In this case, we have used our intuitions about the simplicity of hypotheses to partially reconstruct a P-system on which such intuitions could rest.

It might be useful to reflect for a moment on the circumstances wherein our criterion of simplicity comes to bear in choosing between rival equations. In our outline of a theory of hypothesis choice, simplicity is balanced against support. In choosing between rival equations, interpreting 'support' as meaning 'goodness-of-fit' makes the role of simplicity more intuitive. Consider any n data points gathered from experiments and used as the basis for a general hypothesis about the relationship of the variables involved. Assume that there are two variables and that the data points are ordered pairs of numbers. In general, for any n data points there is a polynomial of order $n - 1$ which has perfect goodness-of-fit for those n points. For example, given two data points, there is a first-order equation (i.e., a straight line) which passes through both of them. Thus, we can always come up with perfect goodness-of-fit by accepting hypotheses of sufficiently high order.

However, even though we desire goodness-of-fit, we also show a preference for lower order equations. In this section, we have seen that the order of a polynomial is inversely related to its simplicity, given our conjecture that simplicity is informativeness. Thus, there is a tension between goodness-of-fit and

---

[32] Note that both questions have very natural physical interpretations where the competition between C and E takes the form of a debate over the orbit path of the earth around the sun.

simplicity. The former pulls towards higher order equations; the latter draws us towards lower order ones.[33] Our rules for hypothesis choice demand that these two tendencies be balanced off. ,

Based on our knowledge of the experimental conditions, we decide that any viable hypothesis must have more than some minimum degree of goodness-of-fit. The relative accuracy of the apparatus used, for example, may lead us to believe that any equation must fit the data points within certain limits. Given that two or more equations fit the data points to a degree greater than the minimum, we then take the simplest. Conversely, if two equations are equally simple, we choose the one which has better goodness-of-fit.

Such considerations relating specifically to equations accord well with our more general conception of how competing hypotheses are evaluated, but in the context of the curve-fitting problem, we do not have to leave the idea of support on a purely intuitive and informal level. Here at least, we can take the theory of hypothesis choice at its word, and it seems reasonable to suppose that our inferential behaviour in this context may be adequately explicated as a policy whose two components are support and simplicity.

The theory of simplicity is open-ended. Presumably, more simplicity judgements on pairs of hypotheses can be mirrored within the theory, and some of these judgements would involve using questions about mathematical properties that go well beyond the few examples (i.e., value of a variable, value of a derivative, radius, curvature) that have actually been mentioned. Although the kinds of examples given in this section are not exhaustive, it would be wrong to think that the theory is adequate only if *every* pair of equations can be definitively compared for simplicity by our theory. Some equations will have such thoroughly different values that the supporting evidence, and not dictates of simplicity, is the relevant standard of choice. Also, some equations are simple because of the laws in which they are embedded, and one cannot expect that this contextual source of simplicity will always manifest itself in the

---

[33] This does not mean that for any set of data points, an equation of order $n + 1$ has better goodness-of-fit than an equation of order n. Sometimes an increase in order will result in worse goodness-of-fit over the short run.

hypotheses considered in isolation. Nevertheless, these caveats do not obscure the fact that the examples given in this section are few and far from diverse. Consequently, the degree to which the theory applies to and illuminates this area remains an open question.

2.7 The Order of Quantifiers

One of the properties of the rules given in Section 1.4 for constructing the contribution that a hypothesis makes to answering a question is that hypotheses that differ only in the order of their quantifiers make the same contribution towards answering a given question. This would suggest that

$$(65) \qquad\qquad (x)(\exists y)(\ldots)$$

would have to be just as simple as

$$(66) \qquad\qquad (\exists y)(x)(\ldots),$$

since they would end up being equally informative. Such a consequence would count against any theory of simplicity, because the order of quantifiers has consequences for the existential commitments of a hypothesis; and surely this is one of the factors that any theory of simplicity should be sensitive to.

However, the theory provides a way to understand the difference in simplicity between hypotheses that differ only with respect to the order of their quantifiers. Let's take (65) and (66) as an example, and consider how they could conceivably differ in truth value. Since (66) implies (65), we must look at the case in which (66) is false and (65) is true. In such a world, there would have to be at least two ys such that (65) is true. On the other hand, in a world where (66) is true (and, hence, (65) is true), we are committed to the existence of only one y. Thus, in so far as (65) and (66) differ, (65) makes more existential commitments than (66). This provides us with a reason—which appeals to our intuitions and is vindicated by the theory—for saying that (66) is simpler than (65).

We can generalize this result by saying that moving an existential quantifier from the right to the left of a universal quantifier yields a gain in simplicity. Of course, some pairs of hypotheses differ only with respect to the order of their quantifiers, yet their simplicity ordering is not determined by this result. For example, how are we to handle

(67) $(x)(\exists y)(w)(z)(\exists v)(\ldots)$

and

(68) $(x)(w)(\exists y)(\exists v)(z)(\ldots)$?

Here, we are faced with another weighting problem. We must decide which is more important, the loss in simplicity that comes from moving the quantifier '$\exists y$' one place to the right or the gain in simplicity that comes from moving the quantifier '$\exists v$' one place to the left. Once we decide this, perhaps by consulting theoretical issues that occur in a wider context, we can compare the simplicity of (67) and (68) as before.

Our conclusion about the order of quantifiers can also be derived via the heuristic device sometimes used to introduce the idea of functional normal forms.[34] The hypotheses

(69a) $(x)(y)(z)(\exists w)(Fxyzw)$

and

(70a) $(x)(\exists w)(y)(z)(Fxyzw)$

differ in that in (69a), one's choice of w turns on one's choice of x, y, and z; while in (70a) one's choice of w turns only on one's choice of x. If we allow the variables 'G' and 'H' to range over functions, we can express this difference as follows:

(69b) $(\exists G)(x)(y)(z)[G(x, y, z) = w \ \& \ Fxyzw]$

(70b) $(\exists H)(x)(y)(z)[H(x) = w \ \& \ Fxyzw]$.

By existential instantiation of (69b) and (70b), we get

(69c) $(x)(y)(z)[g(x, y, z) = w \ \& \ Fxyzw]$

(70c) $(x)(y)(z)[h(x) = w \ \& \ Fxyzw]$.

If we compare the simplicity of (69c) and (70c) relative to the question

What is the value of 'w' in situation s?

(70c) will be simpler. This is an example of the result (obtained in Section 2.4) indicating that the fewer the number of variables in an equation, the simpler it is.

---

[34] See Quine's *Methods of Logic*, p. 186. The line of argument is only heuristic, since it presupposes the axiom of choice.

Taken together, these two arguments make clear how the order of quantifiers affects simplicity. By moving an existential quantifier from the right to the left of a universal quantifier, one reduces one's existential commitments (in the sense indicated) and also reduces the number of previous universal instantiations on which the instantiation of the existential quantifier depends.

2.8 Logical Simplicity

The theory of simplicity applies to hypotheses without regard to their subject matter. Thus, conjectures in mathematics, sufficiently supported by incomplete evidence, could be selected for their simplicity. However, mathematicians at first glance seem not to be particularly interested in choosing mathematical hypotheses in situations of uncertainty on the basis of simplicity. Mathematicians are interested in proofs, and simplicity appears to be used more as a desideratum in the construction of formal systems than as a criterion for accepting hypotheses.

On closer inspection, however, the role of simplicity in mathematics and its role in the rest of science are not so far apart. Although mathematicians are interested in proofs of theorems, their selection of fundamental assumptions is influenced by simplicity just as the scientist's construction of theory is. In both science and mathematics, the basic assumptions of theories are at once rooted in and transcend the evidence. The choice of theoretical postulates, whether it is said to derive from 'scientific method' or from 'mathematical intuition', obeys a simplicity constraint. And not only is it misleading to think that the methodologies of science and mathematics differ in their use of simplicity in choosing basic postulates; but also the very distinction of science and mathematics as separate areas of inquiry is somewhat artificial. Results in each area influence and justify choices in the other.

Thus, simplicity can be a factor governing one's choice of basic beliefs in a given body of mathematical phenomena. But given a set of axioms chosen in this way, judgements of simplicity can occur without serving as reasons for belief. This manifests itself in the fact that at times a proof is said to simplify our view of a body of mathematical phenomena. We did not accept the theorem proved on grounds of simplicity; we accepted it because it was proved. Yet a byproduct of the proof is a gain in simplicity. To show how this is possible, I first want to show why the hypothesis that a sentence s is provable from a set of assumptions P,

(71a) $$\vdash_P s,$$

is simpler than the hypothesis that s is not provable from P,

(72a) $$\nvdash_P s.$$

Put model theoretically, (71a) asserts that s is true in every world w that is a model for P. If we let the predicate 'S' mean 'the sentence s is true in world w', then (71a) may be rewritten as

(71b) $$(w)(Sw).$$

According to (72a), there is at least one model of P in which s comes out false:

(72b) $$(\exists w)(\sim Sw).$$

Now let us compare (71b) and (72b) relative to the question of whether the sentence s is true in a given model of P. Where P is taken to be true, the question might be 'Is s true in the actual world?':

$$(Sa, \sim Sa).$$

(71b) can answer this question without any outside help, whereas (72b) requires some extra information to yield an answer. (71b) is the more informative hypothesis relative to this question, so it is simpler than (72b).

What can we conclude from this difference in simplicity? According to (71a), assuming P renders s redundant; on this view s is derivable from more basic propositions. However, according to (72a), s is *sui generis* relative to the assumptions in P. Now, of course, (71a) and (72a) are incompatible, and a mathematician would choose between them by attempting to prove one or the other. Yet if (71a) were proved, this would mean that if P is a proposed set of axioms for a field of knowledge, the axioms would not have to be augmented to capture the truth of s. On the other hand, if (72a) were proved, the axioms would have to be enlarged to include s, if they are to be adequate for the field being axiomatized. That is, of the two alternatives (71a) and (72a), the proof of the simpler does not force an increase in the axioms, while a proof of the more complex does lead to an increase in the postulated basis.

This mirrors our belief that a contraction in the axiom set is a gain in simplicity. Moreover, a proof that the axioms are mutually independent is a proof that the axiom set is maximally simple; no axiom is redundant. And a proof that the axiom set is complete simplifies our view of the area being axiomatized, for it assures us that relative to the axiom set, every truth is redundant.

These results having to do with axioms can be duplicated for proposed formulations of the primitive predicates of an area of discourse. Given a set P of predicates which is proposed as a formulation of the primitive predicates, showing that a predicate s is definable in terms of P is a simpler outcome than showing that s is not so definable. In the latter case, the set of primitives must be enlarged to accommodate s; in the former case, no such enlargement is required.

Given that an axiom's being redundant is simpler than its being indispensable, we must explain why we want to eliminate redundant statements from the axiom set. In an earlier day, the axioms were supposed to be those truths which were most basic; discovering that a truth was derivable was tantamount to discovering that it was not an axiom. Within our present, more pragmatic epistemology of mathematics, there can be as many different axiom sets as there are purposes in formalizing. Yet even with this tolerant turn, the older policy on redundant axioms persists: Given any selection of truths which are provisionally and pragmatically designated as basic, a truth that is derivable from the set is not itself basic. Mathematicians, like scientists in general, try to minimize unproved assumptions. When postulates are proffered as basic, they assume that no assumption is known to be provable from the rest; if it were, it would not have been designated as basic in the first place.

The conclusions obtained above apply only to cases in which one axiom set or set of primitive predicates is part of another. However, most simplicity judgements on formal systems apply not to this special case but to pairs of sets which at best overlap and often don't even do that. To mirror such intuitions within our theory, I will first show how certain standard logical properties of predicates are related to simplicity and then I will give a more systematic characterization of the logical simplicity of primitive predicates. The simplicity of predicates will be explained in terms of the simplicity of hypotheses that express some of their logical properties, because the theory of simplicity is first and foremost a theory of the simplicity of hypotheses. A similar strategy is used in Chapter 4 where the simplicity of pictures and perceptual judgements is explicated in terms of the simplicity of hypotheses that describe them.

First,

$$(73) \qquad (x)(y)(z)[(Rxy \ \& \ Ryz) \supset Rxz)^{35}$$

is equal in simplicity to

$$(x)(y)(z)[(Rxy \ \& \ Ryz) \supset \sim Rxz]$$

relative to the question

$$(74) \qquad (Rab, \sim Rab).$$

Furthermore, (73) is simpler than its negation relative to question (74). Thus, relative to (74),

(75) R is transitive $=_s R$ is intransitive $>_s R$ is nontransitive.

Similarly, relative to the question

$$(76) \qquad (Raa, \sim Raa),$$

the hypotheses

$$(77) \qquad (x)(Rxx)$$

and

$$(78) \qquad (x)(\sim Rxx)$$

are equally simple. Moreover, (77) and (78) are each simpler than the conjunction of their negations, relative to question (76). Hence,

(79) R is reflexive $=_s R$ is irreflexive $>_s R$ is nonreflexive.

We can prove similar results for symmetry and its kindred relations. The hypothesis

$$(80) \qquad (x)(y)(Rxv \supset Ryx)$$

is just as simple as

$$(81) \qquad (x)(y)(Rxy \supset \sim Ryx)$$

---

[35] MEI construction for most of the remaining hypotheses in this section requires the procedure given in the Appendix, in that the special assumptions of footnote 8 of Chapter 1 do not obtain.

relative to question (74), and relative to the same question (81) is simpler than

(82) $(x)(y)[(Rxy \ \& \ x \neq y) \supset \sim Ryx]$.

Each of (80) to (82) is simpler than the conjunction oɪ their negations, so we have shown that

(83) R is symmetrical $=_s R$ is asymmetrical $>_s R$ is anti-symmetrical $>_s R$ is nonsymmetrical.

One more result of this kind will allow us to compare the simplicity of different orderings that R might impose on a given domain. Since

$$(x)(y)[x \neq y \supset (Rxy \lor Ryx)]$$

is less simple than

$$(x)(y)(Rxy \lor Ryx)$$

relative to question (74), it follows that

(84) R is strongly connected $>_s R$ is connected.

We now give the customary definitions for some kinds of orderings that R might provide for a set.

R is a quasi-ordering $=_{df} R$ is reflexive and transitive.

R is a partial ordering $=_{df} R$ is reflexive, transitive, and antisymmetric.

R is a simple ordering $=_{df} R$ is reflexive, transitive, anti-symmetric, and connected.

R is a strict partial ordering $=_{df} R$ is asymmetrical and transitive.

R is a strict simple ordering $=_{df} R$ is asymmetrical, transitive, and connected.

These definitions allow us to conclude that relative to question (74), the simplicities of these various orderings are related as follows:

(85) R is a simple ordering $>_s R$ is a partial ordering $>_s$ R is a quasi-ordering.

(86) R is a strict simple ordering $>_s R$ is a strict partial ordering.

Evidently, the names 'simple ordering' and 'strict simple ordering' were well chosen.

Notice that all of the conclusions above are simplicity comparisons of the form ' "relation R has property F" is simpler than "relation R has property G" '. We can expand these results in order to compare different predicates for the simplicity of their logical properties, once we recognize what it is for us to be interested in *logical* simplicity. Logical simplicity is the kind of simplicity a predicate has solely in virtue of its logical properties: Any two predicates that have all the same logical properties must be equally simple and may be viewed as identical for the purposes of our theory. If we admit further that the total simplicity of a predicate is a composition of the simplicity of its different logical properties, we may assume that for any two predicates R and S and for any logical property F, 'R has F' is equal in simplicity to 'S has F'. This enables us to show, for example, that one predicate's being symmetrical and another's being nonsymmetrical counts in favour of the greater simplicity of the former. In fact the conclusions on the logical properties of predicates ((75), (79), (83), (84), (85), and (86)), augmented by this postulate of the identity of indiscernibles, allows us to compare the logical simplicity of any two predicates with respect to those logical properties.

Another feature of predicates that seems relevant to assessing their logical simplicity is the number of places that they have. We can use Tarski's idea of a sequence of things *satisfying* a predicate to characterize what it is for a predicate to have n places. We will then show that 'P has n places' is less simple than 'P has $n - 1$ places', and by the kind of argument given in the preceding paragraph we can conclude that 'P has n places' is less simple than 'Q has $n - 1$ places'. We will regard sequences as always having infinite length. The sequence written as ⟨Madison, Wisconsin⟩ can be construed as having infinite length by letting its last member repeat indefinitely. This sequence satisfies the predicate 'x is the capital of y'. Another sequence that satisfies this predicate is ⟨Madison, Wisconsin, Julius Caesar⟩. The predicate has two places in that there are precisely two members of any sequence that matter in determining whether the sequence satisfies the predicate.

Where s and t range over sequences and x_i indicates the ith member of the sequence x, we can represent the claim that P has no more than n places as follows:

(87) $(\exists a_1)(\exists a_2) \ldots (\exists a_n)(s)(t)[(s$ satisfies P &

$\qquad s_{a_1} = t_{a_1}$ & $\ldots$ & $s_{a_n} = t_{a_n}) \supset t$ satisfies $P]$.

Similarly to assert that P has no less than n places is just to say:

(88) $(a_i)(\exists s)(\exists t)\{i \leqslant n \supset [s$ satisfies P &

$\qquad t = \text{Sub} \ (t_{a_i}, s_{a_i}, s)$ & $\sim(t$ satisfies $P)]\}$.

Here 'Sub (x, y, s)' denotes the result of substituting x for y in s. The conjunction of (87) and (88) represents the claim that P has precisely n places. This definition of 'P has n places' mirrors the idea that the number of places a predicate has is the number of places in any sequence that affect whether the sequence satisfies the predicate.

As might be expected, the greater simplicity of 'P has $n - 1$ places' over 'P has n places' is due to the greater simplicity of 'P has no more than $n - 1$ places' over 'P has no more than n places'. 'P has $n - 1$ places' is the simpler hypothesis because it puts a lower ceiling on the number of places in P than does the hypothesis 'P has n places'. To see this, let us compare (87) with the following hypothesis, which says that P has no more than $n - 1$ places:

(89) $(\exists a_1)(\exists a_2) \ldots (\exists a_{n-1})(s)(t)[(s$ satisfies P &

$\qquad s_{a_1} = t_{a_1}$ & $\ldots$ & $s_{a_{n-1}} = t_{a_{n-1}}) \supset t$ satisfies $P]$.

(89) is simpler than (87), relative to the question

$\qquad (a$ satisfies P, a does not satisfy $P)$.

We are now able to compare the logical simplicity of any two predicates with respect to a number of logical properties. Presumably, the number of relevant logical properties could be expanded. For example, it can be shown that a predicate that is self-complete[36] is simpler on that count than one that is not. Yet the kinds of results we have been obtaining are fairly weak. They allow us to compare the simplicity of two predicates with respect to this or that logical property but do not tell us how to calculate the total relative simplicity of two predicates from their simplicity relative to a number of individual logical features. Here again, we encounter a weighting problem (see

[36] See Goodman's *The Structure of Appearance*, Chap. 3, for the definition of 'self-completeness' and other logical properties of predicates. Goodman's calculus of logical simplicity is undoubtedly the most systematic and detailed explication of this concept currently available.

Section 1.8). When we leave the level of individual predicates and proceed to the level of sets of predicates (predicate bases), the same problem occurs. The simplicity of the basis is a function of the simplicity of the member predicates, but some weighting of predicates will usually be needed to make the transition. In all of these respects, it is quite obvious that Goodman's calculus of logical simplicity provides much stronger results than ours does. In Goodman's system, a numerical complexity value is assigned to any predicate basis. It would be interesting to investigate how many of Goodman's comparative judgements are preserved or violated by our proposals, but this would take us too far afield.

2.9 Trade-Offs in Simplicity

Until now we have mainly considered pairs of hypotheses of a very special sort, in that no matter which of several natural-sounding questions was used to assess their relative simplicity, the same result ensued. For example,

$$(90) \qquad\qquad y = x + w$$

is simpler than

$$(91) \qquad\qquad y = x + w + z,$$

no matter which of the following questions is used in comparing the two:

(92)   What is the value of y in situation a?
          What is the value of x in situation a?
          What is the value of w in situation a?

Note that (90) is not defined relative to a question about the value of z, so (90) and (91) are incommensurable relative to that question. Since (90) *dominates* (91) relative to the questions in (92), there is no need to weight the questions in (92) as to their relative impact on the total simplicity of (90) and (91). In this sense, our comparisons of (90) and (91) may be said to be question-invariant. (90) and (91) represent an example of the 'special case' discussed in Section 1.8.

But when hypotheses are not thus isolated from the theoretical context in which they are embedded, such neat results tend to disappear, and one is again faced with a weighting problem. Thus, consider a theory T which has a rather swollen ontology but which posits relatively few changes and hetero-geneities in the universe. Opposing T is a theory T' with a sparser ontology but committed to many changes and hetero-geneities. Here is a case where relative to some predicate families (which focus on the existential commitments of T and T'), T' is simpler than T, but relative to other predicate families (which focus on the heterogeneity and homogeneity hypotheses in T and T'), T is simpler than T'. The two groups of predicate families may both be part of a single coherent P-system. The problem is to weight the dictates of the two groups in order to calculate the relative simplicity of T and T' with respect to the entire P-system.

Thus, the weighting problem is not an idiosyncratic artefact of our theory. Rather, playing off a gain in simplicity in one area against a loss of simplicity in another is at the very heart of the use of simplicity in hypothesis choice. Because of this, the question-relativity of the theory, far from rendering it hopelessly obscure or inapplicable, offers a framework within which these reciprocal and interpenetrating considerations can be understood.

3

Simplicity in Transformational Phonology

3.1 Introduction

In Chapter 2, we tested the theory of simplicity by discerning certain very general policies in our inferential behaviour that seem to be intuitive examples of 'preferring the simpler alternative' and showing that the theory mirrors and explicates these intuitions. Thus far, the interest of the theory lies in its showing how seemingly diverse phenomena have a common logical basis. In this chapter, the theory is used in the service of a slightly different task. Rather than unite disparate details of inferential practice, I want to show how the theory makes clear the substance of one particular debate concerning simplicity that has occurred in science. The objective here is depth rather than breadth; that is, to yield insights into a single strain of theorizing.

The example I have chosen is the attempt by Chomsky and Halle to frame a simplicity criterion for the phonological component of a transformational grammar. Their work has a unique interest for our theory in that it is probably the most detailed attempt by scientists to articulate a simplicity criterion in a form explicit enough to yield unequivocal applications to particular cases. Chomsky and Halle defend their theory by showing that it captures the intuitive simplicity judgements of linguists. Beyond trying to show that their theory coincides with the realities of scientific practice, Chomsky and Halle also argue that their theory of simplicity helps explain related concepts like natural kinds and law-likeness. Thus, their work is of interest to our theory of simplicity for at least two reasons: First, their theory provides a rich range of intuitive simplicity judgements that we can use to test our own theory. Second, in that their theory tries to relate simplicity to other desiderata, mirroring these connections within our own theory of simplicity would enhance the explanatory power of our proposal.

Despite its multifaceted relevance to our theory of simplicity, this body of work by Chomsky and Halle soon reveals some perplexing features. Why, for example, did they bother to explicate simplicity at all, given that scientists usually are quite happy to appeal to simplicity without offering any systematic account of what it is? Another problem is the repeated claim that their notion of simplicity is purely internal to the theory of transformational grammar and need have no significant similarities with the notion of simplicity discussed in philosophy of science. Why did Chomsky make this claim, and how does it bear on our own theory of simplicity? Reflecting on these questions will lead to some practical consequences that our theory might have for work in linguistics.

Before proceeding further, it might be useful for me to give a preliminary indication of the relation I see between Chomsky and Halle's theory and mine. I stressed earlier (in Section 1.8) the reciprocal influence of one's simplicity judgements and one's choice of natural predicates. This relationship is manifest in Chomsky and Halle's discussion, in that they are trying to construct simultaneously a set of natural phonological kinds and an adequate simplicity measure. Yet this affinity helps explain why it would be a mistake to view their proposal and our own conjecture as two alternatives on the same level. From their point of view, ours is only half a theory; we provide an explicit simplicity criterion but fail to provide an enumeration of natural kinds. This omission of natural kinds means that even if our theory is accepted, much linguistics needs to be done before the simplicity criterion can do the theoretical work linguists want it to. On the other hand, our theory's lack of specifically linguistic content means that it is general and can show how the issue of simplicity in linguistics fits into a larger context. This feature has the curious consequence that both the Chomsky–Halle proposal and the proposals of some of their critics (see Section 3.5) can be mirrored in our theory. Thus, our theory of simplicity is offered less as an incompatible alternative to Chomsky and Halle's than as a framework within which their theory can be understood.

In what follows, I explain Chomsky and Halle's view of the role of simplicity in linguistic theory and the details of their simplicity criterion. Then I show how my theory reflects the kinds of intuitions they had about simplicity and how it accounts for most of the particular cases that they thought important. After that, I examine two modifications of Chomsky and Halle's theory suggested by Contreras and Bach and argue that my theory of simplicity mirrors their intuitions as well. Section 3.6 deals with the issue of spurious generalizations and clears up a seemingly paradoxical consequence of my theory. In the conclusion, I discuss what my theory shows about the role of a theory of simplicity in linguistics.

3.2 Chomsky and Halle on the Role of a Simplicity Criterion in Linguistic Theory

Between 1957 and 1968, Chomsky and Halle wrote a series of books and articles in which a recurrent theme was the relationship of a general linguistic theory to the grammar of any particular language. Constant through this period is the belief that a linguistic theory must provide a simplicity measure which ranks alternative grammars according to how well they describe the language in question. Their published views on the role of this simplicity criterion have undergone a subtle change in this period, a change brought about by an alteration in their account of the role of linguistic theory as a whole.[1]

In *Syntactic Structures* (pp. 51 ff.), Chomsky discusses three constraints that might be placed on the relationship between a linguistic theory and the grammar of a particular language. These three possibilities are represented in Figure 6. In all three cases, the box is a linguistic theory containing, among other things, a simplicity criterion.

The strongest requirement that we could place on a linguistic theory is that it provide us with a mechanical method whereby a grammar for a language L is constructed out of a given corpus of utterances from L. This is the requirement that is pictured in

[1] In *Chomsky*, p. 63, Lyons quotes Chomsky as saying that there has been no change in his views on simplicity through the years. Chomsky does say, however, that there has been a shift of emphasis in his published work from weak to strong generative capacity. Perhaps it would be more accurate for us to say that we want to explain this shift in emphasis and its connection with Chomsky's view of linguistic theory as a whole.

(i). A less stringent demand, pictured in (ii), is that a linguistic theory provide a method for saying of a given grammar for L and a corpus of utterances from L whether or not that grammar is the best grammar for L, based on the corpus at hand. The weakest condition, (iii), requires only that the linguistic theory give us a method for saying which of any two proposed grammars is better, relative to the given corpus of utterances. If a linguistic theory satisfies condition (i), it is said to provide a *discovery procedure*; if it satisfies (ii), it is said to provide a *decision*

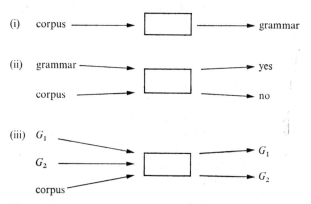

Fig. 6. Three alternative constraints on a linguistic theory (from Chomsky, *Syntactic Structures*, p. 51)

procedure; and if it satisfies (iii), it provides an *evaluation procedure*.

Chomsky then goes on to say that a linguistic theory need only provide us with an evaluation procedure, the other conditions, particularly condition (i), being too demanding, relatively unilluminating, and perhaps unattainable. By 'lowering our sights to this more modest level', Chomsky wanted to bypass the lengthy discussions of discovery procedures that had preoccupied Bloomfieldian linguistics. One was to ignore the problem of how grammars are to be invented. Our interest, as linguists, is confined to evaluating grammars once we have managed to come up with them.

An important reason that Bloomfieldian linguistics had insisted on the formulation of discovery procedures[2] was its

[2] In *Syntactic Structures*, p. 52, Chomsky remarks that many of these attempts to provide discovery procedures at most provide only evaluation procedures.

practical concern with recording the grammars of American Indian languages. These languages were very different from European ones, and it was feared that important ethnocentric biases would enter into their analysis unless methods of discovery were rigorously articulated. Another factor (whether it was a reason or an ideological concomitant is hard to say) in this concern with discovery procedures was the desire to make linguistics 'scientific', which was taken to mean narrowly empirical and behaviourist. The laying down of operational procedures was supposed to purge linguistics of mentalistic and metaphysical obscurity.[3]

Just as Bloomfield's desire for discovery procedures was in keeping with the larger philosophical climate of behaviourism, so Chomsky's eschewing of discovery procedures drew on the familiar philosophical distinction between the context of discovery and the context of justification.[4] The former was regarded with suspicion as a matter for psychology, or worse, as having no interesting general structure (the idea being that somehow there are no interesting regularities underlying how people come to hold a given belief).[5] Philosophers of science, with some exceptions, usually confined their attention to the logic of justification and advised scientists to do likewise. It was argued that one invented theories any way one could; the 'real' problem consisted in evaluating them.

This historical fact helps explain why Chomsky and Halle rejected the goal of discovery procedures,[6] but it fails to help us

[3] This emphasis on detailing methods for constructing a grammar out of a corpus of utterances and a set of elementary speaker judgements is especially prominent in Harris' *Methods in Structural Linguistics*. In 'Some Controversial Questions in Phonological Theory', p. 103, Chomsky and Halle quote Bloomfield as saying that linguistics was the first social science to rid itself of the 'elusive spiritistic–teleologic words of our tribal speech'.

[4] This has been a standard distinction in technical philosophy from Frege on. See, for example, Frege's *Foundations of Arithmetic*, pp. v–x; Reichenbach's *Experience and Prediction*, pp. 6–7; and Hempel's *Philosophy of Natural Science*, pp. 14–18. Quine's 'Epistomology Naturalized' (in *Ontological Relativity*, pp. 69–90) can be seen as an attack on the distinction.

[5] This latter, more radical, claim seems to be implicit in the usual assertion that the incredible diversity of ways in which different people come to believe a given proposition shows that the context of discovery has little to do with the cognitive content or justification of the proposition. In Chapter 4, I argue that the psychology of perceptual knowledge is not idiosyncratic in this way.

[6] In 'Phonology in Generative Grammar', p. 335, Halle imposes the same constraint on linguistic theory.

understand why they thought that a linguistic theory should provide any sort of simplicity measure at all. In presenting a theory, scientists usually leave the standards against which they expect it to be evaluated on a largely imprecise and tacit level. At most, they offer some precise interpretation of 'fitting the data' (e.g., in terms of a goodness-of-fit measure), but they give no formal account of notions like 'simplicity', 'explanatory power', or 'naturalness'. Chomsky realizes the virtual uniqueness of the attention of linguists to evaluation procedures when he says in *Syntactic Structures* (p. 53):

There are few areas of science in which one would seriously consider the possibility of developing a general, practical, mechanical method for choosing among several theories, each compatible with the available data.

It is important to point out that Chomsky's reasons for abandoning discovery procedures in *Syntactic Structures* do not explicitly include mention of any adoption of a mentalistic point of view. Although linguists like Bloomfield and Harris wanted discovery procedures as a hedge against mentalism, the connection between requiring discovery procedures and eschewing mentalism seems somewhat accidental. Moreover, to call *Syntactic Structures* 'mentalistic' would be quite misleading in any case. In fact, Chomsky begins to write that a linguistic theory should provide discovery procedures precisely when he explicitly adopts a more mentalistic point of view.[7] We will leave these questions about Chomsky and Halle's requirement of an evaluation procedure and go on to examine their different attitude towards linguistic theory in two works published in 1965. Then, we will explain the shift in their view by contrasting the relatively formal emphasis of *Syntactic Structures* with the relatively psychological emphasis of their later work.

In Chomsky's *Aspects of the Theory of Syntax* (p. 30) and in Chomsky and Halle's 'Some Controversial Questions in Phonological Theory' (p. 100), the demands on a linguistic theory become much stronger. The requirement in these works is that

---

[7] Although both Bloomfield and Chomsky (in his published writings from about 1965) advocate the search for discovery procedures, the kinds of discovery procedures they wanted were as different as their reasons for wanting them. Thus, I am using 'discovery procedure' to pick out certain formal properties of linguistic theories and not to denote any particular substantive proposal.

a linguistic theory include a method both for constructing alternative grammars compatible with a corpus and for choosing among these alternatives and selecting the best one. That is, Chomsky and Halle seem now to require that a linguistic theory provide a discovery procedure. A justification for this shift becomes obvious if one considers the picture of linguistic theory as a psychological theory that has been so prominent in Chomsky's publications since 1965. In their 1965 paper (p. 100), Chomsky and Halle say that a linguistic theory is to be taken as a model of language acquisition. Just as a child attains competence in a language after hearing only a small and imperfect sample of utterances, so a model of language acquisition must generate a maximally valued grammar based on a finite and incomplete sample corpus. Chomsky and Halle

Fig. 7. Linguistic theory as a language acquisition device (from Chomsky and Halle, 'Some Controversial Questions in Phonological Theory', p. 100)

picture this constraint on the relationship between a linguistic theory and a grammar in a manner closely akin to condition (i) of Figure 6 (see Figure 7).

The acquisition model is usually described as working in two steps. First, it generates a set of alternative grammars, each of which fits the primary linguistic data. Then a simplicity criterion is applied which orders the competitors. The maximally valued grammar (or the grammars tied for first place) among these is the one chosen. The similarity of this set of rules to our own rules for hypothesis choice given in Section 1.9 is interesting. Here, as before, one chooses the simplest from the field of more than minimally supported competitors. Notice also that even though this acquisition model provides a discovery procedure, the simplicity criterion in it provides only an evaluation procedure; that is, it only allows us to compare pairs of hypotheses (grammars) for simplicity.

Given this psychological interpretation of linguistic theory, it is clear why such a theory must provide a discovery procedure rather than just a decision or an evaluation procedure. In both conditions (ii) and (iii) in Figure 6, the grammars considered by a linguistic theory have not been generated by that theory, but are imported fully formed from the outside. This point of view simply does not fit in with a psychological interpretation of linguistic theory as a model of language acquisition. Thus, Chomsky and Halle's psychological interpretation of linguistic theory presupposes the requirement of a discovery procedure. This reinforces our previous conjecture that their eschewing discovery procedures at an earlier date was the result of the influence of contemporary empiricism with its antipsychologism and its devaluation of the context of discovery. To be sure, *Syntactic Structures* characterizes grammar as the end product of language acquisition (p. 15):

Any grammar of a language will *project* the finite and somewhat accidental corpus of observed utterances to a set (presumably infinite) of grammatical utterances. In this respect a grammar mirrors the behavior of the speaker who, on the basis of a finite and accidental experience with language, can produce or understand an indefinite number of new sentences.

However, in spite of this tendency to think of grammars as admitting of an interesting psychological interpretation, Chomsky shows little inclination to treat linguistic theory in the same way.

In *Syntactic Structures*, Chomsky was interested in outlining a linguistic theory within which the notion 'grammatical in *L*' could be defined for any human language *L*. To this end, he considered various ways of representing the syntax of some parts of English, and he eliminated several alternatives by showing that they were inadequate or clumsy. Chomsky used a notion of simplicity to show that his transformational approach yields more perspicuous descriptions of English than do the other alternatives. This notion of simplicity, once explicated, was to form a part of linguistic theory. As such, it was to provide a basis for choosing some grammars over others, and more generally, it was to be a criterion for choosing some ways of representing grammar over others.

Thus, in *Syntactic Structures*, Chomsky conceived of linguistic theory as a metatheory which describes the form of certain formal objects called 'grammars'. Although these grammars describe human behaviour and dispositions, the metatheory is not primarily conceived of as a description of human mental structure. Rather, linguistic theory provides a general standard which allows one to compare the adequacy of pairs of grammars. From this point of view, it makes sense to require of a linguistic theory that it be related to grammars of languages in the same way that any set of conditions of adequacy is related to the theories it is meant to constrain. Condition (iii) of Figure 6, that of evaluation procedures, seemed the most reasonable alternative.

However, by the time of *Aspects of the Theory of Syntax*, both particular grammars and linguistic theory were taken to describe human behaviour and dispositions. This new psychological emphasis made it impossible to merely require of a linguistic theory that it provide an evaluation procedure and made discovery procedures the most reasonable choice. Thus, the goal of a linguistic theory, as it is presented in *Aspects of the Theory of Syntax* and has been elaborated since, is to explicate a certain range of inferential behaviour, namely the process whereby a child acquires competence in a language on the basis of incomplete evidence. It now becomes clear why linguistic theory, so construed, must offer a fully explicit account of simplicity, while a theory of physics, say, may leave the notion of simplicity on a purely intuitive and informal basis. A linguistic theory must do for language acquisition what a theory of scientific inference must do for scientific inference in general. In both cases, 'simplicity' is not just a part of the informal conditions of adequacy we place on our own proposed theories; rather, simplicity forms a part of the phenomenon we have set ourselves the task of explaining.

3.3 Chomsky and Halle's Simplicity Measure

In this section, I describe the simplicity criterion first proposed by Halle and then developed more fully by Chomsky and Halle.[8] This criterion evaluates phonological rules in terms of the number of symbols they contain. I begin with a rough characterization of the phonological component of a transformational grammar.

Suppose that we have a transformational syntax which

---

[8] See Halle's 'On the Role of Simplicity in Linguistic Descriptions', his 'Phonology in Generative Grammar', his 'On the Bases of Phonology', and Chomsky and Halle's *The Sound Pattern of English*.

generates all and only the syntactically well-formed strings in a language. The task of the phonological component is simply to assign phonological interpretations to each syntactic string; that is, to transform syntactic elements into sound.[9] Each syntactic output is a string of formatives, in particular, a labelled bracketing of formatives. Each formative will have certain phonological information about it registered in the lexicon (where resides some basic syntactic and semantic information as well). The phonological component works by consulting the lexicon and extracting information about each formative. Then, on the basis of this information, it subjects the formatives (taken as basic phonological concatenations) to certain transformations whose end result is the phonological interpretation of the string.

This raises the question of what phonological information goes into the lexicon. It might seem that we could trivially pack all of the phonological information into the lexicon and get a phonological representation of a string by using the lexicon like a dictionary. On the other hand, we could leave the lexicon empty and state every phonological fact about the language in terms of a transformation rule. These two extreme policies are rejected by Chomsky and Halle because they want to use the lexicon/phonological rules distinction as a way of separating accidental from law-like facts about the language. The brute givens—the accidental particular facts—are put into the lexicon, and all of the law-like generalities are put into the rules.[10] The obvious question here is how Chomsky and Halle distinguish accidental from law-like facts. This will become clearer after we have gone some way in understanding how their simplicity criterion works.

In 'Phonology in Generative Grammar', Halle characterizes the phonological component of a generative grammar as a set of rules, each having the form

(1) $P \to Q$ in the environment $X\_\_\_Y$,

where P, Q, X, and Y are 'symbols of a particular alphabet or

---

[9] We ignore here the difference between phonetic and phonological representation in order not to complicate the exposition unnecessarily. We also ignore for the moment the explanatory functions of the phonological component. These will be taken up later.

[10] In *Language*, p. 274, Bloomfield distinguishes lexical entries from law-like generalizations in the same way.

zero', and ' → ' means 'is to be rewritten as'. (1) says: Take any item *a*. If *a* is bounded on the left by *X* and on the right by *Y*, and if *a* has the property *P*, then rewrite *a* so that it has the property *Q*. Rules like (1) are subject to certain conventional manipulations. For example, (1) may be collapsed with the rule

(2) $\qquad C \to D$ in the environment $X\underline{\qquad}Y$

to form

(3) $\qquad \left\{ \begin{matrix} P \to Q \\ C \to D \end{matrix} \right\} / X\underline{\qquad}Y.$

In general, 'in the environment' is abbreviated by a slash, '/'; and braces, '{ }', have the force of disjunction. Halle proposes that we explicate simplicity in terms of the number of alphabetical symbols. The complexity of a sentence is assigned a numerical value equal to the number of symbols occurring in its minimum representation. Thus, the numerical value of the conjunction of (1) and (2) would be calculated by counting the symbols in (3), assuming that (3) is the minimum representation of the conjunction.

Halle leaves open what sorts of items *P*, *Q*, *C*, *D*, *X*, and *Y* are. The reason for this initial position of neutrality is important. There has been considerable debate in phonology about whether the basic elements in the phonological part of a grammar are indivisible phonemes or distinctive features such as those described by Jakobson. The intricacies of this debate need not detain us. Suffice it to say that distinctive features are properties of phonemes and that the programme stemming from Jakobson and Halle consists in expressing all phonological rules in terms of these properties. According to this view, a phoneme is nothing more than a distinctive feature matrix, whereas according to the 'indivisible phoneme' point of view, a phoneme is thought of as having an ontological integrity that is obscured by the distinctive feature approach. Notice that this is a debate about which properties are the natural ones in terms of which phonological laws are to be stated.

Halle wants to use his simplicity measure to help settle this debate. He begins with an example that he takes to be self-evident:

(4a) $\qquad\qquad$ a → æ/ $\underline{\qquad}$i

(5a) $\qquad\qquad$ a → æ/ i$\underline{\qquad}$i.

(4a) says that the phoneme /a/ becomes the phoneme /æ/ if it precedes the phoneme /i/. (5a) says that /a/ becomes /æ/ if it precedes and is preceded by /i/. Linguists (with some exceptions) seem to share the intuition that (4a) is simpler than (5a). Note that we have represented (4a) and (5a) in terms of indivisible phonological segments and that the counting measure makes (4a) more highly valued than (5a). Here, our intuitions about simplicity are mirrored by a combination of Halle's simplicity measure and the indivisible phoneme point of view.

If we express (4a) and (5a) in terms of distinctive features, our intuitions also are preserved by the evaluation measure:

(4b)

$$[+\text{grave}] \rightarrow [-\text{grave}] / \begin{bmatrix} \underline{\hspace{2em}} \\ +\text{vocalic} \\ -\text{conson} \\ -\text{diffuse} \\ +\text{compact} \\ -\text{flat} \end{bmatrix} \begin{bmatrix} +\text{vocalic} \\ -\text{conson} \\ +\text{diffuse} \\ -\text{compact} \\ -\text{flat} \\ -\text{grave} \end{bmatrix}$$

(5b)

$$[+\text{grave}] \rightarrow [-\text{grave}] / \begin{bmatrix} +\text{vocalic} \\ -\text{conson} \\ +\text{diffuse} \\ -\text{comp} \\ -\text{flat} \\ -\text{grave} \end{bmatrix} \begin{bmatrix} \underline{\hspace{2em}} \\ +\text{vocalic} \\ -\text{conson} \\ -\text{diffuse} \\ +\text{comp} \\ -\text{flat} \end{bmatrix} \begin{bmatrix} +\text{vocalic} \\ -\text{conson} \\ +\text{diffuse} \\ -\text{comp} \\ -\text{flat} \\ -\text{grave} \end{bmatrix}.$$

Each of the items in the square brackets is a binary distinctive feature. The '+' or '−' before each one tells whether the item in question has the feature or its opposite. The square bracketing indicates conjunction, and the blank to the right of the slash in both (4b) and (5b) has the meaning explained previously. To help the reader grasp this notation, I will translate (4b):

> If the item in question is +vocalic, −consonantal, −diffuse, +compact, and −flat, and if it is followed by an item that is +vocalic, −consonantal, +diffuse, −compact, −flat, and −grave, and if it is +grave, then it is to be rewritten as −grave.

According to Halle's simplicity measure, (4b) comes out simpler than (5b). Thus, whether we represent the two rules in terms of indivisible phonemes or in terms of distinctive features, intuitive results ensue.

Now consider the simplicity of (4a) versus the following:

(6a)
$$a \rightarrow æ/\underline{\hspace{1cm}}\begin{Bmatrix} i \\ e \\ æ \end{Bmatrix}.$$

(6a) says: If the phoneme /a/ is followed by the phonemes /i/, /e/, or /æ/, then it is to be rewritten as /æ/. (6a) is intuitively simpler than (4a). However, by representing (4) and (6) in terms of indivisible phonological segments, we find that Halle's simplicity criterion contradicts our intuitions. According to his counting measure, (4a) should be simpler than (6a). As might be expected, this problem does not arise if we use distinctive feature notation to represent (6a):

(6b)
$$[+\text{grave}] \rightarrow [-\text{grave}]/\begin{bmatrix} \underline{\hspace{1cm}} \\ -\text{cons} \\ -\text{diff} \\ +\text{compact} \\ -\text{flat} \end{bmatrix}\begin{bmatrix} +\text{voc} \\ -\text{cons} \\ -\text{grave} \end{bmatrix}.$$

(6b) contains fewer symbols than (4b) and is simpler according to Halle's criterion. Halle concludes that if we wish to use his simplicity measure, we must 'regard phonological segments as complexes of properties' rather than as indivisible phonemes.[11]

A further vindication of Halle's two-pronged proposal comes from comparing the following rule with (6):

(7)
$$a \rightarrow æ/\underline{\hspace{1cm}}\begin{Bmatrix} i \\ p \\ z \end{Bmatrix}.$$

(6) and (7) come out equally simple when represented in terms of indivisible phonemes. But linguists unhesitatingly regard (6) as simpler than (7), because (6) states a law-like generalization about the front vowels /æ/, /e/, and /i/, while (7) applies to /i/, /p/, and /z/, which comprise 'an odd unsystematic collection of phonemes'.[12] Halle expresses this difference by saying that the front vowels make up a natural

[11] Halle, 'Phonology in Generative Grammar', p. 337.
[12] *Ibid.*, p. 337.

kind while the set /i/, /p/, and /z/ is *ad hoc* and unnatural. The difference between (6) and (7) is mirrored when Halle's simplicity measure is applied to their distinctive feature representations. The distinctive feature representation of (7) would fill an entire page, while (6b), the distinctive feature representation of (6), contains less than a dozen symbols. Once again, Halle's simplicity criterion together with the distinctive feature point of view seem to imply just the judgements we want.

Halle's simplicity measure gives him a handy way of defining the notion of natural kind:

N is a natural kind iff fewer features are required to designate the class N than to designate any individual sound in N.[13]

To evaluate Halle's proposal, it will be helpful to look at the distinctive feature representation of English consonants given in Table 3. In support of his characterization of natural sets,

TABLE 3: *Distinctive feature representation of the con-sonants of English*[14]

	p	b	m	f	v	k	g	t	d	θ	ð	n	s	z	č	ǯ	š	ž
Vocalic	—	—	—	—	—	—	—	—	—	—	—	—	—	—	—	—	—	—
Consonantal	+	+	+	+	+	+	+	+	+	+	+	+	+	+	+	+	+	+
Grave	+	+	+	+	+	+	+	—	—	—	—	—	—	—	—	—	—	—
Diffuse	+	+	+	+	+	—	—	+	+	+	+	+	+	+	—	—	—	—
Strident	—	—	—	+	+	—	—	—	—	—	—	—	+	+	+	+	+	+
Nasal	—	—	+	—	—	—	—	—	—	—	—	+	—	—	—	—	—	—
Continuant	—	—	—	+	+	—	—	—	—	+	+	—	+	+	—	—	+	+
Voiced	—	+	+	—	+	—	+	—	+	—	+	+	—	+	—	+	—	+

Halle points out that the class of consonants [s z š ž č ǯ] is natural, since it can be pinpointed with two distinctive features (nongrave and strident), while any member of the class requires at least three distinctive features to designate it. In contrast, the class [m s] is not natural, because it requires a

---

[13] Halle, 'On the Role of Simplicity in Linguistic Descriptions', p. 90. Although Halle states this characterization as a conditional ('N is a natural kind if . . .') rather than as a biconditional, it seems clear from the examples he cites that he intends to provide a necessary and sufficient condition. He uses the same definition and examples in 'On the Bases of Phonology', p. 328. Notice the affinities of his definition with our discussion of natural sufficient conditions in Section 1.8. In what follows we shall construe Halle's proposal as intended to define what we called *natural sets* and *natural properties* (see Section 1.7).

[14] Halle, 'On the Role of Simplicity in Linguistic Descriptions', p. 90.

rather long list of distinctive features to be characterized, while /m/ can be designated by two distinctive features (grave and nasal), and /s/ can be designated by four (nongrave, diffuse, strident, and nonvoiced).[15]

According to the criterion above, no class containing just one sound counts as natural, because specifying the class requires the same number of distinctive features as specifying the (one) member sound. However, there are both internal and external reasons for wanting to view such unit classes as natural. Within transformational grammar, a class is natural if all its members are subject to the same (or nearly the same) transformation rules. This condition is trivially satisfied by the unit classes. Also, from the broader point of view of our theory of simplicity, we saw in Section 1.8 that every conjunction of natural predicates is itself natural. If we accept the distinctive features as the natural properties for phonology, as Halle would like, it would seen that individual sounds also are natural, since they are then viewed as nothing but conjunctions of distinctive features. If the members of a natural set are unified by the natural properties they share, then the members of the intersection of any natural sets must be unified to an even greater degree. Where the intersection has only one member, the set is unified to the nth degree; all (one) of its members are identical.

A further problem for Halle's criterion is that it conflicts with one of his own examples. The set [p b m f v] is supposed to be natural in that the two features grave and diffuse suffice to specify it; yet, /m/ can be specified with just two features. To remedy this inconsistency and take account of the argument of the previous paragraph, we might revise Halle's criterion to read:

N is a natural set iff no more features are required to designate the class N than to designate any individual sound in N.

This revision fits the examples used by Halle cited above. However, since at least three features are needed to specify each consonant (with the exception of /m/ and /n/), any *disjunction* of two features would have to pick out a natural set according

---

[15] In counting the number of features needed to specify a sound or a class of sounds, we will not count the features +cons, since all of our examples will be taken from the class of consonants anyway.

to the new criterion. Thus the sounds that are nasal or continuant would have to comprise a natural set, as would those that are voiced or strident and those that are grave or voiced. This result seems to be wholly unsatisfactory. The fact that this problem does not seem to arise for sets that are specified as conjunctions of distinctive features reaffirms our previous observation (Section 1.8) that disjunctions seem to be particularly troublesome when it comes to defining the notions of natural set and natural property.

The way around the problem appears to lie in jettisoning Halle's definition and accepting instead the characterization suggested in Section 1.8. Within the distinctive feature framework, the distinctive feature predicates comprise our initial stock of natural predicates. Every conjunction of these is itself natural. A disjunction of natural predicates is natural if it is nomologically equivalent to one of the initial natural predicates or a conjunction of them. That the naturalness of a set is here identified with the dispensability of its disjunctive formulation will be discussed again in Section 3.6.

After offering his definition of 'natural kind', Halle quotes Jakobson as remarking that 'in describing the most varied linguistic facts, we commonly encounter sets of sounds which form natural classes in the distinctive feature framework, and that only rarely does one meet classes of sounds that require long, cumbersome lists of distinctive features for their characterization'.[16] Halle and Chomsky both point to this fact as important. After all, it might have turned out that rules formulated in the distinctive feature framework are quite complex and frequently specify highly contrived sets. That linguistic facts are so simply describable in the Jakobsonian manner seems to show that distinctive features really are the natural properties with which to do phonology. Jakobson's comment is an example of how the fact that a certain vocabulary enables us to obtain a perspicuous representation of a set of truths can serve as a reason for thinking that the vocabulary picks out the natural properties.

The observation that the combined strategy of distinctive feature framework and simplicity measure might not have yielded such neat results brings out two important properties

[16] Halle, 'On the Role of Simplicity in Linguistic Descriptions', p. 90.

that Chomsky and Halle see in their approach. In the first place, they regard their simplicity measure as empirical. A simplicity measure is an explication of our educated intuitions about which transformation rules are simpler than others, and like any other explication, the proposed measure must conserve a significant number of our strong intuitions. However, Chomsky and Halle want to say that the evaluation measure is empirical in another sense. Given a simplicity measure, the choice made between different grammars (or parts of grammars) can have clear testable consequences manifested both in predictions about strings and in deeper hypotheses about competence. We will see an example of this later when we examine how Chomsky and Halle use the simplicity measure to explicate the notion of phonological *deviance*.

Second, Chomsky and Halle view their simplicity measure as *internal* to linguistic theory. They are concerned to forestall irrelevant criticism from those who think they already know what a simplicity criterion should look like. Chomsky and Halle stress that constructing a simplicity criterion is a theoretical task to be evaluated by its consequences within linguistic theory and not by how well it matches our presystematic intuitions about what simplicity 'really is'. Furthermore, Chomsky repeatedly claims that the proposed measure need have no important connection with wider notions of simplicity discussed in philosophy of science. He asserts that not only is the simplicity criterion internal to linguistics, it is internal to the particular linguistic theory that he is considering.[17]

Although Chomsky and Halle's insistence on rigorously formulated and tested explications seems all to the good, one cannot help balking at the claim that a simplicity criterion adequate for transformational grammar need have no wider application. This difficulty is especially pronounced in view of Chomsky and Halle's desire for their simplicity criterion to form part of a linguistic theory that describes human mental structure. Are we to imagine that people use one simplicity criterion in language acquisition and a quite different one when

---

[17] See Chomsky and Halle's criticisms of Householder in 'Some Controversial Questions in Phonological Theory' and Chomsky's *Aspects of the Theory of Syntax*, pp. 38–9. One wonders how simplicity can be internal to linguistic theory and yet be used as it is in *Syntactic Structures* to adjudicate between *kinds* of grammars.

they construct, say, their everyday 'theory' of physical objects? A psychological theory that needs a different simplicity criterion for each area of human cognition surely would be dismissed as *ad hoc* and unnecessarily complex. In the final analysis, we want an adequate simplicity criterion for phonological theory to be a special case of the simplicity criterion used in cognition in general.[18]

3.4 The Relevance of our Theory of Simplicity

An immediately obvious affinity between our simplicity criterion and Chomsky and Halle's is that in both accounts the simplicity of hypotheses is crucially relative to which predicates are regarded as the natural ones. This relativity cuts both ways in Halle's arguments. Intuitions about which hypotheses are simpler than others help determine which predicates are natural, and our confidence that certain predicates are natural constrains which hypotheses we regard as simpler than others.

Beyond this general similarity of approach, our simplicity criterion yields results that are identical to the ones generated by Chomsky and Halle's proposal. Before we can examine some of these points of agreement, it is necessary to explain how to calculate the MEI of a transformation rule. One of the standard conventions for manipulating transformation rules is that we are allowed to move 'any part of the feature complex on the left-hand side of the arrow . . . to the environment'.[19] Thus, we can rewrite (6b) as

$$\emptyset \rightarrow [-\text{grave}]/\begin{bmatrix} \underline{\hspace{1cm}} \\ \begin{bmatrix} +\text{grave} \\ -\text{cons} \\ -\text{diff} \\ +\text{compact} \\ -\text{flat} \end{bmatrix} \begin{bmatrix} +\text{voc} \\ -\text{cons} \\ -\text{grave} \end{bmatrix} \end{bmatrix},$$

where '∅' applies to any segment. In the above reformulation, we have moved into the environment everything that was to

---

[18] This demand for a unified treatment of the role of simplicity in cognition goes counter to the tendency to view the mechanisms of language acquisition as unique. If the unified approach is correct, then we cannot account for whatever special status the use of language might have in our species in terms of the singularity of its manner of acquisition.

[19] Halle, 'Phonology in Generative Grammar', p. 338.

the left of the arrow. We can consider the resulting hypothesis relative to the question

Should phonological segment x be rewritten as —grave?

The MEI of the hypothesis relative to this question is the set to the right of the slash. Manipulating the transformation rule in this way provides an easy method for constructing its MEI set.

Consider (4a), (5a), and (6a) relative to the question

(8)   Should phonological segment x be rewritten as /æ/?

For (5a) to answer this question, we must know that x is /a/ and that it is followed and preceded by /i/. For (4a) to answer (8), we must know that x is /a/ and that it is followed by /i/. And for (6a) to answer (8), we must know that x is /a/ and that it is followed by /i/, /e/, or /æ/. Because (5a) requires more information than (4a), and (4a) requires more information than (6a), relative to question (8), (6a) $>_s$ (4a) $>_s$ (5a).

But as Halle points out, comparing the simplicity of (4), (5), and (6) proceeds smoothly whether one adopts a distinctive feature or an indivisible phoneme approach. It is when we reach examples like (6) and (7) that the difference between these two techniques becomes important. When (6) and (7) are expressed in terms of phonemes, our simplicity criterion seems to be useless. Which requires more information: knowing that a phoneme is in the set [i e æ] or knowing that a phoneme is in the set [i p z]? Specifying these two sets in terms of indivisible phonemes does not reveal that the members of the first have many important properties in common, while the members of the second do not. The significance of the distinctive feature approach in this case is that it makes this fact explicit. Given a phonological segment, one needs to know far less about it to say that it is a member of the first set than to say that it is a member of the second. Thus, within a distinctive feature framework, (6) is demonstrably simpler than (7).

We saw earlier that a phonological theory must assign phonological interpretations to syntactic strings. For Chomsky and Halle, a phonological theory must also meet the requirement of explanatory adequacy. Part of this additional task involves solving the problem of *possible nonexistent forms*. Chomsky

and Halle[20] discuss the fact that English contains the sound
/brik/ ('brick') but not /blik/ or /bnik/. Even though neither
/blik/ nor /bnik/ actually occurs as a formative in English,
most English-speakers would agree that /blik/ is a possible
English sound, while /bnik/ is not. Put another way, the nonoccurrence of /blik/ is an accident, while the nonoccurrence of
/bnik/ is guaranteed by the laws of English sound structure.
The problem posed by nonexistent forms is to find some theoretical explanation of this difference.

This brings us back to the uses that Chomsky and Halle want
to make of the lexicon and the transformation rules: They
want the accidental facts about a language to go into the
lexicon and the phonological laws to be represented by the
transformation rules. Thus, in the example above, Chomsky
and Halle want to exclude /blik/ from the class of actual
English sounds by having it not occur in the lexicon, while
/bnik/ is to be excluded by a phonological law. The following
law excludes /bnik/ but includes both /blik/ and /brik/:

(9)   Consonantal segment → liquid in the context:
        #stop — vowel.

However, compare (9), which satisfies the kind of distinction
between law-likeness and accident that Chomsky and Halle
want to make, with

(10)   Consonantal segment → /r/ in the context: # /b — ik/.

(10) excludes both /blik/ and /bnik/ but includes /brik/ in
the sounds of English.

For Chomsky and Halle to show that the nonoccurrence of
/bnik/ in English is law-like and that the nonoccurrence of
/blik/ is an accident, they must provide a criterion for choosing
(9) over (10). If (9) were adopted, the nonoccurrence of
/blik/ would be registered as an accidental fact in the lexicon.
As might be expected, Chomsky and Halle's simplicity criterion
results in (9) being simpler than (10). Our theory of simplicity
yields the same result, because knowing that a consonantal
segment occurs in the context #stop — vowel requires less

---

[20] Chomsky and Halle, 'Some Controversial Questions in Phonological Theory',
p. 101.

information than knowing that a consonantal segment occurs in the context # /b — ik/.[21]

When we embed this example in the psychological context of language acquisition, another similarity between Chomsky and Halle's measure and our own becomes evident. A child hears neither /blik/ nor /bnik/ in the course of his early training, so all of his primary linguistic data are compatible with generalizations (9) and (10). The child is in a 'situation of indifference', in that the totality of his evidence fits more than one alternative generalization. The rules for hypothesis choice dictate that we choose (9) over (10) because of its simplicity. Thus, the role of simplicity within a psychologically oriented linguistic theory seems similar to the role of simplicity within the context of hypothesis choice in general.

Chomsky and Halle[22] discuss the following two rules in terms of the difference between a natural and an unnatural environment:

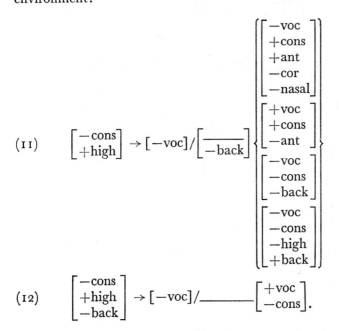

$$(11) \quad \begin{bmatrix} -\text{cons} \\ +\text{high} \end{bmatrix} \rightarrow [-\text{voc}] / \left[\overline{\quad -\text{back} \quad} \right] \left\{ \begin{bmatrix} -\text{voc} \\ +\text{cons} \\ +\text{ant} \\ -\text{cor} \\ -\text{nasal} \end{bmatrix} \begin{bmatrix} +\text{voc} \\ +\text{cons} \\ -\text{ant} \end{bmatrix} \begin{bmatrix} -\text{voc} \\ -\text{cons} \\ -\text{back} \end{bmatrix} \begin{bmatrix} -\text{voc} \\ -\text{cons} \\ -\text{high} \\ +\text{back} \end{bmatrix} \right\}$$

$$(12) \quad \begin{bmatrix} -\text{cons} \\ +\text{high} \\ -\text{back} \end{bmatrix} \rightarrow [-\text{voc}] / \underline{\qquad\qquad} \begin{bmatrix} +\text{voc} \\ -\text{cons} \end{bmatrix}.$$

---

[21] Chomsky and Halle in *The Sound Pattern of English*, p. 417, give a definition of *degree of deviance*: the simpler the rule violated by a sequence, the more deviant it is.
[22] *Ibid.*, p. 340.

(11) says that if a segment has the features −back, −cons, and +high and if it precedes a segment having all of the features specified within any of the square brackets in the braces, then the segment is to be rewritten so that it has the feature −voc. Chomsky and Halle's counting measure clearly yields the result that (12) is simpler than (11).

Our simplicity criterion gives the same result. Consider (11) and (12) relative to the question

(13)   Should segment x be rewritten as −voc?

The MEI of (11) relative to this question is the four-member set

$$(14) \left\{ \begin{array}{l} x \text{ is } \begin{bmatrix} -\text{cons} \\ +\text{high} \\ -\text{back} \end{bmatrix} \text{ and is followed by a segment which is } \begin{bmatrix} -\text{voc} \\ +\text{cons} \\ +\text{ant} \\ -\text{cor} \\ -\text{nasal} \end{bmatrix} \\[4ex] x \text{ is } \begin{bmatrix} -\text{cons} \\ +\text{high} \\ -\text{back} \end{bmatrix} \text{ and is followed by a segment which is } \begin{bmatrix} +\text{voc} \\ +\text{cons} \\ -\text{ant} \end{bmatrix} \\[4ex] x \text{ is } \begin{bmatrix} -\text{cons} \\ +\text{high} \\ -\text{back} \end{bmatrix} \text{ and is followed by a segment which is } \begin{bmatrix} -\text{voc} \\ -\text{cons} \\ -\text{back} \end{bmatrix} \\[4ex] x \text{ is } \begin{bmatrix} -\text{cons} \\ +\text{high} \\ -\text{back} \end{bmatrix} \text{ and is followed by a segment which is } \begin{bmatrix} -\text{voc} \\ -\text{cons} \\ -\text{high} \\ +\text{back} \end{bmatrix} \end{array} \right\} .$$

However, the MEI of (12) relative to question (13) is

$$(15) \quad \left(x \text{ is } \begin{bmatrix} -\text{cons} \\ +\text{high} \\ -\text{back} \end{bmatrix} \text{ and is followed by a segment which is } \begin{bmatrix} +\text{voc} \\ -\text{cons} \end{bmatrix} \right).$$

Since (14) is greater in content than (15), hypothesis (11) requires more extra information to answer question (13) than does hypothesis (12). Therefore, (12) is simpler than (11). Thus, whether we use Chomsky and Halle's counting measure or our criterion in terms of informativeness, (12) is simpler than (11). This result mirrors our strong intuition that an important difference between (11) and (12) is that in (12) 'the environment is a highly natural class of segments, that is, all vowels of the language, whereas the environment [in (11)] ... is a very unnatural class'.[23]

The third example that I want to discuss illustrates the use of variables as feature coefficients in the context of assimilation and dissimilation rules. 'Assimilation is a process in which two segments are made to agree on the value assigned to one or more features, whereas dissimilation is a process in which two segments are made to disagree in the value assigned to one or more features.'[24] The assimilation rule below is taken from Southern Paiute.

$$(16) \quad [+cons] \rightarrow \left\{ \begin{array}{l} \begin{bmatrix} +ant \\ -cor \\ -high \\ -back \end{bmatrix} / \underline{\qquad} + \begin{bmatrix} +ant \\ -cor \\ -high \\ -back \end{bmatrix} \\[4ex] \begin{bmatrix} +ant \\ +cor \\ -high \\ -back \end{bmatrix} / \underline{\qquad} + \begin{bmatrix} +ant \\ +cor \\ -high \\ -back \end{bmatrix} \\[4ex] \begin{bmatrix} -ant \\ -cor \\ +high \\ +back \end{bmatrix} / \underline{\qquad} + \begin{bmatrix} -ant \\ -cor \\ +high \\ +back \end{bmatrix} \end{array} \right\}.$$

Although (16) is highly regular and law-like, according to Halle's counting measure it comes out just as simple as the following monstrosity:

$$(17) \quad [+cons] \rightarrow \left\{ \begin{array}{l} \begin{bmatrix} +ant \\ -cor \\ -high \\ -back \end{bmatrix} / \underline{\qquad} + \begin{bmatrix} -ant \\ +cor \\ -high \\ +back \end{bmatrix} \\[4ex] \begin{bmatrix} +ant \\ +cor \\ -high \\ -back \end{bmatrix} / \underline{\qquad} + \begin{bmatrix} +ant \\ -cor \\ +high \\ +back \end{bmatrix} \\[4ex] \begin{bmatrix} -ant \\ -cor \\ +high \\ +back \end{bmatrix} / \underline{\qquad} + \begin{bmatrix} -ant \\ +cor \\ +high \\ -back \end{bmatrix} \end{array} \right\}.$$

[23] Chomsky and Halle, *The Sound Pattern of English*, p. 340.
[24] *Ibid.*, p. 350.

In (16), but not in (17), there is a perfect correlation between the matrix to the right of the slash and the one to the left. Halle's solution to this problem is to use variables, which in this case can take either '+' or '−' as values. Given this notational convention, (16) can be abbreviated as

$$(18) \quad [+\text{cons}] \rightarrow \left\{ \begin{bmatrix} \alpha\text{ant} \\ \beta\text{cor} \\ \gamma\text{high} \\ \delta\text{back} \end{bmatrix} / \underline{\hspace{2cm}} + \begin{bmatrix} \alpha\text{ant} \\ \beta\text{cor} \\ \gamma\text{high} \\ \delta\text{back} \end{bmatrix} \right\}.$$

Using Halle's counting measure, it turns out that (18) is simpler than (17).[25]

Similarly, consider (17) and (18) relative to the question

(19) What values of the features ±ant, ±cor, ±high, and ±back should x be rewritten as having?

For (17) to answer this question, we must know one of the following:

x is +cons and x is followed by   −ant
                                      +cor
                                      −high
                                      +back

(20) x is +cons and x is followed by   +ant
                                                −cor
                                                +high
                                                +back

          x is +cons and x is followed by   −ant
                                                +cor
                                                +high
                                                −back

For (18) to answer (19), we must know a sentence of the form

(21) x is +cons and x is followed by αant
                                                 βcor
                                                 γhigh
                                                 δback.

---

[25] Strictly speaking, (18) is not equivalent to (16). However, according to Chomsky and Halle, *The Sound Pattern of English*, p. 351, (16) implicitly includes the other permutations of values for the four features mentioned. Once this is spelled out, (18) becomes a straightforward rewrite of (16). In applying the counting measure here, it is assumed that a variable counts as one symbol, just like '+' and '−'.

The set of sentences in (20) has the form

$$\begin{pmatrix} A \\ B \\ C \end{pmatrix},$$

while the set of sentences represented in (21) has the form

$$\begin{pmatrix} A \\ B \\ C \\ D \\ \cdot \\ \cdot \\ \cdot \end{pmatrix},$$

since it includes all of the sentences obtained by permuting the values for α, β, γ, and δ. According to our definition of content, (20) is higher in content than (21). Therefore, (18) is more informative, and hence simpler, than (17).

A final example of an application that Chomsky and Halle make of their simplicity criterion concerns the relationship between the lexical entry of a formative and its final representation. Chomsky and Halle express the intuition that the smaller the amount of change involved in getting from lexical entry to final representation, the better.[26] Thus, they feel that

$$\begin{bmatrix} +\text{voc} \\ -\text{cons} \\ +\text{high} \\ -\text{back} \end{bmatrix} \rightarrow [-\text{voc}]$$

is simpler than

$$\begin{bmatrix} +\text{voc} \\ -\text{cons} \\ +\text{high} \\ -\text{back} \end{bmatrix} \rightarrow \begin{bmatrix} -\text{voc} \\ +\text{back} \end{bmatrix},$$

which in turn is simpler than

$$\begin{bmatrix} +\text{voc} \\ -\text{cons} \\ +\text{high} \\ -\text{back} \end{bmatrix} \rightarrow \begin{bmatrix} +\text{cons} \\ +\text{cor} \\ -\text{high} \end{bmatrix}.$$

[26] Chomsky and Halle, *The Sound Pattern of English*, pp. 337–9.

Clearly, their counting measure preserves these judgements.

They express an allied intuition that the more invariant the formatives of a language, the simpler will be the rules describing their phonological properties.[27] To see what they mean by 'invariant', notice the difference between the phonological representations of 'inn' and 'algebra'. No matter what string of formatives the word 'inn' appears in, its phonological representation in terms of a distinctive feature matrix remains unchanged. However, the same is not true of 'algebra', in that this word has one representation in the sentence 'I like algebra' and quite a different one in 'It is algebraic'. This means that the lexical representation of 'inn' is carried over unchanged into its final representation, while the lexical representation of 'algebra' is not the same as its final representation in certain contexts.[28]

The desire for invariance is a limiting case of the desire to minimize the change between lexical and final representations. If a formative is invariant, then none of its lexical properties are altered in the transformations which produce its final representation. However, this desire to minimize the difference between lexical entry and final representation is not the only ambition we have for our grammar. If it were, we would posit many more formatives than we do, thereby increasing the amount of invariance exhibited by the total description of the language. For example, rather than having a single formative 'algebra' which is not invariant, we might decide to posit two formatives—'algebra' and 'algebraic'—each of which is invariant. As speakers of English, we have strong intuitions that such a move is artificial. But what is the general rationale for avoiding this, if we really do want to maximize invariance? Clearly, counterbalancing this desire for invariance is our desire to maximize law-likeness and thereby minimize the content of the lexical entries.[29]

---

[27] Chomsky and Halle, *The Sound Pattern of English*, pp. 166–8.

[28] We ignore here the import of lexical redundancy rules, since they do not affect this point about invariance. Even so, it is worth mentioning that lexical redundancy rules fit into the desire to minimize the accidental character of a language. These rules guarantee that the lexical entry of a phonological matrix includes only 'accidental facts'; the rest of the matrix is then filled in by phonological laws.

[29] Since both the lexicon and the phonological rules are subject to a simplicity constraint, the problem arises of how to weight the importance of gains in sim-

From our discussions of change/no-change hypotheses and invariance (Sections 2.1 and 2.4), it should be obvious that our theory of simplicity mirrors the intuition that simple grammars minimize the difference between lexical entry and final representation, all else being equal. This desideratum may be traded off for gains in law-likeness, and as we have seen, Chomsky and Halle's notion of law-likeness is also mirrored within our theory. Thus, in evaluating total grammars, we will encounter weighting problems of the kind discussed in Section 2.9.

3.5 The Suggestions of Contreras and Bach

In this section, I examine the recommendations that Contreras[30] and Bach[31] have made for modifying the notation of Chomsky and Halle's distinctive feature framework. These suggestions are similar in spirit to the comments that Chomsky and Halle make at the end of *The Sound Pattern of English*, where they cite examples in which the binary distinctive features used earlier in the book fail to yield correct results when subjected to the counting measure. Like Chomsky and Halle, both Contreras and Bach want to preserve the counting measure, and so they focus their attention on augmenting or altering the predicates regarded as natural. Since the counting measure involves counting symbols, their proposals amount to suggestions of notation. I will not discuss here whether Contreras' or Bach's proposed modifications are true to the linguistic facts, or whether the facts cited really demand a modification in Chomsky and Halle's approach.[32] The goal is

---

plicity in these two areas. McCawley, in *The Phonological Component of a Grammar of Japanese*, pp. 51–2, seems to think that any economy in the rules should take precedence over any economy in the lexicon, and his 'The Accentual System of Standard Japanese', p. 70, attributes this view to Halle as well. In 'The Measurement of Phonological Economy', Harms criticizes this policy and says that the two kinds of economies can be traded off. Zimmer's 'On the Evaluation of Alternative Phonological Descriptions' also questions McCawley's proposal and points to the need for a set of principles that enables us to weight and compare the kinds of economy at issue.

30 Contreras, 'Simplicity, Descriptive Adequacy, and Binary Features'.

31 Bach, 'Two Proposals Concerning the Simplicity Metric in Phonology'.

32 In his 'Resolution of Vocalic Hiatus in Portugese: Diachronic Evidence for Binary Features', Naro takes issue with some of the examples used by Contreras and argues that the relevant facts can be accommodated within a binary distinctive feature framework.

the more modest one of showing how these further simplicity intuitions are captured by our theory.

Contreras considers three possible ways of accommodating the counterexamples he finds to the Chomsky–Halle simplicity measure: (1) rejecting the intuitive simplicity judgements that comprise the counterexamples; (2) rejecting Halle's simplicity measure; (3) rejecting the binary principle (whereby every distinctive feature has just the value '+' or '−', rather than, say, some integer between 0 and 10). Contreras thought that the intuitions were too clear to adopt strategy (1) and that Halle's simplicity criterion works too well elsewhere for (2) to be an option (and Contreras also admits that he has no better alternative to offer). So Contreras chooses (3), and applies the variable notation discussed in Section 3.4 to nonbinary features.

He argues that although

$$(22) \quad [-\text{stress}] \to [-\text{syll}] / \left\{ \begin{array}{cc} \left[\begin{array}{c} \rule{1em}{0.4pt} \\ +\text{diff} \end{array} \right] & \# \left[\begin{array}{c} +\text{syll} \\ -\text{cons} \end{array} \right] \\ \left[\begin{array}{c} \rule{1em}{0.4pt} \\ -\text{diff} \\ -\text{comp} \end{array} \right] & \# \left[\begin{array}{c} +\text{syll} \\ -\text{cons} \\ -\text{diff} \end{array} \right] \end{array} \right\}$$

is intuitively more simple than

$$(23) \quad \left[\begin{array}{c} -\text{comp} \\ -\text{diff} \\ -\text{stress} \end{array} \right] \to [-\text{syll}] / \rule{3em}{0.4pt} \# \left[\begin{array}{c} +\text{syll} \\ -\text{cons} \\ -\text{diff} \end{array} \right],$$

Halle's simplicity measure yields the opposite judgement. In order to compare (22) and (23) from the point of view of our simplicity criterion, first we rewrite (23) equivalently as

$$(24) \quad [-\text{stress}] \to [-\text{syll}] / \left[\begin{array}{c} \rule{1em}{0.4pt} \\ -\text{diff} \\ -\text{comp} \end{array} \right] \# \left[\begin{array}{c} +\text{syll} \\ -\text{cons} \\ -\text{diff} \end{array} \right].$$

Consider (22) and (24) relative to the question

(25)   Should segment x be rewritten as −syll?

For (22) to answer this question, we must know one of the following:

(26) x is −stress and +diff, and is followed by a segment that is +syll and −cons.

x is −stress, −diff, and −comp, and is followed by a segment that is +syll, −cons, and −diff.

On the other hand, for (24) to answer this question, we must know that

(27) x is −stress, −diff, and −comp, and is followed by a segment that is +syll, −cons, and −diff.

(26) has the form $\binom{A}{B}$ while (27) has the form (B). This means that (27) is higher in content than (26), so (22) requires less extra information to answer question (25) than (24) does. Thus, according to our theory, (22) is simpler than (23).

The second example that Contreras brings to bear against Chomsky and Halle's proposal is that

$$(28) \quad [+\text{nasal}] \rightarrow \begin{bmatrix} \alpha\text{ant} \\ \beta\text{cor} \\ \gamma\text{high} \\ \delta\text{low} \\ \varepsilon\text{back} \\ \tau\text{distrib} \end{bmatrix} / \underline{\hspace{1cm}} \begin{bmatrix} \alpha\text{ant} \\ \beta\text{cor} \\ \gamma\text{high} \\ \delta\text{low} \\ \varepsilon\text{back} \\ \tau\text{distrib} \end{bmatrix}$$

and

$$(29) \quad [+\text{nasal}] \rightarrow \begin{bmatrix} +\text{ant} \\ -\text{cor} \\ -\text{high} \\ -\text{low} \\ -\text{back} \\ -\text{distrib} \end{bmatrix} / \underline{\hspace{1cm}} \begin{bmatrix} +\text{ant} \\ -\text{cor} \\ -\text{high} \\ -\text{low} \\ -\text{back} \\ -\text{distrib} \end{bmatrix}$$

are equally simple according to the counting measure, even though (28) is intuitively simpler than (29). However, within our theory, (28) is simpler than (29) relative to the question

(30)   What values of ±ant, ±cor, ±high, ±low, ±back, and ±distrib should segment x be rewritten as having?

Notice that the MEI of (29) relative to this question will have the form (A), while the MEI of (28) will have the form

$$\begin{pmatrix} A \\ B \\ C \\ . \\ . \\ . \end{pmatrix}.$$

Thus, (28) requires less extra information than (29) to answer question (30), and is simpler as a result.

Before presenting the other objections that Contreras raises against Halle's proposal, I should outline how Contreras wants to deal with these problems. Since he wants to continue using Halle's counting measure, Contreras' objective becomes one of formulating a perspicuous notation[33] within which the counting measure yields intuitive results. To this end, Contreras makes use of nonbinary features, and he introduces the following weighting for variable and constant coefficients:

> It seems reasonable to assume that the identification of one out of three elements involves a greater degree of specificity than the identification of one out of two. Therefore, I suggest that the value assigned to integers be a function of the number of integers which are possible for a given feature. Since plusses and minuses may be conceived of as integers for scales having two terms, a uniform measure may be applied to binary and non-binary features. Thus, a variable is assigned the value 1, a plus or minus the value 2, and an integer the value 3, 4, etc., depending on how many integers are possible for the feature in question.[34]

Given this convention, (28) turns out to be simpler than (29) according to the counting measure. But what of (22) and (23)? It still looks as if the counting measure yields the same counter-intuitive result when applied to them.

To solve this problem, Contreras reformulates (22) and (23) as (31) and (32) respectively:

(31) $[-\text{stress}] \rightarrow [-\text{syll}] / \left[\overline{}_{n\text{high}}\right] \# \begin{bmatrix} +\text{syll} \\ -\text{cons} \\ m\text{high} \end{bmatrix}$

Condition: $n \geqslant m$.

(32) $[-\text{stress}] \rightarrow [-\text{syll}] / \left[\overline{}_{2\text{high}}\right] \# \begin{bmatrix} +\text{syll} \\ -\text{cons} \\ n\text{high} \end{bmatrix}$

Condition: $2 \geqslant n$.

---

[33] The Chomsky–Halle programme of developing an adequate counting measure for simplicity embodies the search for perspicuous notation in just the sense that this idea was discussed in Section 2.6. Here, as before, the goal is to so arrange one's technique of representation that 'deep' [properties, like the simplicity of hypotheses, are manifest, in 'surface' properties, like the number of symbols in a sentence.

[34] Contreras, 'Simplicity, Descriptive Adequacy, and Binary Features', p. 4.

Contreras' convention assigns ten points to (31) and twelve points to (32), which is just what is required. Now intuitions and theory agree that (31) is simpler than (32).

Contreras' next criticism of Halle involves the following three rules:

(33) $$[\alpha low] \rightarrow \begin{bmatrix} -low \\ -\alpha low \end{bmatrix}$$

(34) $$[-high] \rightarrow [+high] / \begin{bmatrix} \overline{} \\ -low \end{bmatrix}$$

(35) $$[\alpha low] \rightarrow \begin{bmatrix} -low \\ -\alpha syll \end{bmatrix}$$

Intuitively, we would expect that (33) should be simpler than both (34) and (35). Halle's counting measure and his binary approach yield intuitive results when applied to (33) and (34). However, his strategy seems to go wrong when applied to (33) and (35); in this case, his simplicity criterion says that (33) and (35) are equally simple. However, if these three hypotheses are reformulated in Contreras' nonbinary notation, intuitive results ensue:

(36) $[n high] \rightarrow [n + 1 high]$
Condition: $n < 3$

(37) $[2 high] \rightarrow [3 high]$

(38) $$[1 high] \rightarrow \begin{bmatrix} 2 high \\ -syll \end{bmatrix}.$$

Here, Contreras' proposal implies that (36) is simpler than (37), which in turn is simpler than (38).

It should be obvious that our theory yields the same results. (36) is simpler than (37), since (36) requires less extra information than (37) to answer the question

(39) What degree of height should be given to segment x?

(37) is simpler than (38), since (38) represents a more radical change from input to output than does (37) (see the discussion of invariance in Section 3.4).

Contreras' last example also involves variable notation. This time 'n' ranges over the first n integers and 'α' is a binary variable, as before. As in the previous example,

$$(40) \qquad \begin{bmatrix} +\text{syll} \\ -\text{cons} \end{bmatrix} \rightarrow [\alpha n\text{high}]/\underline{\qquad} \begin{bmatrix} +\text{syll} \\ -\text{cons} \\ \alpha n\text{high} \end{bmatrix}$$

requires less extra information to answer question (39) than

$$\begin{bmatrix} +\text{syll} \\ -\text{cons} \end{bmatrix} \rightarrow [1\text{high}]/\underline{\qquad} \begin{bmatrix} +\text{syll} \\ -\text{cons} \\ 1\text{high} \end{bmatrix},$$

so (40) is simpler.

Bach's proposals on simplicity are similar to Contreras' in that both attempt to augment the notational conventions proposed by Chomsky and Halle in such a way that a counting measure yields intuitive results. Bach begins by noticing that the Chomsky–Halle measure is insensitive to the greater simplicity of (41a) over (42):

$$(41a) \qquad \begin{bmatrix} -\text{cnt} \\ +\text{high} \end{bmatrix} \rightarrow [\alpha\text{grave}]/\left\{ \begin{matrix} \begin{bmatrix} -\text{cons} \\ \alpha\text{grave} \end{bmatrix} \underline{\qquad} \\ \underline{\qquad} \begin{bmatrix} -\text{cons} \\ \alpha\text{grave} \end{bmatrix} \end{matrix} \right\}$$

$$(42) \qquad \begin{bmatrix} -\text{cnt} \\ +\text{high} \end{bmatrix} \rightarrow [\alpha\text{grave}]/\left\{ \begin{matrix} \begin{bmatrix} -\text{cons} \\ \alpha\text{grave} \end{bmatrix} \underline{\qquad} \\ \underline{\qquad} \begin{bmatrix} -\text{cnt} \\ \alpha\text{vce} \end{bmatrix} \end{matrix} \right\}$$

(41a) is the rule for English that determines the front and back allophones of the velar stops. Notice that the two environments represented in the braces in (41a) are mirror images of each other. The rule says that if a $-$cnt $+$high segment is before or after a segment that is $-$cons and αgrave, it is to be rewritten as αgrave. (42) is a hypothetical rule in which there is no important connection between the two possible environments. By ranking the two rules as equally simple, the Chomsky–Halle measure seems to miss the fact that (41a) represents a more significant generalization than (42).

According to the 'neighbourhood convention' that Bach proposes, (41a) could be rewritten as

$$(41b) \qquad \begin{bmatrix} -\text{cnt} \\ +\text{high} \end{bmatrix} \rightarrow [\alpha\text{grave}]/\begin{bmatrix} -\text{cons} \\ \alpha\text{grave} \end{bmatrix}.$$

The omission of the blank in (41b) indicates that the segment described in the environment comes before or after the one described to the left of the arrow. Now intuitions and counting measure concur, because (41b) comes out simpler than (42).

Within our theory of simplicity, we can compare (41b) and (42) relative to the question

What degree of grave should segment x be given?

For (41b) to answer this question, we must know, in addition,

(43) x is —cnt and +high and is before or after a segment that is —cons and αgrave.

For (42) to yield an answer, we must know one of the following:

(44) x is —cnt and +high and is after a segment that is —cons and αgrave.

      x is —cnt and +high and is before a segment that is —cnt and αvce.

If we let '—cons and αgrave' be equal in content to '—cnt and αvce', then (44) comes out higher in content than (43). The idea behind this assumption is that each of the sentences in (44) 'says more' than the sentence in (43). Granting this, our theory implies that (41b) is simpler than (42).

The second situation that Bach considers is 'that in which the determining environment is separated from the segment undergoing the rule by an irrelevant stretch of segments'.[35] Where X indicates such an irrelevant stretch of segments (or no segments at all), we see that

$$(45) \quad \begin{bmatrix} +\text{syll} \\ -\text{grave} \\ -\text{comp} \end{bmatrix} \rightarrow [+\text{high}]/\underline{\hspace{2cm}} \begin{bmatrix} +\text{syll} \\ -\text{grave} \\ +\text{high} \end{bmatrix}$$

is a special case of

$$(46) \quad \begin{bmatrix} +\text{syll} \\ -\text{grave} \\ -\text{comp} \end{bmatrix} \rightarrow [+\text{high}]/\underline{\hspace{2cm}} X \begin{bmatrix} +\text{syll} \\ -\text{grave} \\ +\text{high} \end{bmatrix}.$$

Bach's second convention ensures that (46) comes out simpler

---

[35] Bach, 'Two Proposals Concerning the Simplicity Metric In Phonology', p. 139.

S—E

than (45), which matches our intuitions. Notice that by our criterion (46) is simpler than (45) relative to the question

Should segment x be rewritten as +high?

This is a case when greater generality brings with it greater simplicity. In fact, most of the examples Bach uses could serve as illustrations of the connection between simplicity and generality drawn in Section 2.4.

The suggestions of Contreras and Bach by no means exhaust the attitudes that linguists have to Chomsky and Halle's proposal, nor do they exhaust the recommendations that have been made to modify the simplicity criterion and distinctive feature framework to yield more intuitive results. Yet, the preceding discussion should constitute further evidence that our simplicity criterion mirrors a host of intuitions in transformational grammar and should provide some insight into the kinds of problems faced by the Chomsky–Halle counting measure.

3.6 Spurious Generalizations

One of the principal purposes of a simplicity criterion in linguistics is to distinguish law-like significant generalizations about a language from spurious nonsignificant facts. The examples we have examined thus far show that the dictates of our theory coincide with the intuitions of linguists about this distinction. Yet, one feature of our theory seems to violate these intuitions. According to our proposal,

$$(47a) \qquad A \to B/\underline{\hspace{1.5cm}} \begin{Bmatrix} F \\ G \\ H \end{Bmatrix}$$

is simpler than

$$(48a) \qquad A \to B/\underline{\hspace{1.5cm}} F$$

relative to the question

Should segment x be rewritten as having B?

However, the indispensable use of braces—the disjunction—has been seen by some linguists as a sure sign of a spurious generalization. Lakoff expresses his view of braces quite succinctly:

Devices like curly-brackets may be useful as heuristics when one is trying to organize data at an early stage of one's work, but they are not something to be proud of. Each time one gives a disjunctive list of the environments where a rule applies, one is making a claim that there are no fully general principles determining the application of that rule. Over the years, curly-brackets have had a tendency to disappear as insights were gained into the nature of the phenomena being described.[36]

In Section 2.4, we saw that in general, the hypothesis

(47b) $(x)[(Ax \lor Cx) \supset Bx]$

is simpler than

(48b) $(x)(Ax \supset Bx)$

relative to the question

$$(Ba, \sim Ba),$$

and clearly our judgement on (47a) and (48a) is just an instance of the greater simplicity of (47b) over (48b). I now want to argue that (47) is simpler than (48), although an explanation using (47) as its explanatory law can often be worse than an explanation using (48). That is, hypotheses that use braces are to be eschewed, but on grounds other than simplicity.

Explaining why an individual is B involves placing it in a reference class that is natural (see Section 2.4). Thus, a better explanation for why a melts is that a is a piece of ice in an environment where the temperature is higher than 32°F, rather than that a is either ice or X, where ice and X are completely unrelated except that both melt in environments warmer than 32°F. In transformational grammar, the fact that a given segment having property A is transformed into having B is ex-

---

[36] Lakoff, 'On Generative Semantics', p. 294. In 'Linguistic Universals and Linguistic Change', p. 176, Kiparsky concurs with this judgement. In *A Study of Thinking*, pp. 161–2, Bruner, Goodnow, and Austin give the following historical examples of how the discovery that a disjunctive set can be supplanted by a nondisjunctive one often counts as a theoretical advance. Our understanding of the sensory physiology of the skin was deepened when a nondisjunctive characterization was found for the conditions under which a sensation of cold (or warmth) could be produced. The same thing happened with the discovery of a univocal explanation for why diverse therapeutic techniques can relieve swelling of a bruised joint. In both these cases, a nonnatural category at a macro-level of theory was found to be identical with a natural category at a micro-level. This is the opposite of the kind of situation discussed in Section 1.8 where a natural category at a macro-level was found to be nonnatural at a micro-level.

plained better by saying that the segment precedes a context of kind F than by saying it precedes a context of kind F, or one of kind G, or one of kind H. We see then that our intuition that (47) is a worse explanatory hypothesis than (48) is explicated in terms of our desire for natural reference classes in explanations. Recall that the naturalness of a class is defined in terms of its being equivalent to some intersection of classes that are initially designated as natural (see Section 1.8). Thus, our theory of simplicity substantiates Lakoff's claim that disjunctively characterized sets are natural when their disjunctive characterizations are dispensable, even though the theory violates the intuition that (48) is simpler than (47).

If (47) and (48) are each more than minimally supported by the evidence, the model for hypothesis choice (Section 1.9) dictates that (47) should be chosen on grounds of simplicity. Choosing (47) seems intuitive, because if each hypothesis is a relatively safe bet, what reason could there be for choosing the less general one? The problem here is not which hypothesis is chosen, but the reason for the choice. Granted that (47) is the better hypothesis in this situation, why is it the simpler?

From the discussion of homogeneity in Section 2.1, it seems clear that the simplest possible hypothesis we can make with respect to the predicate family $(B, \sim B)$ has the form '$(x)(\pm Bx)$'. Take

$$(49) \qquad\qquad (x)(Bx)$$

as an example. (49) says the universe is perfectly homogeneous with respect to the predicate family just mentioned. Now consider a universe in which (47b) and (48b) have different truth values. Because (47b) implies (48b), such a universe must be one in which (47b) is false and (48b) is true. In this universe, there must be at least one individual that is both C and not B. Note that if A is nonempty, then the universe has less homogeneity with respect to the predicate family $(B, \sim B)$ than when (47b) is true. That is, in so far as (47b) and (48b) differ, (47b) yields a more homogeneous universe than (48b) does. We can think of (47b) and (48b) as unequal approximations of the maximal simplicity of (49). (47b) puts us one step closer to this goal than (48b) does, and

$$(x)[(Ax \lor Cx \lor Dx) \supset Bx]$$

puts us closer still. In the limit, by sufficiently broadening the class determined by the antecedent, the hypothesis

$$(x)[(Ax \lor Cx \lor Dx \lor \ldots) \supset Bx]$$

is hypothesis (49). This should provide some insight into why the greater generality of (47b) over (48b) is also a greater simplicity.

One result of this discussion, noted in Section 2.4, is to drive a wedge between constraints on accepting hypotheses and constraints on constructing explanations. Even though (47) is a more reasonable choice than (48) when both are more than minimally supported, (48) might better explain why an individual is *B*. We also noticed that acceptance and explanation assign different uses to the notion of support and that two hypotheses can be unequally acceptable but equally explanatory. So even if the theory of simplicity here proposed proves unsatisfactory, sufficient reason remains to regard the desiderata in these two areas as distinct.

This has important consequences for the view that a grammar is at once the accepted output of a language acquisition device and an explanation of the transformations that linguistic units undergo in different contexts. Chomsky and Halle's simplicity measure was supposed simultaneously to model the child's rules for 'accepting' linguistic laws and to prescribe which hypotheses provide the best explanations for linguistic phenomena. However, no single counting measure can do both these jobs, because an ordering of hypotheses in terms of their acceptability is not the same as an ordering of hypotheses in terms of their explanatory adequacy.

Thus, the following argument is not in general warranted: Since a given hypothesis explains the data better than another hypothesis does, we must ensure that the language acquisition device accepts the former hypothesis in preference to the latter. A special version of this argument, however, is suspect for an additional reason. Linguists sometimes argue for the superior explanatory power of a rule by appealing to its symmetry with other transformational rules that already seem reasonable. For a child to be in a position to do the same thing, he must already have internalized the other rules considered. At times, this will be false to his psychological history.

In fact, the impact of the difference between acceptance and explanation is less damaging to the psychological interpretation of linguistic theory than it is to Chomsky and Halle's programme for developing a simplicity measure. It still remains reasonable to suppose that language acquisition involves internalizing rules and that explaining linguistic regularities involves appealing to some of those rules. Moreover, rules of acceptance and explanation both partake of certain constraints, notably simplicity. But constructing explanations is a selective process; we use as explanatory hypotheses only some of the rules internalized during language acquisition. Since acceptance is deciding what to believe and explanation is deciding which beliefs to use for a particular purpose, there seems to be no *prima facie* reason to expect the constraints on the two processes to be the same.

3.7 Conclusion

The discussion of Chomsky and Halle's proposals in the light of our own simplicity criterion has perhaps fostered the impression that linguists largely agree on the role and details of a simplicity criterion in linguistic theory. Nothing could be further from fact. Even among transformational grammarians, the multiplicity of opinion in this area extends right down to fundamentals. Some linguists[37] think that linguistics needs to formulate explicit evaluation procedures only because the subject is not yet mature; once the theory becomes rich enough, such self-conscious attention to criteria for hypothesis choice will naturally pass by the way. Among those linguists who feel that some evaluation procedure is desirable are some who believe that no counting measure can suffice.[38] They would see the weighting of variables and the elaboration of notation discussed in Section 3.5 as an *ad hoc* postulation of epicycles. And even linguists who think that a counting measure is useful do not agree on what conclusions such a measure should yield. For example, Halle's 'Phonology in Generative Grammar' and

[37] See, for example, Botha's *Methodological Aspects of Transformational Generative Phonology*.

[38] In 'On the Functional Unity of Phonological Rules', Kisseberth examines some cases where the usual abbreviatory conventions seem to be insensitive to important theoretical similarities and differences between rules. His article raises the possibility that some fundamentally new standards of evaluation are needed.

Chomsky and Halle's *The Sound Pattern of English* assert that ordered transformation rules should come out simpler than un-ordered ones, but this intuition has been called into question in recent discussion. Moreover, the role of a simplicity measure in diachronic linguistics is a subject of considerable controversy.[39]

How does our discussion affect the general question of whether evaluation procedures are needed in a linguistic theory? It seems clear that if one views linguistic theory as a description of a language acquisition device, then a simplicity criterion is necessary. Yet, our discussion of simplicity throws some doubt on whether any counting measure can explicate simplicity judgements within linguistics or in general. We saw in Chapter 2 that choosing hypotheses on grounds of simplicity often involves a trade-off between a gain in simplicity in one area of theory and a loss in simplicity in another. Moreover, in the previous section and in Section 2.4, we saw that considerations beyond simplicity and support are involved in constructing explanations, and these considerations can often be balanced off against simplicity. The ubiquity of instances of the weighting problem suggests that it may be tremendously difficult to invent a notation in which these complex, inter-related, and theory-wide influences on the simplicity of a hypothesis are all somehow manifest in an 'internal' property of a hypothesis, such as the number of symbols in its minimum representation. In general the global character of a concept mitigates against the possibility of perspicuous notation.

A similarly discouraging conclusion derives from the difference between acceptance and explanation. If the constraints on these two processes are distinct, it seems unlikely that any counting measure can simultaneously mirror a language acquisition device's acceptance policies and linguists' in-tuitions about the relative adequacy of explanations. However, this is a limitation in principle; there are important similarities between our policies of acceptance and explanation, and Chomsky and Halle's proposal reflects many of our intuitions about both areas.

---

[39] See, for example, Yen's 'Two Measures of Economy in Phonological Descrip-tion', Bach's 'Two Proposals Concerning the Simplicity Metric in Phonology', and Kiparsky's 'Linguistic Universals and Linguistic Change'.

Our own simplicity criterion is relatively invariant with respect to notation. Any two logically equivalent hypotheses, no matter how formulated, are equally simple because equally informative. The notational reformations urged by Bach and others, which were required to bring the counting measure in line with considered judgements, are unnecessary when our theory is used to judge the relative simplicity of hypotheses. Notational suggestions, where useful at all, matter to our theory by making the content of hypotheses *explicit*; the actual form of words used in expressing a hypothesis is irrelevant. In the same vein, it is worth recalling that our simplicity criterion is considerably more general than Chomsky and Halle's specifically linguistic proposal. Both of these properties of our theory— its notational invariance and its greater generality—are manifestations of the greater simplicity of our notion of simplicity as informativeness.

In spite of this catalogue of problems for Chomsky and Halle's approach, it is important to emphasize some of the positive lessons of their programme. Their insight into the connection between simplicity judgements and frameworks of natural properties seems fundamentally correct. In addition, their idea of a language acquisition device as involving parameters of simplicity and something like our notion of support shows how language acquisition may obey constraints that also govern the activity of theorizing. In fact, their considerable success in showing that language acquisition can be modelled in terms of a simplicity metric suggests that a similar approach to other areas of cognition may be fruitful. To this task we now turn.

4

Simplicity and Visual Perception

4.1 Introduction

Psychologists and philosophers have frequently stressed the conjectural and active nature of perceiving, likening it to the way we create scientific theories. They have denied that perception consists in the passive assimilation of impressions and have emphasized that in perceiving, we impose our categories and concepts on the sensory stimulations we receive. According to this view, the full spectrum of perceptual and cognitive activities manifests an organizing and meaning-creating quality. All cognition, from the most unreflective recognition of an ordinary object to the most self-conscious and abstract scientific theorizing, essentially involves processing and transformation.

On one level, this analogy between perceiving and theorizing says nothing more than that both processes are active: Sensation underdetermines perception and evidence underdetermines theory. However, some psychologists have made the bolder claim that the mechanisms of perception are identical or strongly analogous to the mechanisms of theorizing.[1] If stated in terms of the flow charts discussed in Chapter 3 (Figures 6 and 7), this thesis would come to the claim that the two boxes in Figure 8 have similar structures. In this chapter, I examine how this general thesis might be substantiated by examining the sense in which simplicity can be said to play a part in perceptual judgements.

We have observed that simplicity becomes a relevant consideration in hypothesis choice when two or more hypotheses fit a given body of evidence but go beyond it in divergent ways.

[1] For example, in *The Intelligent Eye*, Gregory argues for a probabilistic model of perception in which people are taken to perceive the most probable among competing interpretations. Attneave's 'Some Informational Aspects of Visual Perception' discusses some perceptual analogues of the goal in theorizing of seeking out redundancies in the environment. This will be discussed in Sections 4.2 and 4.4.

Simplicity is then used as a criterion for choosing amongst these competitors. Before looking at specific perceptual phenomena, we should consider for a moment what the psychological correlate of this paradigmatic situation might look like. If there were such a thing as a given in perception, we could let it correspond to the evidence, and the component of perception that goes 'beyond the information given' would then correspond to the hypothesis chosen on the basis of simplicity. Within this model, the perceptual given would underdetermine what is perceived, since different perceptual judgements would fit

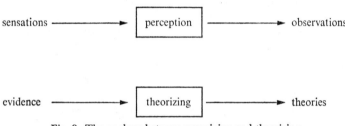

Fig. 8. The analogy between perceiving and theorizing

the given equally well. Simplicity would then be the 'internal criterion' by which these remaining competitors are sorted out.

However, this picture of perception is problematic, since there do not seem to be any givens in perception in the sense that every perception is the result of some degree of cognitive processing. Without the notion of a perceptual given, the psychological correlate of the difference in theorizing between evidence and hypothesis seems impossible to define. The way out of this dilemma begins with the recognition that our picture of theorizing has no truck with the idea that evidence is somehow given in experience or that evidence enjoys some special kind of certainty. The main interest in the analogy is that hypotheses are at once based on and go beyond the evidence. The analogue of the evidence/hypothesis distinction in perception can be made out by discerning two stages. First, we cull certain information from the environment; then we impose an interpretation which subsumes the information first acquired. Neither stage is a passive process; rather, our perceptual judgements are best seen as interpretations imposed upon interpretations.[2]

Another objection that might be raised against the proposed analogy between perceiving and theorizing is that there is no introspective testimony that perception consists of two distinct stages; we simply perceive, without first pondering the evidence and then hazarding a hypothesis. This objection glosses over the fact that we do have some introspective evidence for the existence of stages of processing in perception. For example, in perceiving ambiguous figures (see Section 4.2), we alternatively impose different interpretations (hypotheses) on the same perceived pattern (evidence). But, clearly, the objection based on introspection is mistaken for a more fundamental reason. A distinction between evidence and hypothesis in the theory of theorizing is justified because it helps us make sense of how theorizing works, whether or not we have any introspective evidence that the distinction really exists. Similarly, regardless of the introspective testimony about perceptual judgements, the best justification we could have for making the distinction is that it enables us to construct a better theory of perception. The structure of the mind is not transparent to the inward gaze. Thus, the initial analogy between theorizing and perceiving is nontrivial to the degree that it is substantiated by adequate theories about both. Although the day of such theories is not at hand, it is possible to give some idea of how theorizing and perceiving are analogous, and this will be our task in what follows.

A further objection that might be raised against applying the simplicity criterion to perception is that hypothesizing occurs in language whereas perception does not. Because the theory of simplicity applies first and foremost to sentences, we found it necessary in Section 2.8 to explain the simplicity of predicates in terms of the simplicity of sentences that describe predicates. In this chapter, we will pursue the same kind of programme; we will explain the simplicity of nonsentential objects in terms of sentences that are associated with them.

Perceptions are judgements that a given state of affairs ob-

[2] In his *Aspects of Motion Perception*, Kolers argues persuasively for this stages-of-processing view in the context of apparent motion perception. This will be discussed in Section 4.3.

tains. If a sentence adequately captures the content of such a perception, then the sentence is true of the state of affairs just in case the perceptual judgement it represents is a correct or veridical perception of that state of affairs. Similarly, we will discuss the simplicity of pictures in terms of their corresponding sentences; a sentence adequately captures the content of a picture if the sentence is true of all and only the scenes that the picture represents. To make this idea more precise, we will use a function $R(\ )$ which we will call the method of representation. $R(\ )$ maps pictures or perceptions into sentences. These sentences will be complicated existential hypotheses subject to the constraint that $R(p)$ has a scene (actual or possible) as its verifying instance in just those cases when p pictures the scene or p is a veridical perception of the scene. This allows us to say that a picture is true (or a perception is veridical) just when its corresponding sentence has at least one verifying instance.

The definition of $R(\ )$ provides a partial test for whether a given sentence represents a given picture or perception. In addition, our linguistifying of perception receives a further check from the way it fits in with our theory of simplicity. Given our hypothesis that perception involves a simplicity criterion, it should turn out that in at least some interesting cases where x and y are divergent perceptions each compatible with a given stimulation, we tend to have perception x instead of perception y and $R(x)$ is simpler than $R(y)$. Similarly, if we think that x is a simpler picture than y, then our method of representing pictures in language will be confirmed if it happens that $R(x)$ is simpler than $R(y)$.

This brings us to the question of how we should construct the linguistic representations of pictures and perceptions. We need an enumeration of the natural kind predicates of perception; the linguistic representation of a picture or a perceptual judgement would merely be some logical composition of these predicates. Our theory provides no specification of these natural kinds, just as it fails to provide a set of natural kinds for phonology (see Chapter 3). Psychology fails to do this as well, since at present no comprehensive theory of perception exists. Nevertheless, we can test our conjecture by looking at some experimental work in psychology which has yielded partial successes on circumscribed problems. This will enable us to sketch the likely linguistic representations of certain perceptual judgements.[3]

All of the foregoing can be summarized in terms of a machine model of perception. The machine will have stimulations of its sensory surfaces as inputs and perceptual judgements as outputs. The problem of developing a theory of perception involves specifying an intervening mechanism. The physical cause of a sensation might be a bundle of light rays which excite the machine's receptors. At an early level of processing, the causal impact of this stimulation will be described in some very elementary way, say, by assigning a colour to each square in the mosaic of colours that occurs at the sensory surface. After a sequence of processing on this information, the machine will issue in a perceptual judgement, which typically will be a physical object sentence.[4] This perceptual judgement will be related to the lower-level description as hypothesis to evidence. Moreover, the perceptual judgement often explains the character of the lower-level sentence by locating its causal source in the external world of objects.

To what extent this model can be applied to human perception is a complicated problem. For one thing, we now know that there is no retinal image which consists of a stable mosaic of colours. Thus, if a description of a mosaic of colours plays any role at all in specifying the sensory input, it is constructed from the information yielded as the eye darts about in a series of quick scannings and fixations. When the eye is forced to remain motionless, the retinal image degenerates or disappears altogether.[5] Another problem is to know how seriously to take the model's linguistic quality. I am inclined to regard it as more than a fanciful fiction; the sentences operated upon by this functional model may be thought of as occurring in the language

[3] In 'Epistemology Naturalized', p. 90, Quine suggests that there may be *perceptual norms* that play a role similar to that played by phonemes as linguistic building blocks.

[4] A physical object sentence need not always be the output. Roderick Firth has pointed out to me that conflicting cues can lead the subject to make the more tentative judgement 'I seem to see . . .'. In what follows I will use 'perceptual judgement' to refer both to physical object judgements and to judgements of appearance.

[5] See, for example, Riggs, Ratliff, Cornsweet, and Cornsweet's 'The Disappearance of Steadily Fixated Visual Objects' and Pritchard, Heron, and Hebb's 'Visual Perception Approached by the Method of Stabilized Images'.

of thought—the language in which information is transmitted and processed. I take it that most of the information processing models of cognition considered in cognitive psychology and machine intelligence presuppose a structure of this kind. A *processing* model shows how inputs are transformed into outputs; an *information* processing model shows how objects possessing information (e.g., sentences) are so transformed. If the focus of such models is the *content of representations* and not just the probabilities of states of a system, the idea of information must be *semantic*; for if the syntactic Shannon–Weaver idea is the one used, information is no more central to cognition than to digestion.

4.2 Two- and Three-Dimensional Interpretations of Line Drawings

Many two-dimensional line drawings strike us as being pictures of three-dimensional objects; other two-dimensional line drawings appear flat, not representations of solids at all. Still others strike us as ambiguous, admitting of both kinds of interpretations. If we look a bit more selfconsciously, we notice that most drawings admit of off-beat interpretations. For example, even though a Kopfermann cube is inevitably seen as a cube, it can also be seen as a flat hexagonal figure (see A4 of Figure 9). And although a square can be viewed as a complicated three-dimensional object, it usually is seen as a square. Thus, if we reflect on our unreflective interpretations of such pictures, we realize that although we could interpret a given line drawing in various ways, we typically see it in one way rather than in any of the others.

In what sense might a two-dimensional drawing be seen in different ways? The answer seems to be that the picture underdetermines the object it is taken to be a projection of. Given a line drawing satisfying certain minimum conditions (like closure), an infinity of dissimilar three-dimensional objects can, when suitably oriented, project just that line drawing. Yet, in spite of this underdetermination, we so often manage to single out just one solid as the object depicted by the line drawing. Clearly, 'fitting' the drawing does not uniquely determine the designated interpretation; some other consideration seems to be involved.

This perceptual phenomenon is quite analogous to the paradigmatic situation described earlier in which simplicity judgements are relevant. We know that any acceptable interpretation of a given picture must fit that picture; that is, it must project onto the picture by the method of projection we assume to hold.[6] However, this constraint fails to single out the interpretation that people ordinarily make. According to the rules for hypothesis choice outlined in Section 1.9, we tend to settle on an interpretation that fits the picture and is the simplest alternative.

Before going into the psychological literature on this problem, let us distinguish three questions that might be asked about the regularities underlying a person's choice of two-dimensional versus three-dimensional interpretations of line drawings:

(A) Of two figures, which is more likely to be given a two-dimensional (three-dimensional) interpretation?

(B) Will a figure more likely be given a two-dimensional or a three-dimensional interpretation?

(C) If a figure is given a three-dimensional interpretation, which three-dimensional interpretation will it be given?[7]

The work of Hochberg and his associates provides an answer to question (A).[8] Perkins and Attneave and Frost address question (C).[9] I will indicate how question (B) can be answered by extending the treatment given in the articles that Hochberg co-authored.

The background for much of this work was established in two early papers by Attneave and Hochberg and McAlister.[10] In both papers, an attempt was made to explicate some of the Gestalt qualities of figural goodness in terms of a quantitative definition of information. Although their ideas were inspired

[6] Rectilinear projection is the method that we will consider, although it is not the only method of projection available.

[7] A fourth question falls in with these three: If a figure is given a two-dimensional interpretation, which two-dimensional interpretation will it be given? Although not unproblematic, this question will not be discussed in what follows.

[8] Hochberg and McAlister, 'A Quantitative Approach to Figural "Goodness" '; Hochberg and Brooks, 'The Psychophysics of Form: Reversible Perspective Drawings of Spatial Objects'.

[9] Perkins, 'The Perception of Line Drawings of Simple Space Forms'; Attneave and Frost, 'The Determination of Perceived Tridimensional Orientation by Minimum Criteria'.

[10] Attneave, 'Some Informational Aspects of Visual Perception'; Hochberg and McAlister, ibid.

by Shannon and Weaver's work on information, the authors' proposals by no means constituted uncritical transfers of the engineering notion of information into the domain of perception. According to Hochberg and McAlister (p. 361), when faced with a stimulus that admits of more than one interpretation (as all stimuli in principle do), people tend to perceive the alternative that maximizes certain Gestalt properties. In particular, 'the less the amount of information needed to define a given organization as compared to the other alternatives, the more likely that the figure will be so perceived'. That is, the perceptual system seems to obey a 'minimum principle'; Hochberg later identifies this principle with simplicity.[11]

Note that the minimum principle, thus enunciated, was aimed at solving problem (B). Given a single stimulus, one was to predict the likelihood of a person's making one interpretation rather than another. However, the experimental work in that article, and in the later one by Hochberg and Brooks, really addresses problem (A). The Hochberg–Brooks study (p. 340) proposes to show that 'the relative apparent tridimensionality of each member of a family of reversible-perspective representations of a given three-dimensional object will be a simple function of the geometrical complexity of the two-dimensional figure (as a first approximation)'.

In Hochberg and Brooks' study, the subjects were given each family of figures in Figure 9 and were asked to place the figure that seemed most strongly three-dimensional at 10 on a scale and the one that looked least solid, or 'most flat', at 0 and then to place the rest of the family members in between. The authors devised a series of counting measures on the geometrical figures, such as number of interior angles, number of line-segments, number of points of intersection, and the like. Each drawing was evaluated for each of these measures, and the score of each test was transformed to a 10-point scale, the highest scoring figure within each family being 10, the lowest being 0.

Three different hypotheses were considered which correlated subjects' estimates of three-dimensionality (Y) with the measures on the figures. The single test with the highest correlation was total number of continuous line-segments (T_4), which

<hr />

[11] Hochberg, *Perception*, p. 90.

correlated at 89 per cent. With K a constant very close to 1 and C a constant very close to 0, the conjecture took the form of the equation

(1) $$Y = K(T_4) + C.$$

The second hypothesis considered was the result of a multiple

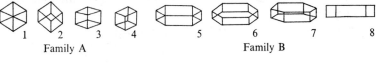

1   2   3   4   5   6   7   8

Family A   Family B

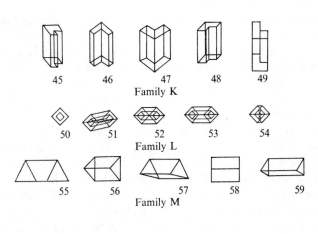

45   46   47   48   49

Family K

50   51   52   53   54

Family L

55   56   57   58   59

Family M

65   66   67   68   69

Family O

Fig. 9. Some figure families used to test the hypothesis that perceived three-dimensionality is a simple function of geometrical properties (from Hochberg and Brooks, 'The Psychophysics of Form: Reversible Perspective Drawings of Spatial Objects', pp. 340, 348)

regression analysis on all seventeen tests. This strategy yielded a monstrous equation (with multiple-R of 0·96, however). It had the form

(2) $$Y = C_1 + C_2(T_2) + \ldots + C_{18}(T_{18}).$$

This alternative was dismissed out of hand, since it failed 'to exhibit any rational pattern', and 'its underlying principles . . . are unclear' (p. 345). Moreover, the weightings reflected in (2) were specific to the figures used and were in fact not verified by the second set of figures examined. The last equation considered, and the one subsequently adopted, related Υ to total number of interior angles (T_2), total number of different angles divided by total number of interior angles (T_{12}), and total number of continuous line-segments (T_4) in the following way:

$$(3) \qquad \Upsilon_i = \frac{(T_2 + T_{12} + 2T_4)_i}{\mathcal{N}_T}.$$

Here, Υ_i is the predicted three-dimensionality score for any figure (on a scale from 0 to 10), and $\mathcal{N}_T$ is the number of tests (with $2T_4$ counting as $\mathcal{N} = 2$) which actually discriminate between the figures of the family being considered. Equation (3) subsequently was verified with a new set of figures.[12]

One cannot help feeling ill at ease with (3) for many of the same reasons that Hochberg and Brooks must have felt ill at ease with (2). Even though (3) fits the data quite well and relies on a relatively small number of parameters, it nevertheless appears rather *ad hoc* in the sense that it does not seem to proceed from any general principle. This comes into focus more clearly when we try to understand (3) as an instance of the minimum principle proposed by Hochberg and McAlister. The information about a figure or object provided by tests T_2, T_{12}, and T_4 does not uniquely specify that figure or object at all; so in what sense does (3) show apparent three-dimensionality to be related to the amount of information needed to describe a figure? Moreover, the minimum principle seems to be quite incapable of providing the theoretical underpinning for hypothesis (3), because the minimum principle concerns question (B), and equation (3) is addressed to answering question (A).

However, neither of these objections is fatal to the programme of Hochberg and his associates, because their research seems to provide the tools necessary for dealing with both of

---

[12] However, Hochberg and Brooks later had to augment equation (3) to include a parameter for perspective. See their 'Compression of Pictorial Space Through Perspective Reversal'.

Hochberg and Brooks' choice between these three hypotheses, each of which fits the data quite well, reflects the rules for hypothesis choice given in Section 1.9. In particular, note that equation (2) was rejected as intolerably complex. According to our theory, (2) is less simple than both (1) and (3), because it has so many more variables in it (see Section 2.4).

them. To begin with, consider the difference between questions (A) and (B). A theory addressed to (A) would merely rank figures according to their relative apparent three-dimensionality. A theory focused on (B) could be built on the shoulders of a theory aimed at (A) merely by specifying a *threshold* such that any figure above that threshold probably would be given a three-dimensional interpretation and any figure below it probably would be given a two-dimensional interpretation.[13]

Take family A of Figure 9 as an example. Subjects ordered these four figures in terms of increasing three-dimensionality as 1, 3, 2, 4. Any theory answering question (A) would merely have to generate this ordering. Now suppose that figures 1 and 3 are usually perceived as two-dimensional, while 2 and 4 are usually perceived as three-dimensional. A theory addressed to question (B) would have to specify a threshold between 3 and 2 as the cut-off between two- and three-dimensional interpretations. But what general principle is available to generate a threshold for every such figure family?

It would seem that an altogether natural solution to this problem is to take the three-dimensional interpretation as specifying the threshold. For example, the three-dimensional alternative in family A is to interpret each figure as a cube, while the two-dimensional alternative is to interpret each figure as a particular kind of hexagon. To decide whether a given figure will be perceived one way or the other, we measure the relevant geometrical properties of the hexagon and compare the results with those yielded by the same measurements on a cube. If the number assigned to the hexagon is greater than the one assigned to the cube, then the figure will be perceived as a cube; if less, then it will be seen as a flat hexagon. A measure on figures and solids which has this property of placing the value of the three-dimensional alternative for each figure family where the threshold for that family should go would provide a solution to question (B).

Imposing one more constraint on this geometrical measure ensures that, besides answering questions (A) and (B), the

---

[13] This difference between questions (A) and (B) is similar to the difference between a probability logic (which defines the relation 'is more probable than' on pairs of hypotheses) and an acceptance logic (which specifies when a hypothesis may be believed in terms of its being more than minimally probable).

result will be an instance of the minimum principle discussed
above. All we need require is that the measure turn on properties of figures and solids which are rich enough to uniquely
specify them. If, for example, the measure were just the number
of different angles, the number of different line-segments, and
the total number of line-segments (say, the ordered triplet of
these three values), it would satisfy our constraint with respect
to a square figure. The value of a square on this measure would
be $\langle 1, 1, 4 \rangle$, and a square is the only plane figure that could
have this value. However, a richer measure would be required
to satisfy our constraint for all straight-edged figures and for
solids in general. Such a measure would be an instance of the
minimum principle, because it would show that a given interpretation of a figure is more likely than an alternative just in
case that interpretation can be specified by fewer facts than the
alternative can. Presumably, the measure would have the
following properties:

- All else being equal, the more nonequivalent angles (line-
  segments) a figure has, the more information is necessary
  to specify it.
- All else being equal, the more angles (line-segments) a
  figure has, the more information is necessary to specify it.

Given Hochberg and Brooks' success in correlating apparent
three-dimensionality with certain simple geometrical properties, it does not seem unreasonable to think that their measure
could be refined in the two ways I have suggested.

This method of understanding the regularities underlying
our two- and three-dimensional interpretations of figures fits
in well with the paradigmatic situation described in Section 4.1,
in that we predict whether a figure will be perceived as three-
dimensional or two-dimensional by evaluating two competing
hypotheses, for example 'It's a cube' and 'It's a hexagon of
such-and-such a kind'. Our theory predicts that people tend to
perceive in accordance with the interpretation which mini-
mizes certain parameters. Notably, we posit that figure or
solid with the fewest number of parts and differences between
parts. In preferring the fewest differences between parts, we
are preferring an interpretation that maximizes homogeneity

(see Section 2.1). In preferring the fewest parts, we are minimizing the existential commitments involved in a given interpretation (see Section 2.2). For if we interpret a given figure p as representing a cube, the linguistic representation of p, via the method of representation $R(\ )$, is the sentence $R(p) =$ 'There exist 12 congruent line-segments and 24 right angles arranged as follows . . .'. Whether p is a perceptual judgement that there is a cube here-now or p is a picture interpreted as a cube, our choice of perceptual judgement or pictorial interpretation, when construed as a kind of hypothesis choice, is influenced by the dictates of a simplicity criterion.

At this point, we must consider the problem raised by question (C): There is no single three-dimensional interpretation of a figure. If we are to give a figure a three-dimensional interpretation, which one are we most likely to choose?

Perkins attacks this problem by considering what geometrical properties of a figure can be used to predict the three-dimensional interpretation that will be attributed to it.[14] His theory is that a straight-line figure tends to be interpreted as '. . . a space form which (1) has planar (not curved) faces, (2) projects to the figure, and (3) satisfies a geometrically maximal combination of constraints from the set of constraints' (p. 24). In explaining what 'projects' comes to, Perkins purposely ignores the influence of perspective on the geometrical properties of the figure; its influence is usually not great and seems to be accommodated best as a second-order effect. The set of geometrical properties that Perkins employs includes sameness of angles, colinearity, rectilinearity, symmetry, and parallelness. Given that each of these is to be optimized, his theory predicts many of the interpretations which we in fact affix to figures. Moreover, his theory often predicts cases in which the maximal interpretation is not unique, where we have the experience of shifting from one interpretation to another. His theory also predicts the opposite situation from ambiguity, namely, the geometrically optimal set of constraints can sometimes preclude the existence of a solid object which satisfies them all. These are cases of perceiving 'impossible' figures. Although Perkins' theory is not perfect because there seem to be some counterexamples and because it is not rigorously quantitative (nor had

[14] Perkins, 'The Perception of Line Drawings of Simple Space Forms'.

it been fully tested at the time of publication), it fits well enough to be highly suggestive.

Perkins' proposal may also be accommodated within our paradigmatic situation. Condition (2) stipulates that the posited object must project to the figure; that is, the hypothesis accepted must fit the evidence. Moreover, the maximally valued interpretation of a figure tends to be one which has the fewest differences and inhomogeneities between constituent parts. For example, one tends to minimize the number of different angles and line-segments. In this sense, condition (3) of Perkins' theory seems to be an instance of a preference for maximally simple interpretations. Perkins' work lends further credence to our claim that the interpretation of these line figures seems to involve the existential positioning of arrays of lines and angles, subject to a minimum principle.

A similar point of view emerges from the work of Attneave and Frost.[15] The variable they investigated was the apparent slant with the frontal plane of line drawings seen as boxes. Attneave and Frost showed that the perceived slant was predicted by the geometrical arrangement in which there was perfect homogeneity of clues on one or more of three variables (angle, length, slope). This case also shows that perceiving involves a preference for interpretations which maximize the homogeneity of certain crucial properties of the posited object.

Even though the details of these theories need to be refined and attention needs to be given to a greater variety of cases, it seems that the success that has been encountered so far is sufficient to show the potential explanatory character of some 'quantitative minimum criterion'. What is needed is some canonical form in which to describe figures and objects (possibly in terms of angles and segments positioned within a visual coordinate system).[16] A simplicity criterion would then be applied which valued interpretations (hypotheses) that posited configurations that are minimal relative to the canonical

[15] Attneave and Frost, 'The Determination of Perceived Tridimensional Orientation by Minimum Criteria'.

[16] An ambitious attempt in this direction which subsumes the Necker cube example as well as many others is Leeuwenberg's *Structural Information of Visual Patterns* and his 'A Perceptual Coding Language for Visual and Auditory Patterns'. Attneave's 'Some Informational Aspects of Visual Perception' also considers some characteristics of the perceptual coding system.

properties. As we have seen, fewer angles (segments) and fewer different angles (segments) would be preferred to more. Such variables as rectilinearity and parallelness clearly are not independent of the other desiderata, and a simplicity criterion applied to an adequate canonical description would have to be sensitive to them as well. It is worth repeating that defining a canonical form in which to describe figures and solids is hardly trivial. There are many different ways of describing figures, and which figures come out more 'minimal' than others crucially depends on which properties are used to describe them. Within the theory of simplicity, this project amounts to constructing a *P*-system for visual forms. Regardless of what the details of this construction turn out to be, it seems clear that the regularities underlying our interpretation of figures are in no way idiosyncratic but constitute an instance of our more general policy of imposing simple hypotheses on the environment.

4.3 Apparent Motion

If two or more figures are flashed onto a screen at properly arranged intervals, durations, distances, and intensities,[17] one will perceive apparent motion between the figures. Depending on how the parameters are set, one can perceive partial apparent motion (where the first figure moves part of the way towards the second and then disappears, and the second figure appears along the path of motion and then moves the rest of the way to 'join itself'), beta motion (where the first figure moves to join the second), or phi motion (usually described as 'pure motion', in which one does not perceive figural characteristics, such as contour). The phenomenon of apparent motion makes movies possible; successive still images are projected on a screen and the viewer fills in the disparities herself. Max Wertheimer was the first to study apparent motion systematically; his study was one of the seminal works of Gestalt psychology.[18]

One of the most striking features of apparent motion is that it is 'rationalizing' in character. For beta motion, the perceiver does not merely fill the intervening space between the flashed

---

[17] The optimal values for these and other parameters and how they are related are discussed in Chap. 3 of Kolers' *Aspects of Motion Perception*.

[18] Wertheimer, 'Experimentelle Studien über das Sehen von Bewegung'.

figures with copies of the first figure. If there is a difference of shape or colour between the first and second figure, the perceiver will transform and deform the first as it moves along the path so that, gradually, it becomes the second. Usually, though not always, the transformation follows a principle of minimal change to resolve disparity; that is, the impletion of images between the two flashed figures seems to rationalize differences in simple ways.[19]

However, as Kolers points out in *Aspects of Motion Perception*, it is difficult to specify what principles these impletions obey. Apparent motion encompasses a multiplicity of effects and seems to turn on a multiplicity of variables. One can perceive plastic and continuous deformations of figures along straight lines, along curves in a plane, and in depth. Also, one can perceive somewhat abrupt contour deformations between figures which intuitively seem to be very different in contour (e.g., the transformation from a circle to a triangle will not be smooth). However, just what this difference in contour amounts to proves to be exasperatingly difficult to explain. Further, certain patterns of apparent motion seem to be impossible to achieve (e.g., one cannot achieve collisions or make figures cross). This staggering variety must be taken seriously, because the effects people experience clearly are not idiosyncratic (in that different people tend to see the same sorts of motion in the same sorts of stimulus situations), nor are they significantly influenced by 'volition, attitude, or expectation'.[20]

In spite of the diversity of effects, the paths followed in apparent motion are rather narrowly constrained. An infinity of impletions could link two flashed points in apparent motion. Yet, which paths are actually seen? Usually one sees a straight line; less often, a smooth curve in the plane[21] or a smooth curve in depth.[22] The same sorts of constraints on the paths seem to apply to three or more points in apparent motion. If the points are colinear, then the path usually seen is a straight line. If the points are not colinear, then we usually see them joined

[19] Kolers, *Aspects of Motion Perception*, pp. 194–6.

[20] ibid., p. 163.

[21] Hall, Earle, and Crookes, 'A Pendulum Phenomenon in the Visual Perception of Apparent Movement'; Johansson, *Configurations in Event Perception*.

[22] Kolers, ibid., pp. 82–95, discusses techniques for obtaining depth apparent movement.

by a smooth curve, often by a circle. Brown and Voth[23] report that four points arranged as a diamond have a circular apparent motion effect, although Sylvester[24] has shown that under some conditions the four points will be linked by four straight lines. Also, if each of three noncolinear points is flashed for a relatively long period while the interstimulus time is relatively short, one sees two straight lines linking the three points. This effect, however, seems to have the form of two separate impletions, rather than a single impletion between three points.

These facts suggest that apparent motion is a kind of perceptual curve-fitting problem. If a scientist is interested in correlating two variables, he plots his evidence, a set of n data points, and then he joins them with a curve. An infinity of curves fits these n points to any desired degree; the scientist will select the simplest curve. Among other things, this preference for simple curves voices itself as a preference for smooth curves, i.e., ones lacking changes and discontinuities (see Section 2.6). Strictly speaking, this conjecture implies that the path perceived in apparent motion between a set of flashed points must be the same as the optimal curve associated with those points in a curve-fitting problem (where perfect goodness-of-fit is required); but this is not true in general. Two points in apparent motion are sometimes seen to be joined by a curve, and three noncolinear points are sometimes seen to be linked by two straight lines rather than by a curve.

At least some of these deviations from the conjecture can be accounted for as second-order effects—the results of intervening variables. Seeing two points in depth apparent motion is sometimes caused by stimulus asynchrony (that is, when points one and two alternate, and the interval between one and two is different from the interval between two and one). This seems to be a case in which the perceiver attributes constant speed and a circular path to the objects to resolve the disparity. The dictates of simplicity are not violated here; rather, the simplest curve is one in which uniform curvature and uniform speed are achieved by moving into three dimensions.[25]

[23] Brown and Voth, 'The Path of Seen Motion as a Function of the Vector-Field'.

[24] Sylvester, 'Apparent Movement and the Brown–Voth Experiment'.

[25] See Kolers' *Aspects of Motion Perception*, Chap. 3, for a discussion of this phenomenon. Kolers doubts that the perceptual system has a primitive speed-

Similarly, the case mentioned earlier in which three noncolinear points are joined by two straight lines seems to be accounted for by the relatively long periods of time that each point is shown. Two curve-fitting problems are being tackled, not one. Initially, the first two points are joined; then the second and third points are joined.

A slightly different difficulty besetting the conjecture that apparent motion is the solution to a perceptual curve-fitting problem is the existence of arrays of points for which it is impossible to achieve a good apparent motion effect. Although there may be apparent motion between two points, introducing a few extra points between the initial two weakens rather than strengthens the effect. However, if many extra points are introduced, the effect can be of good quality. The relationship between number of points and quality of effect seems to graph as a U-shaped curve.[26] Notice that in the two extreme cases where a good effect is possible, the counterpart curve-fitting problem seems to yield results in keeping with our conjecture. When two points are flashed, a straight line occurs (except in the somewhat exceptional cases mentioned before), and a two-point curve-fitting problem has a straight line as its optimal solution. On the other hand, a large number of points arranged in a curve will be seen in curved apparent motion, and the curve-fitting interpolation will also be a smooth curve.

These results suggest that if a pattern of dots is seen in good apparent motion, the path usually obeys the constraints on solving a curve-fitting problem. However, the converse seems not to hold in that there are patterns of dots for which a curve-fitting problem can be solved, and yet there can be no good apparent motion effect between the points. Perhaps the reason for this asymmetry is that curve-fitting is a higher order cognitive process than the perception of apparent motion, and, in general, higher order judgements are more subject to the will than lower order ones are. That is, we can consciously and deliberately impose continuous hypotheses on sets of data, but

---

detecting device and sees the operating principle in terms of time. McKay's 'The Interactive Processes in Visual Perception' suggests that the visual system has a primitive velocity-detecting system.

[26] See Kolers, *Aspects of Motion Perception*, pp. 35 ff.

the same ability seems not to attach to apparent motion perception.[27]

Other facts could be cited in support of this way of looking at apparent motion between points,[28] and other difficulties with our hypothesis could also probably be produced. Clearly, the whole phenomenon of the regularities governing the paths of apparent motion needs more study. However, based on the data now available, it seems reasonable to conjecture tentatively that apparent motion follows simple paths, and the notion of simplicity involved is the same one that applies to scientific hypothesis choice.

4.4 Aesthetic Simplicity

Although discussions of simplicity tend to distinguish routinely between aesthetic simplicity and the kind of 'epistemic' simplicity considered so far,[29] I will argue here that the two kinds of simplicity are in fact one. They share a common logical structure and differ only in the way they are used. Our epistemic policies for choosing hypotheses are based in part on epistemic simplicity, but our aesthetic preferences for pictures do not seem to be as clearly predicated on their aesthetic simplicity. We will take up this question of preference later on. For now, we focus our attention on applying the theory of simplicity to certain elementary judgements of aesthetic simplicity.

Earlier, we used a method of representation $R(\ )$ which translated pictures and perceptual judgements into sentences. It enabled us to compare the simplicity of different pictures and the simplicity of different perceptual judgements by comparing the simplicity of their linguistic representations. We now want to compare the simplicity of different physical objects. To do this, we will use a method of description $D(\ )$ which maps physical objects onto sentences that describe them.

---

[27] In his 'On Perceptual Readiness', p. 8, Bruner notes that perceptual inferences are much less reversible and flexible than higher level ones.

[28] For example, apparent motion seems never to involve 'created corners'. That is, if a corner is perceived at all, it is associated with a flashed point, and is not the result of an impletion. The same applies to the existence of changes in curvature in a smooth apparent motion path.

[29] See, for example, Reichenbach, *Experience and Prediction*, pp. 373 ff., and Popper, *The Logic of Scientific Discovery*, pp. 136-7.

Notice that $D(\ )$ and $R(\ )$ are not the same, although both partake of the linguistifying tactic urged earlier. There are many ways to describe a physical object, so it is important to delimit the kinds of descriptions that $D(\ )$ will provide. The choice of appropriate descriptions can be evaluated on at least two fronts. First, given that we intuitively think that one physical object is simpler than another, does our theory of simplicity mirror this intuition when it is applied to the descriptions that $D(\ )$ yields of the two objects? Second, does the

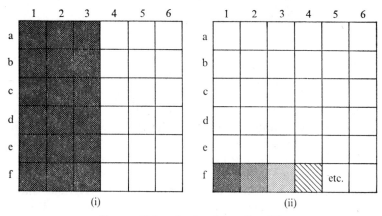

Fig. 10. (i) is a simpler picture than (ii)

description chosen for an object seem to describe fully what we take to be the salient significant properties of the object in the context in which it is discussed? Although these two constraints by no means uniquely fix how objects are to be described, they do provide some check on descriptions assigned to particular objects.

An example shows how our theory draws aesthetic and epistemic simplicity together. Consider the two pictures in Figure 10, each made of a grid of squares with a colour assigned to each square. Picture (i) is half white and half black; picture (ii) has a different colour assigned to each square. We intuitively judge (i) to be aesthetically simpler than (ii). Pictures (i) and (ii) may be described as follows:

(4)   Columns 1, 2, and 3 are black and columns 4, 5, and 6 are white.

(5) Square (1, f) is black, square (2, f) is green, square (3, f) is red, square (4, f) is blue, etc.

Relative to the following question, (4) is more informative and, hence, simpler than (5):

What colour is square x?

Notice that the intuitive aesthetic simplicity of picture (i) over picture (ii) is mirrored by the epistemic simplicity of the canonical description of (i) over the canonical description of (ii).[30]

We might conceive of (i) and (ii) as pictorial representations of two competing hypotheses; for example, they might be incompatible maps of the same terrain. In this case, epistemic simplicity would counsel us to choose (i) over (ii) just as it would dictate our choice of hypothesis (4) over (5). However, if we consider (i) and (ii) as pictures that make no knowledge claims at all, we are not compelled to decide between them on either epistemic or aesthetic grounds. Yet, if we wanted to, we could state an aesthetic preference for one of them. Here, simplicity need not play a decisive role, since we might find (ii) more pleasing than (i). Thus, the use we make of simplicity judgements in aesthetic contexts seems to differ from its use in epistemic contexts; however, if the example of Figure 10 is at all representative, the two kinds of simplicity have a common underlying structure.

In our theory, (4) is a simpler hypothesis than (5) because of its informativeness; that is, because it renders the occurrence of colours in squares more redundant and predictable. Attneave's investigation of the redundancy of grid pictures yields similar results, although he does not couch them in terms of simplicity.[31] Subjects were given a concealed picture divided into squares and were asked to go through the rows in order and guess of each square whether it was black or white. After each guess, the square was uncovered so that the subjects saw

[30] (5) would come out simpler than (4) if they were compared relative to a question about spatial location. This shows that colour, not spatial location, is typical of our simplicity intuitions about (4) and (5) (see Section 1.8 for a discussion of the notion of typicalness). This problem also arises in comparing either (i) or (ii) with a perfectly homogeneous picture.
[31] Attneave, 'Some Informational Aspects of Visual Perception'.

whether their guesses were correct. Attneave found that guessing patterns favoured hypotheses of homogeneity and no-change and that guessing errors clustered around changes in picture pattern. Relative to these guessing policies, pictures can be ranked as more or less redundant, the most redundant picture being one that is all black or all white and the least redundant being one with a random distribution of black and white squares. Attneave's paper examines other cases in which we tend to have expectations of homogeneity and no-change and suggests that the perceptual system aims at detecting redundancies in the environment. Attneave identifies the search for redundancy with the search for law-like connections and explores the analogy between perceiving and theorizing in some detail.[32]

Green and Courtis objected to Attneave's results on the grounds that the results depended on the subjects having to guess the squares' colours in a particular order.[33] It is easy to see how this might be true if we compare picture (i) of Figure 10 with a picture made of an equal number of black and white squares that are randomly distributed. If the subjects were asked to go through both pictures by starting at the lower left and working to the right and then up to the next row and so forth (as they were in Attneave's experiment), they would probably make fewer errors on picture (i) than on the random picture. But suppose that they were asked to guess so that the first half of the squares queried were in fact the black ones of the random picture. In this case, they would probably make fewer mistakes on the random picture than on picture (i) (or at least the difference in the number of errors made on the two pictures would be smaller).

Thus, Attneave's experiments can serve as an explication of pictorial redundancy only if we relativize them to a certain kind of guessing order. Green and Courtis took this relativity as a decisive criticism of Attneave's experiments. However, the guessing pattern Attneave used seems to be a natural one, at least in comparison with the odd guessing sequence contem-

---

[32] Attneave's notion of redundancy is distinct from that given in Garner's *Uncertainty and Structure as Psychological Concepts*, even though the two are related.

[33] Green and Courtis, 'Information Theory and Figure Perception: The Metaphor that Failed'.

plated above. In visual perception, not all groupings of locations in the two-dimensional visual array are equally natural.
Adjacent locations are naturally associated together, whereas
randomly scattered ones are not. That Attneave's results
depend on this difference is not a shortcoming but points once
again to the importance of principles of classification and
organization in perception.

A similar problem besets our explication of simplicity. To
compare picture (i) with the random picture discussed above,
we must compare hypothesis (4), which is the description of (i),
with the hypothesis

(6)   Squares (a, 1), (b, 1), (e, 1), (b, 2), (d, 2), (a, 3),
      (b, 3), (e, 3), (f, 3), (c, 4), (e, 4), (b, 5), (d, 5), (f, 5),
      (a, 6), (b, 6), (d, 6), and (f, 6) are black and all the
      rest are white,

which is the description of the random picture (let us assume),
relative to the question

(7)   What colour is square x?

If we call the set of black squares in (6) 'A' and the set of white
squares in (6) 'B', the MEI of (6) relative to question (7) is
the set

(8) $\begin{pmatrix} x \text{ is in } A \lor x \text{ is black} \\ x \text{ is in } B \lor x \text{ is white} \end{pmatrix}$.

If we call the set of black squares in hypothesis (4) 'left' and the
set of white squares in (4) 'right', the MEI of (4) relative to
question (7) is the set

(9) $\begin{pmatrix} x \text{ is left} \lor x \text{ is black} \\ x \text{ is right} \lor x \text{ is white} \end{pmatrix}$.

To compare the contents of MEIs (8) and (9), we must have
some further information about the relative contents of their
member statements. The set of left-hand squares is a much
more natural spatial grouping than A, which is odd and
artificial. The same applies to the right-hand squares as
opposed to B. Based on this, it seems natural to postulate that
knowing that a given square is on the left requires less information than knowing that it is in set A, and knowing that it is on

the right requires less information than knowing it is in set B. From this, we can deduce that MEI (9) is lower in content than MEI (8), so hypothesis (4) is simpler than hypothesis (6). It follows that picture (i) is simpler than the random picture.

The reason that the unnaturalness of sets A and B led us to say that placing an individual in A requires more information than placing it in the set of left-hand squares derives from a difference between natural and unnatural classes noted earlier (see Section 1.8). If we imagine picture (i) and the random picture to be maps of a city, the source of this asymmetry becomes more apparent. Suppose that the city in question is divided into hostile camps by a wall (falling between columns 3 and 4 on the maps). Under this interpretation, the left-hand squares constitute a natural class in that they comprise one faction's territory. Assuming that A is an unnatural class, it represents a set of spatially scattered locales which our knowledge of the city fails to unite into a law-like category.[34] We can imagine situations in which we know that an individual is in the western half of the city (represented on map (i) in black) but do not know which part of the western half he is in. In contrast, it seems that we can place an individual in A only by knowing which subclass of A he is in. Notice that even though the western half of the city and the locations in A each constitute half of the city's total territory, we must know more about an individual to place him in A than to place him in the western half.

Precisely the same situation obtains in a simplicity comparison between two equations relating x and y that graph as Figure 3 (see p. 70) and Figure 11, respectively. The fact that the equation in Figure 3 is simpler because it posits only one change can be mirrored within our theory only if we can say that the set of x values greater than b is more natural than the set of x values such that $d_1 < x \leqslant d_2$ or $d_3 < x \leqslant d_4$ or $b < x \leqslant d_5$ or $d_6 < x$. Put differently, we need to assume that saying that an individual falls into the former class has less content than saying that it falls into the latter. Granting this,

---

[34] This means that our disjunctive specification of A is indispensable (see Sections 1.8 and 3.6); there is no natural sufficient condition for membership in A that is not also a natural sufficient condition for membership in one of the individual squares in A.

our theory implies that the equation in Figure 3 is simpler than the one in Figure 11 in that it involves fewer changes and heterogeneities.

These observations telescope into our discussion of aesthetic simplicity. The simplicity of two pictures each made of black and white squares can be distinguished only if we can rank different groupings of squares as more or less natural and nonrandom. From the example of picture (i) in Figure 10 and the random picture described in hypothesis (6), we saw that con-

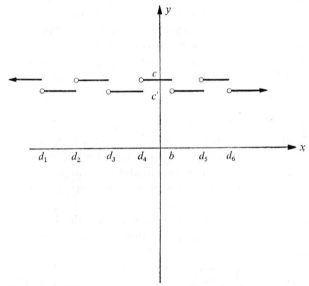

Fig. 11. A multiple change hypothesis

tiguity is an important structural factor. This constraint on the naturalness of ways of grouping squares in a grid picture plays the same role in our theory that the stipulation of a particular kind of guessing pattern plays in Attneave's. In both cases, the constraint is needed if the theory is to explicate the redundancy (simplicity) of pictures.

A crude description of a picture that merely assigns a colour to each square of a grid completely fails to pick out structurally significant properties of organization. We have seen that a set of n contiguous squares is more natural than a set of n randomly scattered ones. A P-system which is insensitive to contiguity as an organizing property would be like a system of phonological description that puts the two sets [i p z] and [i a æ] on the same level because both contain three phonemes (see Section 3.3). The distinctive feature approach to phonology seeks to make relevant groupings of phonemes fully explicit by detailing their basic organizing properties; a similar taxonomy for pictorial organization is needed.

Another study that throws light on aesthetic simplicity is Attneave's 'Physical Determinants of the Judged Complexity of Shapes'. A set of shapes was shown in quick succession to the subjects and then repeated more slowly while the subjects ranked them from 1 to 6 in complexity. There were four different groups of subjects, each given the shapes in a different order. Attneave found that 90 per cent of the responses were predicted by the following generalities: (a) The greater the number of independent turns (curves or angles), the greater the complexity. (b) Symmetrical shapes were more complex than asymmetrical shapes with the number of independent turns held constant, but symmetrical shapes were less complex than asymmetrical shapes with total number of turns held constant. (c) The higher the arithmetic mean of algebraic difference in degrees between successive turns, the greater the complexity.[35]

The factors mentioned in (a) and (c) are similar to the ones Hochberg and his colleagues thought to be predictive of apparent three-dimensionality (see Section 4.2). The second factor Attneave cites—symmetry—is often named as a contributor to simplicity.[36] According to Attneave's experiment, a bilaterally symmetrical ink blot would be judged simpler than an asymmetrical ink blot whose left side was the same as that of the symmetrical ink blot and whose right side had a com-

[35] Attneave's 'Physical Determinants of the Judged Complexity of Shapes' also claims that the matrix grain has no impact on judged complexity nor were curved shapes thought to be more complex than angular ones. Attneave concludes that judged complexity and the amount of information that the psychologist uses to construct his figures need not coincide. For example, more information is needed to specify a curved shape $(x, y$ and the radius of curvature) than to specify an angular shape (x, y). Note that neither of these results jars with our explication of simplicity.

[36] See, for example, Birkhoff's *Aesthetic Measures*. Weyl's *Symmetry* gives an interesting overview of some uses that have been made of symmetry in the visual arts and provides a mathematical characterization of symmetry in terms of transformational invariance.

pletely different pattern (although the same number of turns). Notice that Attneave's guessing experiment would probably yield the result that subjects make fewer errors on the symmetrical ink blot than on the asymmetrical one. In another experiment, Attneave showed that a symmetrical picture is easier to remember than an asymmetrical one occupying the same number of cells.[37]

Within our theory, bilateral symmetry contributes to the simplicity of a form by making one side of a figure highly predictable from our knowledge of the other. More precisely, the transformations that carry each side into the other are simpler functions for a symmetrical form than for an asymmetrical form with the same number of angles or curves. To see this, imagine transformations for each of the two ink blots just mentioned, which carry one side of the ink blot into the other. Let the axis of symmetry be the y-axis. For the symmetrical ink blot, all we need know about an arbitrary point p to answer the question 'What is the image of p?' is the distance between p and the axis of symmetry. To calculate this, we need know only the ordinate of the coordinate of p. However, for the asymmetrical ink blot, we must know more about p than its distance from the y-axis if we are to be able to answer the question. Bilateral symmetry contributes to simplicity because the equation defining one side of a symmetrical figure in terms of the other is simpler than the counterpart equation which describes an asymmetrical figure with the same number of turns. Similar considerations would account for rotational symmetry as a simplifying factor.

We have concentrated so far on the aesthetic simplicity of 'meaningless' patterns. The difference in simplicity that we saw between the two pictures in Figure 10 could apply just as easily to two bolts of cloth and has nothing to do with taking these two pictures to be representations of the world. We might say that we compared them as physical objects rather than as messages or hypotheses. I now want to consider the simplicity of pictures as meaningful representations. Using the method

[37] Attneave, 'Symmetry, Information, and Memory for Patterns'. In this experiment, each square of a grid either contained one dot or was blank. Attneave also found that random patterns were harder to remember the more cells they occupied and that symmetrical patterns were no easier to remember than asymmetrical ones with the same information content.

of representation $R(\ )$, we can work backwards from pairs of hypotheses h and h', such that we have strong intuitions that h is simpler than h', to pairs of pictures p and p', such that $R(p) = h$ and $R(p') = h'$. Here are two likely pairs of examples: a picture of a crowd of men each wearing wildly different coloured clothing and each engaged in a different activity and a picture of a few men wearing the same clothing and doing the same thing; an architectural plan of a building which is richly ornamented and an architectural plan of the same building without its ornaments. The counterpart sentence for each picture is a conjunction of existential hypotheses. By Russell's razor (Section 2.2), the former of each pair is simpler.

We began this section by noting that simplicity is put to different uses in aesthetic and epistemic contexts. We choose hypotheses in part for their simplicity, where 'choose' means 'reasonably regard as true'. However, the role of simplicity in aesthetic 'choice' is very poorly understood; presumably, the notion of choice involved here is something like 'aesthetically prefer'. In spite of the little that is known about the role of simplicity in aesthetic valuations, two very extreme cases seem to exist in which human preferences are rather clear. Dember has argued that we show a marked taste for complexity; we tend to avoid environments which are too homogeneous and impoverished of sensation.[38] Conversely, it seems obvious that we avoid environments that are too chaotic and rich in surprises. Attneave has noted that a very fine-grained picture made of random scatterings of black and white dots tends to be viewed as perfectly homogeneous; here, the tremendous information overload is 'averaged out'.[39] Presumably, these two tendencies exist side by side, and we seek some middle ground. Between the two extremes of perfect randomness and perfect homogeneity, different people tend to seek different optimal arrangements.[40]

Our discussion of aesthetic simplicity has been sketchy, but

[38] Dember, *The Psychology of Perception*.

[39] Attneave, 'Informational Aspects of Visual Perception', p. 188.

[40] In *The Psychology of Perception*, p. 360, Dember discusses the ideal complexity level for a person at a given time with respect to a given stimulus. In 'Pattern Preference as a Function of Pattern Uncertainty', Dorfman and McKenna argue along similar lines that a person's pattern preferences reveal an ideal complexity level which they define in terms of the fineness of the matrix grain.

I hope it has been suggestive of how the relative simplicity of pairs of aesthetic objects can be modelled within our theory. Our simplicity judgements in aesthetics frequently turn on the qualities that were discussed in Chapter 2 as applying to hypotheses. Functions $D(\ )$ and $R(\ )$ provide an aesthetic object with a linguistic counterpart, and the simplicity of the object is then explained in terms of the simplicity of the corresponding sentence. Much care must be taken in choosing the appropriate linguistic surrogate for the aesthetic object; the simplicity criterion can mirror no more than is fully explicit in the sentences to which it is applied. This suggests why it is difficult to imagine how the greater complexity of Mannerist over Renaissance painting could be explained in the facile fashion we explained the relative simplicity of the pictures in Figure 10. When simplicity comparisons are meant to be subtle, subtle descriptions of the objects compared must be provided.

4.5 Perspicuity

In this chapter, we have used the ideas of a method of representation $R(\ )$ and a method of description $D(\ )$ to talk about the simplicity of pictures. $R(p)$ is true of any scene that p pictures and $D(p)$ describes p. $R(p)$ and $D(p)$, both being hypotheses, can be subjected to the simplicity criterion. The question arises of how these two functions are related. That is, given two pictures or sentences[41] p and p', can one predict the relative simplicity of $R(p)$ and $R(p')$ from that of $D(p)$ and $D(p')$ or vice versa?

In Sections 2.6 and 3.5, we noticed that a system of notation is perspicuous if the simplicity of hypotheses is manifest in the surface properties of the notation. The functions $D(\ )$ and $R(\ )$ enable us to define perspicuity as follows:

A system S is perspicuous iff for any p, p' formulatable in S, $D(p) >_s D(p')$ iff $R(p) >_s R(p')$.

Thus, when the system considered is perspicuous, the answer to the question of the previous paragraph is yes. If S is a system of notation and p and p' are sentences, then 'formulatable in S'

---

[41] If p is a sentence, then $R(p) = p$.

merely means constructable via the basic vocabulary and the formation rules of S. If S is a system of representation and p and p' are pictures, the meaning of 'formulatable in S' is less easily specified. Roughly, S will include a potential infinity of pictures each subject to certain general constraints (possibly including a family of kinds of perspective). For our purposes, S may be thought of as composed of all pictures that we would intuitively take to be representational.

One way a system of notation can be perspicuous is if the simplicity of hypotheses is manifested in the length of their minimum representations (which is exactly what Chomsky and Halle were trying to achieve; see Chapter 3). For example, according to our theory

$$(10) \qquad\qquad (x)(Fx)$$

is simpler than

$$(11a) \qquad\qquad (x)(Gx \supset Fx).$$

Now let us suppose that the respective relevant descriptions of (10) and (11a) are:

(12) There is a line of type containing just seven inscriptions.

(13) There is a line of type containing just ten inscriptions.

(12) is simpler than (13) because (12) more closely approximates the optimally simple case in which *all* the spaces in a line of type are blank (see Section 2.2 on the relationship between simplicity, perfect homogeneity, and the way hypotheses can approximate perfect homogeneity). If this parity between the simplicity of hypotheses and the simplicity of their relevant descriptions could be maintained for every pair of hypotheses formulatable in a given notation, the notation would be perspicuous.[42]

Developing a perspicuous notation for any reasonably expressive language would be a formidable task. Since (10) is simpler than its negation, universal and existential hypotheses might be expressed as $(x)(. . .)$ and $\sim(x)(. . .)$, respectively. Furthermore, in Section 3.6 we argued that

$$(14a) \qquad\qquad (x)[(Gx \vee Hx) \supset Fx]$$

---

[42] Notice that if S were a system of descriptions made of elementary descriptions plus rules for building up compounds, then S would be perspicuous if simple properties were given short names.

is simpler than (11a). To allow a counting measure to reflect this, we might introduce a predicate 'I' which is defined as equivalent to 'G or H'. (11a) and (14a) would then be reformulated as

(11b) $(x)[(Ix \& \sim Hx) \supset Fx]$

and

(14b) $(x)(Ix \supset Fx)$.

Now the counting measure yields intuitive results.

However, this notational convention brings with it as many problems as it solves. Given that we intuitively believe that

(15a) $(x)(Gx)$

is simpler than

(16a) $(x)(Gx \lor Hx)$,

reformulating (16a) in terms of 'I' leads the counting measure astray:

(16b) $(x)(Ix)$.

Similar problems arise when we try to mirror the intuition that (11a) is less simple than $(x)(Gx \equiv Fx)$.

This raises the question of whether there could be a perfectly perspicuous system of representation. Our rather discouraging comments on the possibility of perfect perspicuity for a language carry over to the case of representational pictures. In our discussion in Section 4.2 we saw that members of various figure families in Figure 9 are not equally simple when taken as two-dimensional drawings, although many of them have the same three-dimensional interpretations. These examples defeat the claim to perfect perspicuity by providing pairs of pictures p and p' such that $D(p) >_s D(p')$ and $R(p) =_s R(p')$. Just as the set of all sentences must be narrowly restricted if perspicuity is to be possible, so the set of all representational line drawings must be substantially limited if there is to be any hope of defining a perfectly perspicuous system of representation. In both cases, it seems somewhat unlikely that perfect perspicuity is attainable for any moderately rich representational system.

Other qualities of hypotheses and their representations can be relevant to the perspicuity of a system of notation. Thus, our characterization of perspicuity in terms of simplicity is less a definition than an example of how a system can be perspicuous. Onomatopoeia constitutes a further example. In a poem, if a theme of violence and conflict is mirrored in the sounds of the words, the harmony of form and content exemplifies perspicuous representation. Here, as in our example having to do with simplicity, properties of what the message says (There is conflict . . .) are mirrored in properties of how the message says it (harsh sounds). Within standard musical notation, pitch is perspicuously represented while tempo and rhythm are not. Thus, as might be expected, a system of notation may be perspicuous in some respects but not perspicuous in others.

In the light of these diverse considerations, we can modify and generalize our initial definition of perspicuity. Where ϕ is a measure of a semantic property (like how simple a hypothesis is) and F is a measure of a syntactic property (like how many inscriptions there are in a minimum representation of a hypothesis) within a system of representation S, we can say that ϕ is perspicuously represented in S by F just in case

For any p, p' formulatable in S, $\phi(p) > \phi(p')$ iff $F(p) > F(p')$.

4.6 Conclusion

Much work remains to be done on the psychological phenomena touched on in this chapter and on other phenomena as well. For example, the often-referred-to connection between simplicity and difficulty needs to be worked out. Using the framework of experiments developed by Bruner, Goodnow, and Austin,[43] we might conjecture that the connection runs something like this: A subject would be told to guess a predetermined concept by choosing objects one at a time from a group of objects and asking whether the item he has chosen falls under the concept or not. After learning from the experimenter whether or not the chosen item falls under the concept, the subject would try to guess what the concept is. The sequence would be repeated until the subject attains the concept. The hypothesis would be that the longer on average it takes subjects to guess the concept, the less natural the concept is. This connection between simplicity and difficulty seems clearest in

[43] Bruner, Goodnow, and Austin, *A Study of Thinking.*

the case of disjunctive categories; the more unrelated categories strung together in a disjunction, the longer it would take to guess the concept. However, the conjunctively defined concept A & B & C seems at times to be more difficult to attain than the concept A, where A, B, and C are logically independent natural concepts. If we accept the claim of Section 1.8 that A & B & C is no less natural than A, this would be a case where difficulty and naturalness part ways. Similar problems occur when the concept to be attained is a natural one in virtue of a theory that the subject believes but does not immediately call to mind. In this case, a disjunctive set which is not natural might be attained more easily than a natural one. These difficulties do not vitiate the possible significance of some connection between naturalness and difficulty but merely define some of the parameters that a study of the connection might take into account.[44]

Further instances of elementary inference-making might be fruitfully seen from the point of view of a theory of simplicity. Given our general tendency to favour no-change hypotheses (see Section 2.1), the child's development of the concepts of object permanence[45] and conservation of liquids[46] can be regarded as involving a preference for simplicity. The advent in the child of both of these cognitive capacities might be explained in terms of the child's applying an already present simplicity criterion to new properties and transformations rather than in terms of the acquisition of some fundamentally new thought schema.[47] Similarly, the philosophically interesting phenomenon of continuing the series might profitably be conceived

[44] Attneave's 'Physical Determinants of the Judged Complexity of Shapes' claims that complex visual objects are harder to reproduce from memory, to name, and to match. His 'Symmetry, Information, and Memory for Patterns' shows that a symmetrical pattern is remembered more easily than an asymmetrical one occupying the same number of cells. Rosch's 'Natural Categories' uses the difficulty of learning certain concepts as evidence for their unnaturalness.

[45] See, for example, Bower's 'The Development of Object Permanence: Some Studies of Existence Constancy', his 'The Object in the World of the Infant', Bower and Patterson's 'Stages in the Development of the Object Concept', and Piaget's *The Construction of Reality in the Child*, pp. 1–96.

[46] See, for example, Piaget's *The Child's Concept of Number*, Chaps. 1 and 2, and Bruner, Oliver, and Greenfield's *Studies in Cognitive Growth*, Chaps. 9 and 10.

[47] In 'Interactive Processes in Visual Perception', p. 353, Mackay says: 'The perceptual mechanism functions on the principle of Fisher's null hypothesis— taking stability as the norm, and demanding adequate evidence before making any

of as involving a simplicity criterion. The conjecture would in part be that a person's choice of the next member of a series is dictated by the simplest general rule. For example, in the series 1, 1, 1, 1, ____, the next number chosen will be 1 rather than, say, 3, since 1 is generated by a rule that is simpler than any rule that generates 3.

Investigations along these lines as well as more detailed work on the areas already discussed constitute one half of the programme of discovering what interesting content there might be in our initial conjecture that perceiving and theorizing obey a simplicity criterion. The other half of the programme consists in work on the nature of theorizing itself. Both the psychological hypotheses and the views of theorizing cited here should be taken as preliminary and incomplete. But from this merely temporary vantage point, it seems reasonable to think that the different levels of cognitive processing have similar structures.

---

change in the world-as-perceived, and in every case making the minimal change (however surprising) that will match such new evidence as may arise.' See also Mackay's 'The Stabilisation of Perception during Voluntary Activity'. Quine's principle of minimum mutilation says that the same constraint applies to theorizing. See, for example, his *Philosophy of Logic*, p. 7.

5

Justification

5.1 Justification and Description

The theory that I have been elaborating and defending can be said to justify the use of simplicity in hypothesis choice on the grounds that informativeness is one of our goals in choosing hypotheses and, according to the theory, simplicity is informativeness. But what justifies the theory of simplicity? Since it is a *theory* like any other, its justification derives from its being sufficiently supported and simple. That is, we should assess the adequacy of the theory by subjecting it to the canons of hypothesis choice outlined in Section 1.9. In part, this involves applying the theory to itself. To give substance to the dual claim that the use of simplicity is justified relative to our theory and that our theory is justified relative to the rules of hypothesis choice, we must first give some account of what a justification is. I will do this by examining Goodman's views on the relationship between justifying induction and describing it.[1] His position is built on a fundamentally correct analogy between deductive and inductive inference. The view I will present differs from Goodman's while remaining true to the spirit of his analogy.

Traditionally, philosophers have viewed the tasks of justifying induction and describing it as being quite separate. Conceivably, one could have a descriptively adequate account of our inductive practice that fails to provide a justification of that practice. Conversely, one could have a justification of induction without having more than an intuitive grasp of what our inductive practice is. The former might result in an anthropological theory that describes certain forms of thought and behaviour; the latter might provide us with a licence for

[1] Goodman's account of this relationship constitutes a considerable part of the novelty of his new riddle of induction, which is presented in his *Fact, Fiction, and Forecast*, Chap. 3.

following our inductive intuitions without giving us any deep insight into how those intuitions work.

That justification and description are independent in this way is rejected by Goodman in the strongest terms:

> Principles of deductive inference are justified by their conformity with accepted deductive practice. Their validity depends upon accordance with the particular deductive inferences we actually make and sanction. If a rule yields inacceptable inferences, we drop it as invalid. Justification of general rules thus derives from judgments rejecting or accepting particular deductive inferences.
> This looks flagrantly circular. . . . But this circle is a virtuous one. The point is that rules and particular inferences alike are justified by being brought into agreement with each other. . . . The process of justification is the delicate one of making mutual adjustments between rules and accepted inferences; and in the agreement lies the only justification needed for either.
> All this applies equally well to induction. An inductive inference, too, is justified by conformity to general rules, and a general rule by conformity to accepted inductive inferences. Predictions are justified if they conform to valid canons of induction; and the canons are valid if they accurately codify accepted inductive practice.[2]

An illuminating way to evaluate Goodman's analysis is to pursue his analogy between deductive and inductive inference. We can view a set of syntactic rules for propositional inference as fulfilling a *descriptive* function; it explicates our intuitions that some inferences are reasonable in a way that others clearly are not. That is, within a restricted but potentially infinite class of arguments, we can informally divide the arguments into two groups, and the syntactic rules replicate this sorting process by providing a test which separates the arguments in (approximately) the same way.

Now suppose that we want to choose between making an inference I and an inference I', where I conforms with these syntactic rules and I' violates them. If we decide to make inference I, the justification would take the following form: By following the syntactic rules, we ensure that our inference is valid in the sense that *true* premises guarantee *true* conclusions. Since we can readily identify validity as one of our goals in this

---

[2] Goodman, *Fact, Fiction, and Forecast*, pp. 63–4; quoted in Scheffler, *The Anatomy of Inquiry*, pp. 316–17.

particular inference situation, following the dictates of the propositional calculus is justified, so we make inference *I*. This justification has two components. On the one hand, we were able to identify certain (semantic) purposes which we had in the particular inference situation; on the other hand, we were able to show (by the familiar truth table method, say) that this goal is achievable by following certain (syntactic) rules.[3] Thus, by identifying a goal and showing that a given method will achieve that goal, we succeed in justifying that method as a method for reaching the desired end.

In the case just described, we might have decided not to conform to the rules of the propositional calculus, perhaps because we wanted to infer beyond the data (i.e., to make a nondeductive inference). This ambition requires that we not follow the dictates of a deductive logic, and so the propositional calculus, for all of its descriptive adequacy, has no normative impact on our decision. Thus, in cases where we do obey the canons of propositional logic, our inference is not justified merely because it conforms with the propositional calculus. The inference is justified because conforming with the propositional calculus guarantees that the inference has certain properties that we regard as desirable.

Applying this lesson to nondeductive inference, we see that the fact that general rules fit particular inferences is not sufficient to justify any inference. A descriptively adequate account of our inferential practice provides a justification of that practice only if it embodies parameters that we can take as goals in hypothesis choice. The precise desiderata of non-deductive inference are currently a matter of conjecture. But suppose we had a descriptively adequate theory of nondeduc-tive inference based on simplicity and evidential support of the kind outlined in Section 1.9. By this I mean that the theory accounts for the vast majority of our intuitions that a given hypothesis is more reasonable than another by showing that the former is in some sense simpler or better supported than the latter. We could then justify a particular inference by showing (1) that it conforms with the rules of this theory and (2) that in

---

[3] I am ignoring here the nontrivial problem of saying how the truth table method 'shows' that following certain rules 'ensures' valid arguments. This will not affect the force of the analogy between deductive and nondeductive inference.

making this particular inference we want to maximize simplicity and support.

The inevitable response to such a suggestion is to demand a justification of our desire for hypotheses that are supported and simple. Our desire for support—however this key notion is finally explicated—seems to derive from our wanting hypotheses to be relatively safe bets, given the evidence on which they are based. Similarly, the explication of simplicity I have offered allows us to explain why simplicity is desirable in terms of our wanting theories to anticipate nature, to render experience redundant. In fact, the way in which the theory of simplicity shows how diverse desiderata are reducible to simplicity makes it plausible to say that our desire for *theories* is in fact a desire for simplicity. Of course, one might go on to ask why we should want our theories to be relatively safe and informative. One might just as well demand a justification for wanting the arguments to which we apply deductive canons of inference to be truth-preserving. Justification is always relative to a goal, and one may always go on to ask for a justification of a goal. But no matter how far back one pushes these questions, no pristine justification will be uncovered which is goal-independent. Support and simplicity are as manifestly desirable in nondeductive inferences as truth-preservation is in deductive inferences. So the persistent question of 'Why *this* goal?' is as much and as little an objection to a justification of induction as it is an objection to a justification of deduction. Notice that this argument does not justify induction so much as show how an adequate description of our inferential behaviour could begin to provide such a justification.

In contrast to the above theory of inference with its combined policy of simplicity and support, let us assume that our intuitive judgements about the reasonableness of hypotheses are explicated in terms of the optimization of some set of properties P. Suppose further that we could not identify the properties contained in P as goals that we have in our inductive practice. In this case, we would have a description of induction that failed to justify any inductive inference. If we fill in the set of properties P with support and entrenchment, we see why it is that some people balk at accepting entrenchment as a solution to the (old) problem of induction, even if it does happen to provide an adequate description of our inductive practice.[4] The basis of this hesitation is that some people are reluctant to identify entrenchment as a goal in inductive inference.[5] If the task of describing induction and the task of justifying induction were the same, then the problem of motivating entrenchment would never arise.[6]

Thus, it is at least possible to obtain an adequate description of inductive practice that fails to justify any inductive inference. On the other hand, any general and fully explicit justification of inductive practice must be preceded by a description of what inductive practice is, because an attempted justification that lacks a general description is in the position of not being able to say what it is that stands in need of justification. Goodman's attempt to collapse justification into description fails because it glosses over the fact that description becomes justification only when parameters in the description align themselves with goals that we designate as desirable. Goodman sees his views on justification as harking back to Hume. Ironically, the analysis of justification that I am offering also finds its origins in Hume, but I am applying Hume's idea of justification in ethics to the problem of justification in epistemology.[7]

---

[4] See Goodman, *Fact, Fiction, and Forecast*, Chap. 3, for Goodman's distinction between the old and the new problem of induction and Chap. 4 for a discussion of the notion of entrenchment.

[5] Scheffler's *The Anatomy of Inquiry*, pp. 314–26, and Grunstra's 'The Plausibility of the Entrenchment Concept' try to overcome this reluctance by showing how entrenchment may be seen as desirable.

[6] The goals we have in theorizing, although now imperfectly understood, are themselves governed by second-level desires about what our goals in theorizing should and should not be. That our first-level goals are not *sui generis* but are subject to higher constraints explains how a description of practice can sometimes undermine the justification of that practice. Nietzsche tried to base his normative critique of morality on a description of the goals and motives underlying moral practice. He relied on our wanting our ethical judgements not to be based on weakness, mediocrity, and resentment. Nietzsche hoped to use this second-level assumption of ours to make the transition from an allegedly correct description of moral practice to a discrediting of that practice.

[7] Goodman's identification of justification and description is in harmony with his rejection of intensional notions. For if there is a descriptive predicate that picks out all and only the ordered pairs of beliefs and contexts such that each belief is justified in the context associated with it, then the strict extensionalist will claim that the distinction between the property designated by the descriptive predicate and the property of being justified is a distinction without a difference. Thus, rejecting Goodman's notion of justification commits one to thinking that it makes sense to say that two coextensive predicates can pick out different properties.

5.2 Justifying Simplicity

From the vantage point of this account of justification, it becomes clear why the following demand is wholly misplaced: 'Choosing simple theories over more complex ones is justified only if simple theories are more likely to be true than complex ones.' This position on what is required to justify simplicity I will call 'probabilism'.[8] A theory of hypothesis choice based on high probability alone is not even descriptively adequate (as argued in Section 1.9), and identifying justified theories with maximally probable ones is tantamount to a form of scepticism that refuses to venture beyond the evidence and its consequences. If it is granted that other parameters besides high probability are relevant in hypothesis choice, then the demand that simplicity be justified in terms of high probability seems to be an odd fixation. What would be wrong with justifying simplicity in terms of other desiderata (e.g., in terms of informativeness)?

Unless he is a sceptic, the probabilist is usually under the illusion that simpler theories *are* in general more likely to be true. However, this supposition is incorrect. A theory that goes beyond the evidence by systematizing what appear to be unrelated data is simpler, and less probable, than the evidence itself.[9] Here simplicity and support are at odds with each other and our policies of hypothesis choice at times favour accepting a loss in support if it means a gain in simplicity.

Perhaps the probabilist's position can be reformulated. Take two theories that seem to be equally supported by the evidence. What reason is there to suppose that the simpler of the two is more likely to be true? An example of such a case might be the curve-fitting problem. Two different curves are defined at all points and pass exactly through each data point. Why should we think that the smooth curve is more probably true? To answer the probabilist here, let us first compare this case to the

---

[8] My comments on probabilism are to some extent recapitulations of what should be familiar Popperian themes. See Popper's *Logic of Scientific Discovery*. In *Gambling with Truth*, Levi recognizes that there is a parameter in hypothesis choice that goes beyond the desire for truth. The analysis of justification that I have given is in harmony with his picture of hypothesis choice as a goal-directed activity.

[9] Moreover, it is a property of our theory that if $T \to T'$, then $T \geqslant_s T'$.

one just discussed. Formerly, we were quite willing to sacrifice support to gain simplicity, and none but the sceptic would say that such a trade-off is unjustified. In the second case, no trade-off is required. We can take the simpler hypothesis without any loss in support. Surely if the first choice is justified, the second one is too. Simplicity seems to have a binding force above and beyond any link it may have with probability.

Experience might nevertheless reveal that of two equally supported hypotheses, the simpler one more often turns out to be false. Based on this induction over past inductions, we might decide to countermand our disposition to opt for simple theories. However, this decision would not represent a rejection of simplicity altogether; in this case, we have decided in our second-level induction to view our sample of past inductions as representative of what will happen in future cases of inference. That is, we make use of a simplicity criterion which bids us view the sample class as typical of the total class. From this meta point of view, it is simpler to reject simple object theories. However, after this initial decision, we would try to find out why our inductions usually turned out false. This might lead us to revise our set of natural predicates (our P-system) in such a way that simplicity remains a criterion in hypothesis choice, although now simplicity judgements would be relative to a different set of natural predicates.[10]

In the idea of a second-level induction over past inductions lies the key to the ounce of truth that probabilism contains. Our model of hypothesis choice combines desiderata of support and simplicity. Choosing the manner in which one wields a simplicity criterion may itself be viewed as a problem in hypothesis choice, to be decided by examining past cases of application. If past cases of application tend to yield satisfactory results, we apply our second-level simplicity criterion and decide to act in the future as we have in the past. If past cases of application tend to yield unsatisfactory results, we likewise apply our second-level simplicity criterion and decide to modify our policies in the future, since if we did not, past shortcomings would continue into the future. Thus, our decision on how to apply simplicity considerations in hypothesis choice is

---

[10] It is difficult to imagine a coherent nonsceptical system of hypothesis choice in which simplicity is consistently violated.

influenced by past experience. But simplicity has a deeper claim on our inductive practice than probabilism would suggest. The very way in which we look to past success and failure embodies a simplicity criterion; the paths of coherent revision in method that past experience suggests will involve the use of simplicity to varying degrees and relative to modified systems of natural predicates.

Thus, the position I am defending at once acknowledges that simpler theories are more likely to be true (in the sense explained previously) and denies that the justification of simplicity depends on this fact. This might seem paradoxical in view of the use made of the likelihood of simple theories. We sometimes throw out anomalous data in order to obtain simpler theories, and surely we are justified in regarding such ostensible pieces of evidence as false only if simpler theories are more probable. But as we have seen, our somewhat attenuated admission that simpler theories are more likely is itself inferred from past theorizing, and the inferential policy used itself includes a simplicity constraint. That simplicity is irreducible and *sui generis* may seem less paradoxical once we recall that our desire for *theories* in large measure reduces to a desire for simplicity. Diverse desiderata like accuracy, generality, and univocal treatment of disparate phenomena reduce to simplicity as we have explicated it. And as we have seen, we are interested in theories in spite of their being less probable than some weaker but less satisfying alternatives.

Thus, it is no more reasonable to claim that simplicity is justified because simple theories are more likely than it is to claim that likelihood is justified because likely theories are more simple. Support and simplicity are irreducibly distinct goals in hypothesis choice. Yet, our search for simplicity is not immune to the corrective lessons which we can draw from examining the reliability of past practice. The point is that simplicity is so central to hypothesis choice that even when we use our past experience with simplicity as a guide to future applications, our efforts presuppose the applicability of canons of simplicity. Past experience is not *irrelevant* to the justification of simplicity; rather, all the facts of past experience together with the goal of support are *insufficient* to justify simplicity.

Probabilism pales in comparison with its robust ancestor, the principle of the uniformity of nature. Where probabilism tried to forge a link between simplicity and truth by asserting that the simpler of two hypotheses is more likely to be true, the principle of the uniformity of nature tries to connect simplicity and truth by claiming that the world really is simple. This principle runs foul of the fact that the world can be described in a variety of ways, all equally true but unequally simple. To which of these descriptions corresponds *the* simplicity of the world? Perhaps we can identify the simplicity of the world with the simplicity of its simplest (and reasonably complete) description. We can then formulate the position on justification associated with the principle: Using simplicity in hypothesis choice is justified only if there exists a true (and reasonably complete) description of the world that is more than minimally simple.

Thus formulated, the principle fails. In any world, no matter how complex, we should like as simple a (true) description of that world as possible. Granting that our hypotheses should not be simpler than the world they describe, we grant only a truism: Our hypotheses should not be simpler than the simplest true description of the world; i.e., our hypotheses should not be false. Thus, our desire for simple theories persists even in the face of complex phenomena. The relative complexity of the world cannot account for this goal. The goal is a property of our theorizing which claims our allegiance regardless of how complex the world may be.

With the removal of the objections that probabilism and the principle of the uniformity of nature can make to our justification of simplicity in terms of informativeness, it only remains to justify our theory, which equates simplicity and informativeness. According to our account of what a justification is, we must discern our goals in creating a theory of simplicity and show that the theory achieves them. These goals are precisely those of all theorizing. The theory of simplicity, to be an acceptable theory, must be sufficiently simple and supported.

The support of our theory is the degree to which it fits the facts of our inferential practice. We have seen how the theory captures many preferences and policies that intuitively seem to be instances of 'choosing the simpler alternative'. In Chapter 2, I argued that some desiderata (such as accuracy and good extra logical strength) which appear to be quite distinct from simplicity are in fact reducible to simplicity. It is an open question how much of the rich fabric of our simplicity intuitions can be mirrored within the theory and how many other desiderata of hypotheses can be explicated by the theory of hypothesis choice. For example, we devoted comparatively little attention to different kinds of mathematical equations, so it remains to be seen how the simplicity of other kinds of equations can be accommodated in the theory. Besides capturing notions of simplicity that have to do with inferential policies, the theory also unites epistemic simplicity with formal and asethetic simplicity. Furthermore, connections were made with properties lying beyond simplicity—for example, with naturalness and perspicuity. Thus, the theory seems to apply to facts about cognition that extend beyond the domain of what we initially thought to be simplicity judgements.

That the theory unites diverse intuitions about simplicity within a common logical structure means that it would be simpler than one which requires different *explicans* for different varieties of simplicity judgements. Yet the question of the simplicity of our theory of simplicity is not of decisive importance. At this stage in the development of theories of simplicity, we would be well advised to accept a theory that is somewhat less simple than the one I have proposed if it were better supported by the facts of our inferential practice. Within our theory of hypothesis choice, this means that theories of simplicity are still struggling to push their support above the requisite minimum. Once this is achieved, competitors may then be chosen for their relative simplicity.

One of the main problems for our theory is explaining the notion of support that is simplicity's partner in the rules for hypothesis choice. We have assumed only that if one hypothesis implies another, the former is not more supported than the latter. This stipulation is consistent with explicating support in terms of probability. It is, of course, possible that once an adequate theory of support is provided, no separate constraint of simplicity will be required, since the model will already include those preferences which now go under the rubric of simplicity. Such an outcome would not show that simplicity is superfluous; rather, the problems of explaining and justifying simplicity would be assimilated into the theory of support.

The applications we made of the theory of simplicity occasionally led us to revise some of our initial intuitions. That not all of our pretheoretical judgements are preserved in theory is no novelty for philosophical explications or for science in general. Moreover, the fact that such revision is possible and even necessary has important consequences for the kinds of criticisms of a theory that can count as important. The best criticism of the present theory of simplicity would be a better theory; the worst would be some scattered and idiosyncratic intuitions that are not richly connected in the nexus of our theoretical judgements. This is not to say that violated intuitions provide no basis for criticism, but only that their significance is to be pondered seriously. In advance of a better theory, intuitive judgements will provide bases for criticism to the degree that they are systematic and central.

5.3 Simplicity and Realism

Past discussions of simplicity have often involved an unhappy alliance between methodology and metaphysics. Conventionalists, instrumentalists, and verificationists often cited the importance of simplicity in hypothesis choice as substantiating their antirealist view of theories. A realist might draw the wrong lesson from this proposed connection and try to support realism by arguing against the importance of simplicity in hypothesis choice. Both of these strategies are misguided; there *is* a connection between the use of simplicity in hypothesis choice and a realistic view of the hypotheses so chosen, but the connection is not a simple one.

Conventionalism, instrumentalism, and verificationism agree that two observationally equivalent theories cannot be incompatible. If two theories have all the same predictions in observations, then whatever choice there is between them is a choice between equally true but (perhaps) unequally convenient alternatives. Realism parts ways with these views in its insistence that two observationally equivalent theories may differ in such a way that one is true and the other is false.

A methodology provides a set of reasons for choosing between alternative hypotheses and differentially attributing truth and falsity to them. We will call a methodology *complete* if, for any two hypotheses, the methodology provides a ground for regarding one as true and the other as false just in case the two hypotheses are incompatible. Complete methodologies may allow that there are circumstances in which one cannot choose between incompatible alternatives. For example, insufficient evidence may prevent one from making a unique choice. Yet, for a complete methodology this agnostic stance is in principle only temporary; if two hypotheses are incompatible, then one can specify a condition which, if satisfied, would provide a sufficient reason for making the choice.

Metaphysics and methodology are connected by this idea of completeness. If realism is true, a complete methodology must provide a basis for choosing between some observationally equivalent theories and regarding some as true and others as false. If realism is false, then a complete methodology must not provide such a basis. Thus, a complete realist methodology will (1) distinguish between some observationally equivalent theories in such a way that (2) the basis for the distinction justifies differential attributions of truth. We now must examine our theory of simplicity to see (1) under what conditions it equates the simplicity of two hypotheses and when it distinguishes them, and (2) when such simplicity judgements can serve as a reason for regarding some hypotheses as true and others as false. Determining these properties of our simplicity criterion will allow us to see whether it favours one metaphysical position more than another.

Our account of simplicity organizes hypotheses into equivalence classes, where the equivalence relation is *logical* equivalence. Two logically equivalent hypotheses must be equal in (epistemic) simplicity. They may differ in aesthetic simplicity, but that is just to say that their descriptions (perhaps in terms of the number of inscriptions they contain) differ in epistemic simplicity. Just as the lengths of the words 'caterpillar' and 'dog' are irrelevant to deciding whether caterpillars are longer than dogs, so too is aesthetic simplicity irrelevant to epistemic simplicity and to hypothesis choice in general. Our theory of simplicity explains the difference between aesthetic and epistemic simplicity; it explains *away* the faulty intuition that aesthetic simplicity is involved in hypothesis choice. As we have seen, only in the context of a perspicuous notation would there be any correlation between epistemic and aesthetic simplicity. But the prospects for perfect perspicuity are dim.

Although logically equivalent hypotheses must be equal in simplicity, observationally equivalent hypotheses need not be. It is this fact that makes it possible for our account to be assimilated into a realistic methodology. Of course, this proposed assimilation would be blocked if it could be shown that simplicity is not a ground for differential attributions of truth and falsity. But as we have argued before, simplicity is as serious a ground as there can be for regarding some hypotheses as true and others as false. Simplicity is a ground for attributions of truth and falsity, not because simple hypotheses are more likely to be true, but because our goals in accepting and rejecting hypotheses as true or false involve a commitment to constructing informative hypotheses.

Yet, the suspicion may linger that simplicity is really not a ground for attributions of truth and falsity because simplicity is subjective, mind-dependent, or 'relative to our conceptual scheme'. This kind of devaluation of simplicity can be blocked by pointing to the deep affinities we saw between simplicity and support. The simplicity of a hypothesis is relative to a stock of predicates; the support of a hypothesis is relative to a body of evidence. Some evidential statements are true and are relevant to choosing between competing hypotheses; some predicates really do pick out natural properties and are likewise relevant to choosing between hypotheses. Our goal of making reliable and fruitful conjectures involves seeking out such evidence and predicate systems. This parity between simplicity and support means that an objective attitude towards one should bring with it an objective attitude towards the other.

As we have seen, simplicity can be crucial in choosing between low-level *observational* generalizations. If the choice between two observational hypotheses at least partially hinges on simplicity, and if one views the difference between observational hypotheses realistically, then one must regard simplicity as constituting a legitimate ground for differential attributions of truth and falsity. But this very same criterion for hypothesis choice can be applied to *theories*. There is nothing in the simplicity criterion that sanctions the first application but proscribes the second. Any methodology that wishes to regard choice between observational generalizations as properly involving accepting one hypothesis as true and rejecting the other hypothesis as false but wishes to treat choice between theories as involving choices between equivalent alternatives must superimpose an additional story on all that we have said about simplicity. The simplicity criterion is blind to any alleged difference between theories and observations.

Similar comments apply to those who wish realism to be subject matter specific. For example, if one wishes to hold that observationally equivalent theories in physics can be incompatible but that observationally equivalent theories in psychology cannot be incompatible, our account of simplicity will not provide him with any arguments. Again, this is because our account of simplicity is largely *formal*. In general, if h is simpler than h' relative to predicate family p, the result of judiciously substituting some predicates for others (in conformity with footnote 2 of Chapter 1) will preserve this simplicity ordering. The simplicity criterion is blind to differences in subject matter.

According to our explication of simplicity, a simplicity criterion distinguishes between observationally equivalent theories. According to our justification of simplicity, a difference in simplicity between two hypotheses counts as a reason for differential attributions of truth and falsity. These two facts place our account of simplicity within a realist methodology. An antirealist would be untroubled by our claim that simplicity distinguishes between observationally equivalent hypotheses; indeed, conventionalists have insisted on this all along. The antirealist would reject our proposed justification. Although he might allow that simplicity is a reason for differential attributions of truth and falsity in the realm of observational generalizations, he would deny that it is such a ground in the case of observationally equivalent theories.

The antirealist's attitude towards a simplicity criterion which distinguishes between observationally equivalent theories has important ramifications for how such a criterion is to be assimilated into a complete antirealist methodology. The antirealist must so arrange the rules of hypothesis choice that they do not overstep what he takes to be the bounds of truth;

the rules must never differentially attribute truth and falsity in cases where there is no difference in truth value to be divined. If the methodology is to treat pairs of hypotheses differently according to whether they are observationally equivalent or not, or according to whether they are observational or theoretical, or according to their subject matter, further constraints must be placed on the simplicity criterion, since the criterion is blind to just these differences, as noted earlier.

Adding such further constraints is possible, but as we have seen (e.g., in Section 2.1) there is always a presumption against distinctions and divisions. One treats the choice between two observational hypotheses, the choice between two observationally nonequivalent theories, and the choice between two observationally equivalent theories *alike* unless one can find compelling reason to treat them differently. It is *simpler* to give all hypotheses equal treatment under the rules for hypothesis choice and to leave the rules for hypothesis choice unfettered by these further constraints.

The methodology of realism allows canons of simplicity, as well as other principles of hypothesis choice, a perfectly universal application over the domain of hypotheses; any difference that these canons detect between hypotheses counts as a reason for regarding some hypotheses as true and others as false. The methodology of antirealism must either limit the application of rules for hypothesis choice to less than the full domain of sentences, or it must claim that the results of some applications count as grounds for attribution of truth while others do not. In either event, the methodology of antirealism emerges as less simple than the methodology of realism. Although not decisive in itself, this is a considerable advantage that realism can claim.

Rules for Constructing the Contribution a Hypothesis Makes to Answering a Question

THE contribution a hypothesis makes to answering a question contains all the information about the individuals and properties queried that the hypothesis provides. The contribution can be thought of as the last line of a deduction which begins with the hypothesis itself and aims at yielding an answer to the question; the contribution is as close as the hypothesis can come to yielding an answer. In Section 1.4, rules were given for constructing the contribution, H^*; but these rules applied only in special cases where two assumptions (given in footnote 8) held sway. The following is a completely general set of rules for constructing H^*. We assume that a hypothesis H in prenex normal form is formally relevant to a question Q in that an answer predicate in Q essentially occurs in H. This predicate is attached to constants as it occurs in the answer and is attached to bound variables as it occurs in H. When the question is identified with its (single) answer schema, H^* is constructed by treating the dummy constant(s) in the answer schema as real constant(s).

1. If H has an initial existential quantifier, instantiate it with 'q_k' where k is the lowest number such that 'q_k' has not been used before. Repeat this step until the first quantifier is not existential.
2. Choose an answer predicate P in question Q (not previously selected) such that P essentially occurs in H.
3. Choose an essential occurrence of P in H (not previously selected).
4. Assign distinct numbers i from 1 to n to the argument places of P in Q (in an order not previously selected).
5. Take the ith numbered place $i = 1, 2, \ldots, n$ (not previously selected) of P in Q. Find the corresponding place in the occurrence of P in H (that was selected in 3).
6. If the variable in that place is bound to a universal quantifier and has not already been instantiated, instantiate it uniformly with the constant in the ith place of the answer predicate.

7. If the variable in that place is bound to an existential quantifier and has not already been instantiated, instantiate it uniformly with the constant 'q_k', where k is the lowest number such that 'q_k' has not been used before.

8. Repeat 5 through 7 until every constant in the series of constants attached to P in Q has been selected and every variable in the corresponding series of variables in H has been instantiated.

9. At this point j distinct constants have been used; some or all of the quantifiers in H have been instantiated. Now start with the left-most quantifier remaining. If it is universal, form $j + 1$ instantiations, using the j names already used and one new one as the replacing constants. If the left-most quantifier is existential, form one instantiation using 'q_k', where k is the lowest number such that 'q_k' has not been used before. Repeat this procedure until all the quantifiers have been eliminated and r quantifier free instantiations of H have been formed. Conjoin these together and call the conjunction 'H_k^+', where k is the lowest number such that 'H_k^+' has not been used before.

10. Write H_k^+ in a shortest conjunctive normal form and cross out the clauses that are neither formally relevant to Q nor formally relevant to a clause in H_k^+ that is formally relevant to Q, nor formally relevant to a clause that is formally relevant to a clause that is formally relevant to Q, etc. Call what remains 'H_k^*' where k is the lowest number such that 'H_k^*' has not been used before.

11. Repeat 4 through 10 until every way of numbering the argument places of P in Q has been selected.

12. Repeat 3 through 11 until each essential occurrence of P in H has been selected.

13. Repeat 2 through 12 until each answer predicate that essentially occurs in H has been selected.

14. Conjoin all of the H^*s thus formed. This conjunction is the contribution H^* that H makes to answering Q.

These rules satisfy the self-sufficiency condition (see p. 10). That is, if H implies an answer A_i, so does H^*. To see this, notice first of all that if H^+ (i.e., the conjunction of H^+s formed by rule 9) implies A_i, so does H^*. This follows from the fact that H^* is constructed from H^+ by crossing out clauses in a conjunctive normal form representation of H^+ that cannot help those clauses in H^+ that are formally relevant to A_i to yield A_i (see rule 10). It remains to show that if H implies A_i, so does H^+. At this point we appeal to Quine's main method[1] wherein we can show that a quantified hypothesis H

---

[1] Quine, *Methods of Logic*, pp. 161–4.

implies an unquantified hypothesis A_i by forming a set of instantiations of H. The adequacy of this method guarantees that if H implies A_i, so does a finite conjunction of instances of H. Our H^+ is a conjunction of instances obtainable by the main method; moreover, the instances of H that are excluded from H^+ would not help the instances in H^+ to imply A_i; they would just contain more new names (i.e., not occurring in A_i) than those used in rule 9. To see that the instances constructed via our rules together imply A_i if any conjunction of instances does, consider the hypothesis

$$(\exists y)(\exists z)(x)(w)\{Fx \ \& \ [(Fy \ \& \ Fz) \supset Gw]\}$$

relative to the question $(Ga, \sim Ga)$. The two instances of H that together suffice to imply an answer to Q are

$$Fq_1 \ \& \ [(Fq_1 \ \& \ Fq_2) \supset Ga]$$
$$Fq_2 \ \& \ [(Fq_1 \ \& \ Fq_2) \supset Ga].$$

Of course, there are further instances of H generated by returning to the variables 'x' and 'w'. These further instances play no role in guaranteeing the self-sufficiency of H with respect to Q; all but two of these further instances are excluded from H^+. Although there may be infinitely many names that are candidates for replacing constants, the fact that A_i contains a finite number of names and H a finite number of bound variables guarantees that if H implies A_i, a finite conjunction of instances of H (constructed by letting the names in A_i serve as replacing constants and then using a limited number of new names) will also imply A_i.

A further example may help show how these rules work. We will construct H^* for the hypothesis that says that the relation R is transitive (see p. 81),

$$(x)(y)(z)[(Rxy \ \& \ Ryz) \supset Rxz],$$

relative to the question $(Rab, \sim Rab)$. Notice that there are three occurrences of the answer predicate 'R' in the hypothesis, each linked to a different series of variables. Following rule 12, we must focus on each of these occurrences in turn, yielding the following three partial instantiations:

$$(z)[(Rab \ \& \ Rbz) \supset Raz]$$
$$(x)[(Rxa \ \& \ Rab) \supset Rxb]$$
$$(y)[(Ray \ \& \ Ryb) \supset Rab].$$

Each of these partial instantiations has one bound variable left, and according to rule 9, each must be instantiated three times: with 'a', with 'b', and with the new name 'c'. That makes nine full instantiations. Each of these H^+s contains no irrelevant clauses (see rule 10), so the conjunction of these nine is H^*.

These rules will generate an H^+ containing more than one instance of H when a predicate in H essentially occurs more than once and is linked to different series of variables at its several occurrences. This is illustrated by the above two examples. H^+ will also contain more than one instance of H when repetitions in the series of variables attached to P in H fail to match repetitions in the series of constants attached to P in Q. For example, the H^+ of the hypothesis

$$(x)(Rxx)$$

relative to the question $(Rab, \sim Rab)$ is

$$Raa \,\&\, Rbb,$$

although relative to the question $(Raa, \sim Raa)$, its H^+ is simply 'Raa'.

Bibliography

In addition to containing works referenced in the text, this bibliography includes some others that I have found useful.

ACKERMANN, R., 'Inductive Simplicity', *Philosophy of Science*, 28(2), 1961, pp. 152–61. Reprinted in M. H. Foster and M. L. Martin (eds.), *Probability, Confirmation, and Simplicity*.

ATTNEAVE, F., *Applications of Information Theory to Psychology: A Summary of Basic Concepts, Methods and Results*, Henry Holt and Co., New York, 1959.

ATTNEAVE, F., 'Physical Determinants of the Judged Complexity of Shapes', *Journal of Experimental Psychology*, 53, 1957, pp. 221–7.

ATTNEAVE, F., 'Some Informational Aspects of Visual Perception', *Psychological Review*, 61(3), 1954, pp. 183–93.

ATTNEAVE, F., 'Symmetry, Information, and Memory for Patterns', *American Journal of Psychology*, 68, 1955, pp. 209–22.

ATTNEAVE, F. and FROST, R., 'The Determination of Perceived Tridimensional Orientation by Minimum Criteria', *Perception and Psychophysics*, 6(6B), 1969, pp. 391–6.

BACH, E., *An Introduction to Transformational Grammar*, Holt, Rinehart, and Winston, New York, 1964.

BACH, E., 'Two Proposals Concerning the Simplicity Metric in Phonology', *Glossa*, 2(2), 1969, pp. 128–49.

BAR-HILLEL, Y. and CARNAP, R., 'An Outline of a Theory of Semantic Information', in Y. Bar-Hillel (ed.), *Language and Information*, Addison-Wesley, Reading, Mass., 1964, pp. 221–75.

BARKER, S. F., *Induction and Hypothesis*, Cornell University Press, Ithaca, N.Y., 1957.

BARKER, S. F., 'On Simplicity in Empirical Hypotheses', *Philosophy of Science*, 28(2), 1961, pp. 162–71. Reprinted in M. H. Foster and M. L. Martin (eds.), *Probability, Confirmation, and Simplicity*.

BARKER, S. F. and ACHINSTEIN, P., 'On the New Riddle of Induction', *Philosophical Review*, 69, 1960, pp. 511–22.

BIRKHOFF, G. D., *Aesthetic Measures*, Harvard University Press, Cambridge, Mass., 1933.

BLACKBURN, S. W., 'Goodman's Paradox', in N. Rescher (ed.), *Studies in the Philosophy of Science*, American Philosophical Quarterly Publication No. 3, 1969, pp. 128–42.

BLOOMFIELD, L., *Language*, Holt, Rinehart, and Winston, New York, 1933.

BOEHNER, P. (ed.), *Ockham: Philosophical Writings*, Thomas Nelson and Sons, Edinburgh, 1957.

BOTHA, R. P., *Methodological Aspects of Transformational Generative Phonology*, Mouton, The Hague, 1971.

BOWER, T. G. R., 'The Development of Objective Permanence: Some Studies in Existence Constancy', *Perception and Psychophysics*, 2(9), 1967, pp. 411–18.

BOWER, T. G. R., 'The Object in the World of the Infant', *Scientific American*, 225(4), 1971, pp. 30–8.

BOWER, T. G. R. and PATTERSON, J. G., 'Stages in the Development of the Object Concept', *Cognition*, 1(1), 1972, pp. 47–55.

BROWN, J. F. and VOTH, A. C., 'The Path of Seen Motion as a Function of the Vector-Field', *American Journal of Psychology*, 49, 1937, pp. 543-63.

BRUNER, J. S. 'On Going Beyond the Information Given', in J. Bruner *et al.*, *Contemporary Approaches to Cognition*, Harvard University Press, Cambridge, Mass., 1957, pp. 41-69. Reprinted in J. M. Anglin (ed.), *Beyond the Information Given*, W. W. Norton, New York, 1973, pp. 218-40.

BRUNER, J. S., 'On Perceptual Readiness', in J. M. Anglin (ed.), *Beyond the Information Given*, W. W. Norton, New York, 1973, pp. 7-42.

BRUNER, J. S., GOODNOW, J. J., and AUSTIN, G. A., *A Study of Thinking*, Wiley, New York, 1956.

BRUNER, J. S., OLIVER, R. R., and GREENFIELD, P. M. *et al.*, *Studies in Cognitive Growth*, Wiley, New York, 1966.

BUNGE, M., *The Myth of Simplicity*, Prentice-Hall, Englewood Cliffs, N.J., 1963.

BUNGE, M., 'The Weight of Simplicity in the Construction and Assaying of Scientific Theories', *Philosophy of Science*, 28(2), 1961, pp. 120-49. Reprinted in M. H. Foster and M. L. Martin (eds.), *Probability, Confirmation, and Simplicity*.

CARNAP, R., *Continuum of Inductive Methods*, University of Chicago Press, Chicago, 1952.

CARNAP, R., *Logical Foundations of Probability*, University of Chicago Press, Chicago, 1962.

CARNAP, R., 'On the Application of Inductive Logic', *Philosophy and Phenomenological Research*, 8, 1947, pp. 133-47.

CARNAP, R., 'Probability and Content Measure', in P. Feyerabend and G. Maxwell (eds.), *Mind, Matter, and Method*, University of Minnesota Press, Minneapolis, 1966, pp. 248-61.

CHOMSKY, N., *Aspects of the Theory of Syntax*, M.I.T. Press, Cambridge, Mass., 1965.

CHOMSKY, N., 'Current Issues in Linguistic Theory', in J. Fodor and J. Katz (eds.), *The Structure of Language*, Prentice-Hall, Englewood Cliffs, N.J., 1964, pp. 50-118.

CHOMSKY, N., *Syntactic Structures*, Mouton, The Hague, 1957.

CHOMSKY, N., 'Topics in the Theory of Generative Grammar', in J. Searle (ed.), *The Philosophy of Language*, Oxford University Press, London, 1971, pp. 71-82.

CHOMSKY, N. and HALLE, M., 'Some Controversial Questions in Phonological Theory', *Journal of Linguistics*, 1(2), 1965, pp. 97-214.

CHOMSKY, N. and HALLE, M., *The Sound Pattern of English*, Harper and Row, New York, 1968.

CONTRERAS, H., 'Simplicity, Descriptive Adequacy, and Binary Features', *Language*, 45(1), 1969, pp. 1-8.

DAVIDSON, D., 'Mental Events', in L. Foster and J. W. Swanson (eds.), *Experience and Theory*, University of Massachusetts Press, 1970, pp. 79-103.

DEMBER, W. N., *The Psychology of Perception*, Holt, Rinehart, and Winston, London, 1960.

DORFMAN, D. D. and McKENNA, H., 'Pattern Preference as a Function of Pattern Uncertainty', *Canadian Journal of Psychology*, 20, 1966, pp. 143-53.

DUHEM, P., *The Aim and Structure of Physical Theory*, Atheneum, New York, 1962.

EINSTEIN, A., 'On the Electrodynamics of Moving Bodies', in H. A. Lorentz, A. Einstein, *et al.*, *The Principle of Relativity*, Dover, New York, 1952, pp. 35-65.

FODOR, J. and KATZ, J. (eds.), *The Structure of Language*, Prentice-Hall, Englewood Cliffs, N.J., 1964.

FOSTER, M. H. and MARTIN, M. L. (eds.), *Probability, Confirmation, and Simplicity*, Odyssey Press, New York, 1966.

FREGE, G., *The Foundations of Arithmetic*, Basil Blackwell, Oxford, 1968.

FRIEDMAN, K., 'Empirical Simplicity as Testability', *British Journal for the Philosophy of Science*, 23, 1972, pp. 25–33.

GARNER, W. R., *Uncertainty and Structure as Psychological Concepts*, Wiley, New York, 1962.

GOODMAN, N., *Fact, Fiction, and Forecast*, 2nd edn., Bobbs-Merrill, Indianapolis, 1965.

GOODMAN, N., 'On Infirmities of Confirmation Theory', *Philosophy and Phenomenological Research*, 8, 1947, pp. 149–51. Reprinted in N. Goodman, *Problems and Projects*.

GOODMAN, N., *Languages of Art*, Bobbs-Merrill, Indianapolis, 1968.

GOODMAN, N., 'Positionality and Pictures', *Philosophical Review*, 69, 1960, pp. 523–5. Reprinted in N. Goodman, *Problems and Projects*.

GOODMAN, N., *Problems and Projects*, Bobbs-Merrill, Indianapolis, 1972.

GOODMAN, N., 'Safety, Strength, Simplicity', *Philosophy of Science*, 28, 1961, pp. 150–1. Reprinted in N. Goodman, *Problems and Projects*.

GOODMAN, N., 'Seven Strictures on Similarity' in N. Goodman, *Problems and Projects*, pp. 437–48.

GOODMAN, N., *The Structure of Appearance*, 2nd edn., Bobbs-Merrill, Indianapolis, 1966.

GREEN, R. T. and COURTIS, M. C., 'Information Theory and Figure Perception: The Metaphor that Failed', *Acta Psychologica*, 25, 1966, pp. 12–36.

GREENO, J. G., 'Explanation and Information', in W. C. Salmon (ed.), *Statistical Explanation and Statistical Relevance*, University of Pittsburgh Press, Pittsburgh, Pa., 1971, pp. 89–104.

GREGORY, R. L., *Eye and Brain*, Weidenfeld and Nicolson, London, 1966.

GREGORY, R. L., *The Intelligent Eye*, Weidenfeld and Nicolson, London, 1970.

GRUNSTRA, B., 'The Plausibility of the Entrenchment Concept', in N. Rescher (ed.), *Studies in the Philosophy of Science*, American Philosophical Quarterly Publication No. 3, 1969, pp. 100–27.

HALL, K. R. L., EARLE, A. E., and CROOKES, T. G., 'A Pendulum Phenomenon in the Visual Perception of Apparent Movement', *Quarterly Journal of Experimental Psychology*, 4, 1952, pp. 109–20.

HALLE, M., 'On the Bases of Phonology', in J. Fodor and J. Katz (eds.), *The Structure of Language*, Prentice-Hall, Englewood Cliffs, N.J., 1964, pp. 324–33.

HALLE, M., 'On the Role of Simplicity in Linguistic Descriptions', *Proceedings of Symposia in Applied Mathematics*, 12 (Structure of Language and its Mathematical Aspects), 1961, pp. 89–94. Also, Bobbs-Merrill Reprint Series in Language and Linguistics, No. 35.

HALLE, M., 'Phonology in Generative Grammar', in J. Fodor and J. Katz (eds.), *The Structure of Language*, Prentice-Hall, Englewood Cliffs, N.J., pp. 334–52.

HARMS, R. T., 'The Measurement of Phonological Economy', *Language*, 42(3), 1966, pp. 602–11.

HARRIS, Z., *Methods in Structural Linguistics*, University of Chicago Press, Chicago, 1951.

HEMPEL, C. G., 'Inductive Inconsistencies', in C. G. Hempel, *Aspects of Scientific Explanation*, Free Press, New York, 1965, pp. 53–80.

HEMPEL, C. G., *Philosophy of Natural Science*, Prentice-Hall, Englewood Cliffs, N.J., 1966.

HESSE, M. B., 'Ramifications of "Grue"', *British Journal for the Philosophy of Science*, 20, 1969, pp. 13–25.

HESSE, M. B., 'Simplicity', in P. Edwards (ed.), *Encyclopedia of Philosophy*, vol. 7, Macmillan, New York, 1967, pp. 445–9.

HESSE, M. B., *The Structure of Scientific Inference*, Macmillan, London, 1973.

HINTIKKA, J., 'On Semantic Information', in J. Hintikka and P. Suppes (eds.), *Information and Inference*, Reidel Publishing Co., Dordrecht, Holland, 1970, pp. 3–26.

HOCHBERG, J. E., *Perception*, Prentice-Hall, Englewood Cliffs, N.J., 1964.

HOCHBERG, J. E. and BROOKS, V., 'Compression of Pictorial Space Through Perspective Reversal', *Perceptual and Motor Skills*, 16, 1963, p. 262.

HOCHBERG, J. E. and BROOKS, V., 'The Psychophysics of Form: Reversible Perspective Drawings of Spatial Objects', *American Journal of Psychology*, 73(3), 1960, pp. 337–54.

HOCHBERG, J. E. and MCALISTER, E., 'A Quantitative Approach to Figural "Goodness"', *Journal of Experimental Psychology*, 46(5), 1953, pp. 361–4.

HUNT, G. M. K., 'A Conditional Vindication of the Straight Rule', *British Journal for the Philosophy of Science*, 21, 1970, pp. 198–9.

JEFFREY, R., 'Statistical Explanation vs. Statistical Inference', in W. Salmon (ed.), *Statistical Explanation and Statistical Relevance*, University of Pittsburgh Press, Pittsburgh, Pa., 1971, pp. 19–28.

JEFFREYS, H., *Scientific Inference*, Cambridge University Press, Cambridge, 1937.

JOHANSSON, G., *Configurations in Event Perception*, Almqvist and Wilsell, Uppsala, 1950.

KEMENY, J. G., 'Two Measures of Complexity', *Journal of Philosophy*, 52, 1955, pp. 722–33.

KEMENY, J. G., 'The Use of Simplicity in Induction', *Philosophical Review*, 62, 1953, pp. 391–408.

KIPARSKY, P., 'Linguistic Universals and Linguistic Change', in E. Bach and R. T. Harms (eds.), *Universals in Linguistic Theory*, Holt, Rinehart, and Winston, New York, 1968, pp. 171–202.

KISSEBERTH, C. W., 'On the Functional Unity of Phonological Rules', *Linguistic Inquiry*, 1(3), 1970, pp. 291–306.

KNEALE, W., *Probability and Induction*, Clarendon Press, Oxford, 1966.

KOLERS, P. A., 'Apparent Motion of a Necker Cube', *American Journal of Psychology*, 77, 1964, pp. 220–30.

KOLERS, P. A., *Aspects of Motion Perception*, Pergamon Press, Oxford, 1972.

KOLERS, P. A., 'The Illusion of Movement', *Scientific American*, Vol. 211, No. 4, 1964, pp. 98–106.

KRIPKE, S., 'Naming and Necessity', in D. Davidson and G. Harman (eds.)., *Semantics for Natural Languages*, D. Reidel Publishing Co., Dordrecht, Holland, 1969.

LAKATOS, I., 'Proofs and Refutations', *British Journal for the Philosophy of Science*, 14, 1963–4, pp. 1–25, 120–39, 221–43, 296–342.

LAKOFF, G., 'On Generative Semantics', in D. D. Steinberg and L. A. Jakobovits (eds.), *Semantics*, Cambridge University Press, Cambridge, 1971, pp. 232–96.

LEEUWENBERG, E. L. J., 'A Perceptual Coding Language for Visual and Auditory Patterns', *American Journal of Psychology*, 84(3), 1971, pp. 307–50.

LEEUWENBERG, E. L. J., *Structural Information of Visual Patterns*, Mouton, The Hague, 1968.

LEVI, I., *Gambling with Truth*, Routledge and Kegan Paul, London, 1967.

LYONS, J., *Chomsky*, Fontana, London, 1970.

LYONS, J., *Introduction to Theoretical Linguistics*, Cambridge University Press, Cambridge, 1969.

MCCAWLEY, J., 'The Accentual System of Standard Japanese', Ph.D. dissertation, M.I.T., 1965.

MCCAWLEY, J., *The Phonological Component of a Grammar of Japanese*, Monographs on Linguistic Analysis, No. 2, Mouton, The Hague, 1968.

MACKAY, D. M., 'Interactive Processes in Visual Perception', in W. A. Rosenblith (ed.), *Sensory Communication*, M.I.T. Press, Cambridge, Mass., 1961.

MACKAY, D. M., 'The Stabilization of Perception during Voluntary Activity', *Fifteenth International Congress of Psychology*, Brussels, 1959, pp. 284–5.

MILL, J. S., *A System of Logic, Ratiocinative and Inductive*, Harper Bros., New York, 1887.

MOODY, E. A., 'William of Ockham' in P. Edwards (ed.), *Encyclopedia of Philosophy*, vol. 8, Macmillan, New York, 1967, 306–17.

NAGEL, E., *The Structure of Science*, Harcourt, Brace, and World, New York, 1961.

NARO, A. J., 'Resolution of Vocalic Hiatus in Portuguese: Diachronic Evidence for Binary Features', *Language*, 47(2), 1971, pp. 381–93.

PERKINS, D., 'The Perception of Line Drawings of Simple Space Forms', in D. Perkins, *Geometry and the Perception of Pictures: Three Studies*, Technical Report No. 5, Harvard Project Zero, Cambridge, Mass., 1971.

PIAGET, J., *The Child's Conception of Number*, Norton, New York, 1965.

PIAGET, J., *The Construction of Reality in the Child*, Basic Books, New York, 1954.

POPPER, K. R., *Conjectures and Refutations*, Routledge and Kegan Paul, London, 1969.

POPPER, K. R., *Logic of Scientific Discovery*, Hutchinson, London, 1968.

POST, H. R., 'A Criticism of Popper's Theory of Simplicity', *British Journal for the Philosophy of Science*, 12, 1961, pp. 328–31.

POST, H. R., 'Simplicity and Scientific Theories', *British Journal for the Philosophy of Science*, 11, 1960, pp. 32–41.

PRITCHARD, R. M., HERON, W., and HEBB, D. O., 'Visual Perception Approached by the Method of Stabilized Images', *Canadian Journal of Psychology*, 14, 1960, pp. 67–77.

PUTNAM, H., 'The Analytic and the Synthetic', in H. Feigl and G. Maxwell (eds.), *Minnesota Studies in the Philosophy of Science*, vol. 3, University of Minnesota Press, Minneapolis, 1962, pp. 358–97.

PUTNAM, H., 'Formalization of the Concept of "About"', *Philosophy of Science*, 25(2), 1958, pp. 125–30.

PUTNAM, H., 'The Meaning of "Meaning"', in K. Gunderson (ed.), *Minnesota Studies in the Philosophy of Science*, vol. 7, University of Minnesota Press, Minneapolis, forthcoming.

PUTNAM, H., 'Reductionism and the Nature of Psychology', *Cognition*, 2, 1, 1973, pp. 131–46.

QUINE, W. V. O., 'Existence', in W. Yourgrau and A. D. Breck (eds.), *Physics, Logic, and History*, Plenum Press, New York, 1970, pp. 89–104.

QUINE, W. V. O., *Methods of Logic*, 3rd edn., Holt, Rinehart, and Winston, New York, 1972.

QUINE, W. V. O., 'Natural Kinds', in W. V. O. Quine, *Ontological Relativity*, Columbia University Press, New York, 1969, pp. 114–38.

QUINE, W. V. O., 'On Cores and Prime Implicants of Truth Functions', in W. V. O. Quine, *Selected Logic Papers*, Random House, New York, 1966, pp. 164–71.

QUINE, W. V. O., *Philosophy of Logic*, Prentice-Hall, Englewood Cliffs, N.J., 1970.

QUINE, W. V. O., 'The Scope and Language of Science', in W. V. O. Quine, *The Ways of Paradox*, pp. 215–32.

QUINE, W. V. O., 'Simple Theories of a Complex World', in W. V. O. Quine, *The Ways of Paradox*, pp. 242–6. Reprinted in M. H. Foster and M. L. Martin (eds.), *Probability, Confirmation, and Simplicity*.

QUINE, W. V. O., 'Truth by Convention', in W. V. O. Quine, *The Ways of Paradox*, pp. 70–99.

QUINE, W. V. O., 'Two Dogmas of Empiricism', in W. V. O. Quine, *From a Logical Point of View*, Harper Torchbooks, New York, 1963, pp. 20–46.

QUINE, W. V. O., *The Ways of Paradox*, Random House, New York, 1966.

QUINE, W. V. O., *Word and Object*, M.I.T. Press, Cambridge, Mass., 1960.

REICHENBACH, H., *Experience and Prediction*, University of Chicago Press, Chicago, 1938.

REICHENBACH, H., *Nomological Statements and Admissible Operations*, North-Holland Publishing Co., Amsterdam, 1954.

REICHENBACH, H., *The Theory of Probability*, University of California Press, Berkeley, 1949.

RIGGS, L., RATLIFF, F., CORNSWEET, J., and CORNSWEET, T., 'The Disappearance of Steadily Fixated Visual Objects', *Journal of the Optical Society of America*, 43, 1953, pp. 495–501.

ROSCH, E. H., 'Natural Categories', *Cognition*, 4(3), 1973, pp. 338–50.

RUDNER, R., 'An Introduction to Simplicity', *Philosophy of Science*, 28(2), 1961, pp. 109–19.

RUSSELL, B., *My Philosophical Development*, George Allen and Unwin, London, 1959.

RUSSELL, B., 'The Relation of Sense Data to Physics', in B. Russell, *Mysticism and Logic*, Penguin Books, Baltimore, Md., 1953.

RUSSELL, B., 'Reply to Criticisms', in P. Schilpp (ed.), *Philosophy of Bertrand Russell*, Tudor, New York, 1951, pp. 679–742.

SALMON, W. C., *The Foundations of Scientific Inference*, University of Pittsburgh Press, Pittsburgh, Pa., 1967.

SALMON, W. C., 'Statistical Explanation', in W. C. Salmon (ed.), *Statistical Explanation and Statistical Relevance*, University of Pittsburgh Press, Pittsburgh, Pa., 1971, pp. 29–88.

SCHEFFLER, I., *The Anatomy of Inquiry*, Routledge and Kegan Paul, London, 1964.

SYLVESTER, J., 'Apparent Movement and the Brown–Voth Experiment', *Quarterly Journal of Experimental Psychology*, 12, 1960, pp. 231–6.

TARSKI, A., 'The Concept of Truth in Formalized Languages', in A. Tarski, *Logic, Semantics, Metamathematics*, Oxford University Press, Oxford, 1969.

THORBURN, W. M., 'The Myth of Ockham's Razor', *Mind*, July 1918, pp. 345–53.

WERTHEIMER, M., 'Experimentelle Studien über das Sehen von Bewegung', *Zeitschrift für Psychologie*, 61, 1912, pp. 161–265. Excerpted and translated in T. Shipley (ed.), *Classics in Psychology*, Philosophical Library, New York, 1961.

WEYL, H., *Philosophy of Mathematics and Natural Science*, Princeton University Press, Princeton, N.J., 1949.

WEYL, H., *Symmetry*, Princeton University Press, Princeton, N.J., 1952.

YEN, S. L., 'Two Measures of Economy in Phonological Description', *Foundations of Language*, 4, 1968, pp. 58–69.

ZIMMER, K. E., 'On the Evaluation of Alternative Phonological Descriptions' *Journal of Linguistics*, 6, 1969, pp. 89–98.

Index